Making More Sense of How to Sing

MULTISENSORY TECHNIQUES
FOR VOICE LESSONS AND
CHOIR REHEARSALS

Alan J. Gumm

Published by
Meredith Music Publications
a division of G.W. Music, Inc.
4899 Lerch Creek Ct., Galesville, MD 20765
http://www.meredithmusic.com

MEREDITH MUSIC PUBLICATIONS and its stylized double M logo are
trademarks of
MEREDITH MUSIC PUBLICATIONS, a division of G.W. Music, Inc.

No part of this book may be reproduced or transmitted in any form or by
any means, electronic or mechanical, including photocopying,
recording, or by any informational storage or retrieval system
without permission in writing from the publisher.

Text and cover design: Shawn Girsberger

Copyright © 2009 MEREDITH MUSIC PUBLICATIONS
International Copyright Secured • All Rights Reserved
First Edition
July 2009

International Standard Book Number: 978-1-57463-152-4
Cataloging-in-Publication Data is on file with the Library of Congress.
Library of Congress Control Number: 2009929136
Printed and bound in U.S.A.

CONTENTS

Tables and Figures iv
Preface vii
Acknowledgments ix

INTRODUCTION 1

CHAPTER 1 | Breath Energy that Supports Vocal Tone 17
Posture 17
Abdominal Breathing 20
Diaphragmatic Breathing 34
Ribcage Expansion and Costal Breathing 42

CHAPTER 2 | Accurate, Relaxed, and Vibrant Vocal Tone 51
Acoustics: Frequency 51
Pitch Accuracy 59
Lower Larynx 66
Open and Relaxed Throat and Glottis 68
Vocal Fold Pressure 73
Vocal Registers 79
Effects of Posture on Phonation 83

CHAPTER 3 | Focused, Lifted, and Resonant Tone 89
Acoustics: Timbre and Harmonics 89
Raised and Open Soft Palate 98
Beyond the Palate 101
From the Oropharynx to the Nasopharynx 105
Deeper and Wider Sinus Resonance 108
Vowel and Register Resonance 113
Effects of Posture on Resonance 120

CHAPTER 4 | Projection and Release of Sound 131
Acoustics: Amplitude 131
Moving Sound Beyond the Resonators 137
Learning to Hear Sound in a Room 142
Choral Applications: No One is Heard, Everyone is Heard . . 146

CHAPTER 5 | Freedom of Articulators from Other Functions . . 159
Clear and Distinct Vowels 159
Separate Function of the Tongue 166
Free and Quick-Moving Jaw 175
Loose and Responsive Cheeks and Lips 178
Putting It All Together 180

References 187

Tables and Figures

Table 0.1	Two Pronunciation Systems.	9
Figure 0.1	Chapters are organized to show how tone is supported, produced, resonated, projected, and kept separate from articulation.	15
Figure 1.1	Blowing an imaginary candle at a distance helps in sensing abdominal movement.	21
Figure 1.2	Hands used to indicate direction of abdominal muscle movement.	23
Figure 1.3	Fists used to accentuate abdominal flex.	23
Figure 1.4	Voice teacher's abdominal push on top of the singer's own hand.	25
Figure 1.5	Hands used to indicate breath noise along the mouth and throat.	27
Figure 1.6	Basic pant-sing exercise.	30
Figure 1.7	Path of singing tone.	31
Figure 1.8	Blowing into a cupped hand replaces resistance in the vocal cords and throat.	32
Figure 1.9	Diaphragm-hand position.	35
Figure 1.10	The dome of the diaphragm follows the curve of the ribs.	38
Figure 1.11	The upward hand guides a strong lift of breath, the downward hand guides resistance for efficient use of breath.	40
Figure 1.12	Rib-touch hand positions before and after inhalation.	44
Figure 1.13	Rib expansion arm movement.	45
Figure 1.14	Thumbs represent the hinge at the spine; fingers represent ribs expanding out.	46
Figure 2.1	Ball throws: fast for a high-pitched tone, slow for a low-pitched tone.	51
Figure 2.2	Higher pitches have frequencies that are faster and closer together; lower pitches are slower and farther apart.	54
Figure 2.3	Matching the speed and shape of a sound wave with the hand.	55
Figure 2.4	Pant sing scale exercise. 1. Five-note rise and fall. 2. Extended-range thirds. Note that commas and rests indicate to breathe after each pitched tone.	60
Figure 2.5	A simple interval pattern to practice multisensory solfége syllables and hand signs.	62
Figure 2.6	Signal the division of the half step between *ti* and *do* into 1/4 steps and smaller; do the same for other half step intervals.	65
Figure 2.7	A falling gesture down to a low, comfortable pitch is used to guide the same comfortable sensation on high notes.	68
Figure 2.8	Pretending to be a sword swallower to open the glottis and lower the larynx.	69
Figure 2.9	Floppy hands to guide an open, relaxed position for singing.	70
Figure 2.10	Upside-down funnel hand gestures open on top as pitch rises to open the pharynx and sinuses to sound.	71
Figure 2.11	Closed and open glottis hand movements train attention to starting sound on a stream of air rather than with tension and pressure around the vocal cords.	74
Figure 2.12	Hands in a V, on the left the direction of effort aims toward the narrower opening at the front of the vocal cords; and on the right the direction of effort is toward the back, which swings wider and narrower in forming a sound wave.	76
Figure 2.13	Arms trapped to the sides, pushing out, then let go to raise with no added effort.	78

Figure 2.14	Developing consistent tone by buzzing across paper	79
Figure 2.15	Thumbs represent the use of the thicker portion of the vocal folds in chest voice; index fingers represent the thinner surface of the vocal folds that vibrate more quickly in falsetto register.	80
Figure 2.16	Moving from a forward-leaning posture (left) to an up-and-out posture (right)	84
Figure 2.17	The head aligns with the vocal cords with a push back and up against a teacher's hand; a slight push forward by the teacher triggers a release of vibrant tone.	86
Figure 3.1	Sonar hands help detect the primary source of sound coming out of the body	89
Figure 3.2	Resonant spaces	91
Figure 3.3	Harmonic series: the fundamental pitch and overtones	95
Figure 3.4	Frequencies in the harmonic series change by singing in and through different resonant spaces, which changes the timbre of the voice	96
Figure 3.5	Buckteeth finger position to trigger a raised soft palate	99
Figure 3.6	Placing a thumbprint on the soft palate	100
Figure 3.7	Resonating sound out through the mouth (left); resonating sound through the sinuses and nasal cavity (right)	101
Figure 3.8	Palate-hand position	104
Figure 3.9	Aim sound behind and above the palate before turning the corner forward	106
Figure 3.10	Smelling an imaginary rose opens the resonators up to the olfactory area	108
Figure 3.11	Hand motion to draw tone across the width of the sinuses	110
Figure 3.12	Hold the arm down and sing on the release for a surprisingly tension-free tone.	112
Figure 3.13	Borrow the first vowel sensation to sing a more resonant second vowel.	113
Figure 3.14	Imagining pulling a bucket up by a rope brings balance and deep supported tone	120
Figure 3.15	A tilted position releases tension and allows a deeply supported release of resonant tone.	124
Figure 3.16	Targeting sound different directions out of the head.	127
Figure 4.1	The height of the amplitude of a sound wave determines loudness	132
Figure 4.2	Narrow hands for a quiet tone and tall hands for a loud tone.	133
Figure 4.3	Tall and short hands used to execute dynamics accurately and freely	135
Figure 4.4	Draw-tone-out hand gesture	138
Figure 4.5	A telescope-hands position gives a sense of direction and shape to tone across open space	140
Figure 4.6	Highlighted quartet starts the process, each singer matches until all sing as one.	149
Figure 4.7	Making choir sections audible by using the resonance and overtones of different underlying vowels.	153
Figure 4.8	Multisensory synesthesia-like perceptions: seeing choral sound within the choir (top), around the choir (middle), and at distances away from the choir (bottom).	156
Figure 5.1	Arm shapes to guide vowel shapes and colors	160
Figure 5.2	Pant-sing exercise on different vowels and syllables.	161

Figure 5.3	A tall hand signals the resonators to stay open across the length of a vowel.	164
Figure 5.4	Hold your tongue to detect and release tension.	167
Figure 5.5	Tongue curl and fat "L" tongue positions	170
Figure 5.6	The bubble hand on top guides resonance, the rocking hand on bottom guides the tongue.	171
Figure 5.7	Different overtones are highlighted due to vowel shape (left) and slight changes in the shape of the oropharynx (right)	174
Figure 5.8	A jutting position of the jaw (left) changes to correct rotation (right).	175
Figure 5.9	Correct jaw rotation.	176
Figure 5.10	The combination of wide intervals and changing syllables develops quicker and freer movement of articulators	177
Figure 5.11	Separation of a lift in the cheek muscles and a relaxed rotation of the jaw.	178
Figure 5.12	Release of the arm to external control guides release of tension in singing.	181
Figure 5.13	Hand and finger gestures help guide consonants: voiced (left), plosive and brief sustained (middle), and aspirated (right).	183

PREFACE

Somewhere deep inside voice teachers and choral conductors lies the knowledge that we should be using movement to improve our students' singing. The companion to that knowledge is a feeling that since we don't have specialized training in movement-based pedagogy—such as Dalcroze Eurhythmics—we are not qualified to direct movement activities. Worse, we will probably be wasting valuable rehearsal time because the students will resist because they (and perhaps we?) see no direct connection between singing and movement.

Writing as a Dalcroze teacher, this is patent nonsense. The body and physical movement is the basis for all music that humans make. Yet we as teachers and conductors continue to act as if the brain and vocal apparatus were somehow detached from the rest of the body, as if our students and ensembles could produce lively music with inert bodies.

The teaching of vocal technique—a subject that is fraught with contention among voice teachers—is usually one of the most deadening of activities since it is almost always removed from movement. Alan Gumm understands this. In *Making More Sense of How to Sing*, he has produced a well-organized, heuristic approach to applying movement directly to vocal technique, and has filled the book with suggestions about the kind and quality of gestures that have served him well in teaching singers and directing ensembles.

Dr. Gumm is a colleague of mine, and I have had occasion not only to hear his ensembles but also to sit in on his rehearsals. I have been impressed by his passion for using the rehearsals to actually educate the students to be better musicians and singers, and not merely use the time to prepare them for the next concert.

Our profession would benefit if there were more "Alan Gumms." However, since his talents do not extend to cloning himself, he has done the next best thing: written a book that shares his passion and insights. I hope his work will lead you to your own insights into the bonds between music and the body.

J. Timothy Caldwell
author, *Expressive Singing: Dalcroze Eurhythmics for Voice*
Professor of Voice, Central Michigan University

ACKNOWLEDGMENTS

My gratitude starts with voice teachers who made a difference in my singing: Ken Forsyth, Stephanie Graber, Jonah Kliewer, and David Rasmussen. Thanks also to my voice faculty colleagues—Roland Bentley, Carol McAmis, Randie Blooding, Patrice Pastore, David Parks, Tim Caldwell, Cora Enman, Jeffrey Foote, Mary Stewart Kiesgen, Eric Tucker and others—whose varying approaches pointed out both our distinctions and our common aims. Special thanks to Barbara Burdick for giving the book her expert review, and to Tim Caldwell for a Preface that challenges us all to connect music with movement and insightfully captures the purpose and benefit of this book. My thanks extends to choral directors with substantial influence to this book, particularly John Cooksey, Ed Thompson, Janet Galván, Larry Doebler, and Bob Zazzara, and to Virginia Kerwin whose response to these techniques as our choirs sang together motivated my commitment to the book, and for testing and reviewing an early draft. Special thanks to Nina Nash-Robertson whose choir is pictured in this book. Also to the abundance of unnamed directors witnessed to ignore vocal problems, turn away those with vocal problems, lack solutions for vocal problems, add to vocal problems, and most of all to strongly desire to find solutions to vocal problems—you provided perhaps my greatest motivation to share techniques that make more sense in deciding who can sing and how to sing.

Of the thousands of general music, choral, vocal, music education, and elementary education students on whom I honed these strategies and who put me to the test in applying my belief that anybody can learn to sing, I particularly thank Ryan Mackey, the Horton sisters Allison and Staci, Janelle Flory, Danny Ramsey, Mark Godfrey, Amy Fast, Deborah Polkinghorn, Darren Hendricks and others from McPherson College. From Central Michigan University: Michelle Miller whose triumph in learning to sing and subsequent commitment to inspired teaching fed my commitment to this book, Brandi Brauker whose quick grasp confirmed how others could readily benefit from this approach, and Nick Stokes for reviewing the book from a budding teacher's point of view and who is found in pictures in this book. And thanks to others who allowed their image to appear in this book: Maika, Alexander, Savannah, Nicholas, Bob, Jayna, Rebecca, John Paul, Cristen, Stephanie, Megan, Danielle, Angela, Charlotte, Ashley, and Erin. Also to my sons Jordan and Brandon, who are also pictured in this book.

Thanks to physical therapists Mark Stansberry and Peter Loubert, radiologist George Polanco, and psychologist Bob Van Ooserhout for the discovery of common principles and practices underlying our varied fields. And to David Gillingham and the Mountain

Town Singers—for me the book will remain linked with our joyous experiences of singing together. Thanks to colleagues, clinicians, conductors, and authors whose solutions were collected as examples of multisensory techniques and are further recognized in the body and bibliography of this book.

And finally, thanks to Central Michigan University for the sabbatical leave to put these multisensory techniques into words and graphics. Special thanks to Scott Burgess and Randi L'Hommedieu for the technical support needed to complete this book project.

INTRODUCTION

Anybody with a healthy voice can learn to sing and improve singing far into old age. The truth of this often-argued statement is witnessed in the rise of an excited voice, the low tones of a sad or tired voice, and the wavering of a laugh or cry. The specific aim and purpose with which vocal pitch is varied in everyday lives suggest that these efforts could be redirected and increasingly expanded for purposes of singing.

But there are certain limitations that get in the way of learning to sing, both for beginning and experienced singers. Many of the mechanisms of the voice are inside the body and cannot be readily sensed or directed. Unlike a musical instrument that can be held, observed, and manipulated externally, much of singing remains beyond obvious perception. Even after extensive explanation, hard effort, and lengthy practice, the skills of singing can remain confusing, frustrating, complicated, and hard to pin down.

What makes matters worse is the tendency to judge those who have difficulties in learning to sing as entirely unable to sing or to improve their singing any further. Whether coming from a friend, relative, casual observer, or worst from a choir director or voice teacher with trusted expertise on the subject, such passing judgments can be self-fulfilling prophecies that end progress merely because the singer believes it and stops trying. However, like Michael Jordan who failed to make his high school basketball team yet went on to be perhaps the greatest player ever in the sport, a passing judgment on a singer does not predict the potential to sing or learn to sing. Such a judgment is more a failure of the person who made the judgment to see beyond a singer's current limitations as it is a failure of the singer.

Most anybody can tell when singing does or does not sound good, so it takes more than this to realize future possibilities of a singer. It is one thing to choose singers who can currently sing and use them to advantage in choir or solo situations; it is yet another to help all singers work beyond their current limitations and learn to sing better.

The underlying problem in learning to sing at any level of talent or experience is that *people learn differently*. Beyond knowledge of the voice, voice teachers and choir directors need to have knowledge of how singers learn and have effective strategies to match the different learning styles and life experiences of potential singers. Instead of concluding that someone can or cannot sing or improve in singing, teachers need to tap into the various ways that people learn. Instead of giving up when a singer finds it difficult to learn or improve, methods can be found that both match a singer's current learning strengths and help the singer adapt to new ways of learning.

The Unique Purpose and Approach of This Book

The purpose of this book is to help make singing more tangible and understandable for singers and more externally perceptible and assessable for teachers of singing. This purpose is met in a set of techniques that involve the same external sense of sight, sound, and touch as in learning a mechanical musical instrument, a sport, craft, or other skill.

Using combinations of sight, sound, and touch, and at times the senses of taste and smell, most anybody can learn to sing. With such a multisensory approach, music teachers can learn to teach most anybody.

Learning by Sight

Sight is a strong sense in learning, especially in this visually oriented era of television, computers, video games, and increasing varieties of video devices. However, only some singing efforts can be easily seen, such as posture, facial movement, and the larger motions of breathing. Many of the functions of singing have a small range of motion or are inside the body. To address these problems, physical techniques presented in this book help make small and internal aspects of singing more observable for both teacher and student.

Teaching singing in a choir is even more difficult by sight because of the number of people to observe and the obstructed view of singers standing in a group. Techniques presented in this book are intended to be obvious enough to see at a glance and large enough to see in all singers in a group.

To keep techniques visually learnable, and for those who learn best visually, a variety of graphically enhanced photographs and images are provided. Such images also help those with other learning strengths to develop a better visual sense of learning. Graphics are designed to help visualize objects, sounds, sensations, and directions of movement and sound, and to picture things that typically remain hidden or invisible.

Vocal techniques and method books commonly include images of the structures of the body, ranging from scientifically accurate and detailed illustrations to cartoon-like drawings that get across the general point (Bunch & Vaughn 2004, Paton 2006, Ware 2004). Perhaps the most authoritative visual displays of the physiology of singing are presented in McKinney's (1994) *The Diagnosis & Correction of Vocal Faults* and in his teacher Vennard's (1967) *Singing: The Mechanism and Technic*. However, without a connection to common experiences and sensible solutions, by themselves such images can remain abstract and static, and therefore do not promote a sense of tangible function.

The visual approach to this book is not to fully detail the physiology of the body, which has already been done exceptionally well in other sources, but to support tangible exercises and strategies with a type of visual information that helps make more sense of how to sing. The unique visual approach is to merge pictures of where things are on the inside relative to what things look like and sound like on the outside. This blending places meaningful images in the mind on top of real live events during singing, and is intended to lead to more precise problem solving in learning to sing. A visual sense of movement of body and sound is also attempted in certain images. Picturing the direction and shape of sounds provides powerful insight into the direction of physical efforts and mental decisions during singing. Book images become mental images that help singers visualize sounds that are otherwise invisible and add a sense of sight to what could not be felt.

Learning by Sound

The *sound* of the voice is a primary way to know if a voice is improving. After all, the improved sound of the voice is the main point of learning to sing.

However, judging the voice by its sound only indirectly suggests how to physically improve. Telling a singer to make the voice sound fuller, richer, sweeter, more emotional, like some non-vocal sound, or like one singer or another tells nothing about what it takes to produce that sound with a healthy technique.

Learning to sing by the sound of the voice is a trial and error process in which different solutions are attempted until a desirable sound is produced, which is not a very concrete or objective way to solve problems. Singing primarily by sound may lead to short cuts that involve incorrect and damaging vocal techniques. As the great soprano Beverly Sills said, "There are no short cuts to any place worth going."

Learning to sing by the sound of the voice is a subjective process. Preferences for how a voice should sound vary between and within musical styles and genres, and even from person to person. There are preferences for different vocal sounds within country, jazz, folk, or rock music, and even in the more enduring tradition of operatic singing there are camps and schools of thought as to how the voice should sound. Likewise, there are certain vocal tone qualities implied in this book, but be assured that *the goal is to create options for the voice, to focus on healthy singing in any choice of styles, and to leave the final choice of vocal tone open* to those who use this book.

It is important for teachers and singers to discuss specific preferences for vocal tone. A singer cannot hear what singing sounds like to others, and yet may have strong preferences for the sound that is produced. A singer with a preference for one tone or musical style may find a mismatch with a teacher who directs the voice to sound like another tone or style, and may choose to quit lessons or choir due to this mismatch. Or a singer may simply not be willing to give up control over the direction of vocal sound and therefore resist any outsider's point of view.

A bigger problem than guiding vocal techniques based on the sound of an individual singer is to guide several singers in a choir. A conductor cannot easily hear to get an audible sense of each individual's vocal tone. As the overall choral tone is guided to meet a conductor's preferred tone, it may come at the cost of overexertion and incorrect habits in some singers to balance the lesser efforts and qualities of others. Therefore, exercises presented in this book help conductors localize individual singers' sounds and to hear the effects of individuals on the whole sound, and to allow all singers to achieve a healthful approach to singing.

What is more, this book attempts to make the hearing of vocal sound more concrete and objective. Singing is judged by the specific source, size, and direction of the sound produced instead of by a preferred color of the voice. Exercises lead singers to make objective decisions for the improvement of their own singing. This involves hearing the voice in new ways, for instance listening (a) with both the outer ear and inner ear, (b) for sounds coming out of more places in the body, and (c) to the acoustical results in a room. Such efforts make singing easier instead of fighting to fit the voice to a certain conception of sound.

Learning by Touch

More than other senses, this book focuses on the kinesthetic and tactile sense of *touch*. The most unique feature of the book is to put knowledge of the voice into more tangible action. Learning about the parts of the body that are involved in singing does not teach someone how to sing; it is the movement and result of movement of these parts that need to be experienced, not the labels of the parts. For this reason, photographs, graphics, and written descriptions all aim to get the singer to sense what singing feels like, not merely to see what the physical body looks like during singing.

On the topic of touch, voice teachers commonly touch students to guide and manipulate the techniques of singing. The problem in modern times is that certain interpersonal, moral, and legal implications—and consequences—have led to greater caution and restraint in the teaching of singing. This book addresses this problem in three ways. First, the hands-on approach of this book gets students to more effectively feel for themselves how singing works. Second, students show what is going on during singing using observable movements that guide the student's efforts more concretely and show a voice teacher or choir director what is going on in the student's mind and body. Third, exercises that do require touching a student limit contact to less intrusive areas such as hands, arms, the back of the head, or the upper back, with student permission suggested in each case. Though contact is limited, it still is of a type that has a deep affect on breathing muscles, skeletal position, sense of balance, and overall sensation of singing. Exercises that require contact or the assistance of a teacher or helper are far fewer than exercises that have the singer sense things personally—after all, the point of an education is for students to continue what they have learned without assistance, so it is best to work for independence from the start.

Several approaches to movement have been developed or adapted that meet different problems in learning to sing. The Alexander Technique and its offshoot of Body Mapping are approaches for learning how to move in physiologically correct ways overall, and have been adapted to assist singers to stand and move correctly during singing (Conable 2000, Conable & Conable 2000, Heirich 2005). The Feldenkrais (1972) method of Awareness Through Movement is also a general physiological approach, but uses guided exploration to discover possible movements rather than prescriptions of how the body is to move, and has also been adapted for learning to sing (Nelson & Blades-Zeller 2002). Laban Movement Analysis documents the movement of the body by its effort and shape, and has been used to show how movement helps in choral situations (Hibbard 1994, Holt 1992). An approach originally developed for actors and athletes is Lessac Body Wisdom (Lessac, 1979), which was adapted to guide the kinesthetic senses of relaxation and energy—NRG as he puts it—in learning to use the voice (Lessac, 1997). The Dalcroze Eurythmics approach uniquely uses movement for the purpose of helping people be more musically expressive, and was applied to singing by Caldwell (1994). Cooksey (1999, 2006), a foremost expert on male voice maturation, broadly adapted movement for both vocalises and rehearsal singing, for both creative and efficient body responses to music, to reflect both the technical and expressive aspects of music, and to internalize both the physical and emotional experiences of singing.

This book would not have been written except in finding the set of movements in this multisensory approach to be unique. The book presents the benefits of both exploratory and prescriptive strategies to coordinate observable external movements with internal efforts as well. Though movement is used in finding the unique expressive power of the singing voice, musical interpretation and expression is left for existing approaches to solve. Movements developed for this book are intended simply to make more sense of how to sing.

Learning by Smell and Taste

Smell and *taste* are not typically involved in formal education. However, smell is a powerful sense that is used in this book to more extensively guide efforts of singing. The sense of smell overlaps with other sensations of singing, and therefore is both a barrier and solution to learning how to sing. Taste, which is linked to the sense of smell, is added in select instances to heighten the sensation of internal structures and movements involved in singing.

Learning Through Words

There is another mode of learning unmentioned so far—verbal learning, or learning through words. This includes the preference to learn by being told, the preference for written words, and the ability to visualize words in the mind somewhat like a photographic memory. While being told involves hearing, it is not the same as hearing how something sounds, such as in a recording or a voice teacher providing a vocal example; and while seeing words involves visual learning, it is not the same as seeing something in action, such as a voice teacher demonstrating a technique.

Too often, voice students are taught by talking the singer through the process. Talk should be used with greater caution than other modes of learning because words merely symbolize the actual experiences of singing. Labels, terminology, and descriptions of experiences are merely abstract representations of actual experiences. Further, words are only as meaningful as the experiences associated with the words. Therefore, it is important that words do not guide experiences, but instead that experiences guide the choice of words. This balance was well described by Benjamin Franklin, who said, "Well done is better than well said," and by the composer Virgil Thomson, who said, "The whole point of being a serious musician is to avoid verbalization whenever you can."

As in any professional field, standard terminology of vocal techniques has been developed that represents the agreed upon jargon for the subject matter. However, using correct terminology does not guarantee successful results, or else everybody who reads one of the many expertly written books on vocal techniques would be a successful singer without ever singing a note. Even the most correct and authoritative terminology is not useful when associated with faulty experiences or not connected to sensory experiences at all.

Using verbal descriptions of singing is especially a problem in a choir. Verbal directions would need to be followed by a physical check of how individuals translate terminology into personal sensations of singing. Unless steps are taken to verify how each singer responds, verbally guided exercises will lead to unknown results in each singer's experience.

Even so, instead of limiting the use of terminology, multisensory techniques open up the possibility to use most any terminology as long as successful experiences and sensations come first. This is the logic and psychology of multisensory vocal techniques, and the reason why exercises in this book are listed first and then are supported by background information. The solution presented here is to experience sensations of singing first and allow terminology to flow from the experience, even to allow for the singer to share a personal choice of words before making the connection to "correct" technical terms. The solution is not to define or debate terminology but instead to bring the terminology to life by describing ways to sense, perceive, feel, visualize, hear, and thereby learn how to sing more successfully. The strategy is to *begin directly with physical vocal techniques and label the experiences—if at all—only after having experienced correct singing.*

Learning Through Other Symbol Systems

Beyond the use of spoken and written words, coding systems have been developed to interpret the distinct sounds of pitch, rhythm, and text. The coding systems are adapted to focus attention to the various specific properties involved in music.

Pitch is coded in ways that focus attention to the eight pitches of a major or minor scale, as well as to pitches in between in the chromatic scale and ascending or descending pitches before or after a specific pitch such as a glissando or jazz smear. Numbers one through eight are used to designate each major-scale pitch as it climbs the scale. Pitches are visually associated with lines and spaces up and down a musical staff with appropriate flat and sharp signs for chromatic pitches, and in verbal or written form with letters A through G on a musical staff. Alternatively, generic labels for pitch are provided in the solfége syllable system: *do-re-mi-fa-so-la-ti-do* for the major scale, *do-re-me-fa-so-le-te-do* for a natural parallel minor scale starting on the same *do* pitch, *la-ti-do-re-mi-fa-so-la* for a relative natural minor scale that starts two pitches lower than *do*, and by other various options including the fixed *do* system in which the syllables *do-di-re-ri-mi-fa-fi-so-si-la-li-ti-do* are always associated with the same pitch in the chromatic scale with *do* always associated with the pitch of C.

In rhythm there are systems that assign different syllables to different types of rhythms, such as *Ta Ta* for quarter notes, *ti-ti ti-ti* for eighth notes, *ti-ri-ti-ri ti-ri-ti-ri* for sixteenth notes, and *Trip-e-let* for beats divided three ways. There are systems that use numbers to designate the beat within a metered measure and syllables to divide each beat either four ways, 1-ee-&-a 2-ee-&-a 3-ee-&-a, or three ways, 1-lah-lee 2-la-lee 3-la-lee. Other systems keep syllables consistent for each position in a duple and triple division of a beat, such as Edwin Gordon's *du-ta-de-ta* and *du-da-di* (Dalby, 2005) or *Takadimi* and *Takida* (Ester and others, 2006; Hoffman and others, 1996).

Of course text is designated by alphabetical symbols strung together into words, but this is fraught with problems due to different spellings and pronunciations within English and between different languages. For example, in English the word *pie* rhymes with the words shy and eye, in spite of three different spellings for the same double-vowel sound, but in Latin the same word *pie* has the same pronunciation as in naming the letters P-A and rhymes with the words see-say.

Throughout this book, two systems are used to indicate pronunciations of vowels, consonants, syllables, and words. The first is written in all capital letters and uses commonly understood spellings in the English language (see Table 0.1). This system is used so that most anybody who can read English can figure out the sounds intended by the capital-lettered spellings. The system is adapted from the one used by Royal Stanton in his two publications, *Steps for Singing for Voice Class* (2000) and *The Dynamic Choral Director* (1979). The system is similar to the lower-case tone syllables promoted by Fred Waring (1951), who was known for his professional ensemble The Pennsylvanians, the impeccable diction of his choirs, and his choral publications with these diction spellings written under the text. The second system uses the symbols agreed upon by language experts, the International Phonetics Alphabet (IPA; see examples in Table 0.1; a full chart and description is available free on the Internet, one source being http://www.arts.gla.ac.uk/IPA/ipachart.html). Many of the letters used for pronunciation in IPA are not the ones used in the English language, for example the letter *i* used to indicate the vowel sound in the word *shy* instead of being pronounced as in the English words *pick* or *ill*. In IPA, however, the spellings remain consistent when interpreting the sounds of any language. Just as solfége associates a unique syllable with each pitch, IPA uses a distinct symbol consistently for each sound, so once you learn the system you can pronounce anything that is translated into IPA. Throughout the book, both systems will be listed side by side, such as AH [ɑ], which may take some getting used to.

So why not keep things simple and choose one system as is common in singing technique books (Bunch & Vaughn 2004, Paton 2006, Ware 2004)? Readers who are not familiar with IPA are given the chance to learn more easily at first using the English system, and then to compare back and forth enough to eventually use IPA more on its own. IPA is still there for those who already know it. Also, two systems are more multisensory in that multiple systems require the use of more of the senses.

Combining the Senses Together

By addressing each of the senses in voice lessons and choir rehearsals, learning comes more readily and deeply for singers, and singers end up being more powerful *learners*. From the teacher's perspective, using teaching strategies that address different sensory learning modes sharpens perceptual abilities across a fuller range of senses, and teachers end up being more powerful *teachers*. Every movement can be seen to reveal what the singer is paying attention to and how the singer thinks singing works. A singer's thinking can then be efficiently redirected toward more effective efforts. Movement can even be seen to predict the sound that a singer is about to make, before sound actually comes out. Every perception is merged into a powerful problem-solving tool, with the ability to see and feel sound, see and hear movement, and feel and hear what is seen.

TABLE 0.1 Two Pronunciation Systems

Different English Spellings	English System	International System (IPA)
Vowels		
father, log, heart	AH	[ɑ]
bought, nautical, warm, saw	AW	[ɔ]
pet, friend, heaven	EH	[ɛ]
pit, thing, year, before, devote	IH	[ɪ]
hooray, taste, steak, soufflé, toupee	AY	[e]
free, she, the, steam	EE	[i]
stone, boat, bough, beau	OH	[o]
fruit, room, flu, flue, through	OO	[u]
foot, put	OŎ	[ʊ]
but, rough, the—or—about, potato	UH	[ʌ] or [ə]
grass, ask (long) or at (short)	AE or AH̆	long [a] or short [æ]
Diphthongs		
say, taste, grey	AY or EH+EE	/ei/ or /ɛi/
toy, spoil	OY or OH+EE	/oi/
few, fuel, butane	EW or EE+OO	/iu/
pie, shy, bye	IE or AH+EE	/ai/
so, know	OH or OH+OO	/ou/
now, about	OW or AH+OO	/au/
Examples of Consonants		
cow, kick, quit, torque	K	[k]
chicken, kitchen, kitsch	CH	[tʃ]
sing	NG	[ŋ]
rich	R	[r]
never, pleasure, sir	ER	[ɚ]
burden, early, nerve, birth, world	UR	[ɜ˞]
sir, circus, nurse	S	[s]
sheriff, sure, Schmidt, ocean	SH	[ʃ]
thing	TH	[θ]
those	TH	[ð]
yes	Y	[j]
zenith, jewels, nose	Z	[z]
azure, measure	ZH	[ʒ]

Principles of a Multisensory Approach

More than a set of disconnected strategies, this multisensory approach is grounded in a distinct set of guiding principles. It is more educationally sound to guide your many actions based on a coherent set of principles than to apply many disconnected actions. Understanding the principles upon which this book was developed gives you, the reader, the freedom to think of the vocal techniques presented as samples of a larger potential pool of techniques and strategies. This way, you can more critically consider any vocal and choral technique you may come across through the lens of multisensory learning. You can choose those techniques and strategies from the book that make most sense to you, or find and create others that support these underlying principles. Toward helping you apply these principles, a place to include one of your own exercises is provided at the end of each chapter.

Allow Sound Out

A general guiding principle is that *sound needs to be allowed to come out rather than made to come out*. Incorrect singing often occurs because we try too hard, which brings interfering muscles into the process. More often than not, less effort produces more sound. Therefore, a lot of learning to sing is learning to let go of control, to allow sound to flow without the restrictions that come through our efforts to control singing.

Guided by this principle, exercises are intended to lead to easier singing, a release of sound energy, and a more physically fit and healthy approach. Exercises aim attention to where efforts need to be placed and away from where efforts get in the way.

Sound Goes to What Moves

A second general principle is that *sound goes to what moves*. It fills the spaces we open up, gets trapped in the spaces we close off, pressurizes behind objects that block the path, detours through the spaces we bend, and compacts in the spaces we squeeze.

Because movement on the inside has a way of connecting with the way we look on the outside, and the way we look on the outside has a way of influencing movements on the inside, *we sound like we look like* when we sing. Smile and singing can sound bright and happy, frown and singing can sound hollow and dull, scrunch up and singing can sound tight and stressed, stand tall and wide and singing can sound more uplifting and open. Open the mouth wide and sound spreads wide as it comes out of the mouth, tense the tongue and sound is channeled across the tongue, bend the neck out of line and the path of tone gets cut short, and lift a cheek and sound will lift.

Such connections between physiology and acoustics are behind strategies across this book. Exercises are designed to help the singer become aware of what moves and the sounds that follow. New sounds are discovered by selecting one movement over another, exaggerating a new movement to override an old movement, and by practicing a new movement until it replaces old habits of movement. Same as the old adage, "you become what you practice," your singing improves by practicing what to move.

Taking this principle into choral situations, gestures and movements in the conductor transfer to movements in singers. As a result *a choir sounds like the conductor looks like*. A lazy conducting stance leads to sluggish singers and an unruly tone, an unbalanced conductor stance leads to tilted singers and an unsupported sound, tense conducting gestures leads to stiff singers and a strained tone. In a specific example, signaling the end of a phrase with a finger-pinched cut off can influence singers to close off sound in the throat, whereas a smooth and lifting release can stop sound within a healthy breathing technique. Therefore, develop conducting gestures that promote healthy singing techniques.

Redirect the Senses

A third principle is that *to improve singing is to redirect the senses*. This principle is crucial because our sensory perceptions are limited, because we come to rely on particular senses over others, and because we have no idea what it would be like to sense things differently. Following this principle, exercises refocus senses in new directions and isolate one sense over another until new sensations are discovered in the process of learning to sing. Some of the limitations to be explored, along with suggested directional changes in our efforts, include the following.

1. Singing can sound ugly to the ear as internal vibrations interfere with external hearing, and so *sing by how it feels and not by how it sounds*.

2. Most of our senses point forward, which can aim our singing efforts excessively forward, and so consciously *aim the flow of singing energy backward to compensate for our forward-pointed senses*.

3. The downward pressure of gravity confounds efforts and perceptions of singing, therefore consciously *aim singing efforts upwards, or upside down, to counteract the pressure of gravity*.

4. Much of singing involves internal efforts that are difficult to sense, therefore *use external movements to reveal what is perceived internally and to monitor and guide internal functions*.

5. Our perceptions focus primarily on sensations in and close to the body, therefore *aim singing efforts through and beyond the body to help singing tone travel to a distant destination*.

Sensations and Movements are Linked

A fourth principle is that *a sensation or movement in one part of the body overrides and guides those in another part of the body*. There is constant communication and feedback between different systems of the body. Patterns of movement often work in a highly coordinated fashion, sometimes involving very distant parts of the body. The problem is that conflict can occur between two different patterns, with the conflict causing tension within and across entire systems of the body.

This is a wide-ranging principle of motor learning found in the fields of psychology, physical therapy, biomechanics, kinesiology, neurophysiology, neuroscience, physical medicine, and sports medicine. Physical therapists, for example, work on a problem in one part of the body knowing that the cause may be elsewhere or that it may solve problems in other parts of the body. Medically, this principle explains why a heart attack is felt down an arm or up the neck, why a cold drink or food in the mouth can result in a "brain freeze" headache higher up and forward in the head, and why visual information is needed to maintain balance and coordination.

The principle is also the same as applied in yoga, biofeedback, and many other fields dedicated to improving the body's functioning. For example, yoga uses stretching postures and breathing to help attain a relaxed body, unstressed nervous system, and calm state of mind. Using the example of Awareness Through Movement (Feldenkrais 1972; Nelson & Blades-Zeller 2002), movement explorations are commonly restricted to a joint or area on one side of the body to affect the entire sensation on that side, which then travels to the other side of the body for an extraordinary sense of release, effortless functioning, and well being. A guided imagery example demonstrates that movement is not even necessary for one part of the body to affect another—it is possible to reduce headache symptoms simply by imagining the sensations of submerging a hand in a warm basin of water, the imagined sensation stimulating blood flow to the hand and so reducing the pressure felt in the head.

The principle behind these examples is the same as applied in this book to control intricate patterns of motor learning in singing.

Teach Less and Learn More

Beyond principles that guide singing is an educational principle to guide the teaching of singing. Simply put, *less teaching leads to more learning*. This conclusion comes out of an extensive line of research that is more thoroughly explained in the book *Music Teaching Style* (Gumm 2003a). Other findings that support this basic less-is-more principle include the following:

1. The more time the teacher takes to teach, the less time is allowed for students to be involved in the act of learning.

2. The quicker the pace of learning activity, the more gets done yet at a shallower level of understanding.

3. The more the student is expected to focus externally on the teacher, the less the student focuses on internal and personal sensations and insights.

4. By doing most of the observing, thinking, and deciding, music teachers leave singers merely to act upon the decisions made for them.

5. The tighter the teacher's extrinsic or external control over learning, the less intrinsically students are motivated, the more narrowly learning is confined, the less sense the experience makes to students, and the less insightfully singers think and act on their own.

6. A traditional conductor-decision centered choir mostly attracts singers who already prefer to learn by following a leader's decisions, and to a lesser extent attracts or meets the learning needs of singers who prefer to learn by observation, self-reflection, or personal problem solving.

7. The more singers observe their own progress, reflect on their own experience, and make decisions for themselves, the more they develop learning skills needed for continued self-directed learning beyond formal education.

A traditional teacher-oriented approach neglects sensory learning experiences of students. A full enough variety of learnable teaching skills has been identified that music teachers no longer have an excuse to stick to teaching traditions that only meet the needs of particular types of learners. In this book are provided specific student learning oriented strategies to complement and expand any voice teacher's or conductor's existing teaching style.

Finding Your Own Principles

Principles guide people's actions whether they are consciously in mind or not. For instance, "I love life" is more than a passing sentiment for those whose love of life leads them to be regularly joyous, outgoing, or kind to others. "I'm no good" is a principle that leads many to unnecessary failure. The ideas we believe explain many of the patterns of behavior in our everyday lives. To understand our everyday patterns of behavior requires us to face our principles.

To improve as a singer, voice teacher, or choir conductor requires a critical consideration of the principles behind chosen actions. To help reveal some of your personal principles, skim back through the ideas presented so far in this book, figure out when you agree and disagree, and ask why. The answers to why you agree or disagree put you face to face with your principles. Continue to check when you agree and disagree—and why—as you read the rest of the book.

Fully defining your personal principles is beyond the purposes of this book. However, there are exercises and further discussion of this important topic provided in *Music Teaching Style* (Gumm 2003a). The aim is to help each individual find what works—what makes most sense—in learning and teaching how to sing, and perhaps to find the reasons behind what works for one person or another.

Organization of the Book

This book is divided into five chapters with topics similar to typical vocal techniques books. In multisensory fashion, however, the titles are more than labels. They suggest the active purpose, direction, or function for each vocal-techniques topic.

- Chapter 1, **Breath Energy that Supports Vocal Tone**, provides movement, mental imagery, and scale-singing exercises to guide and assess the functions of the diaphragm, ribcage, and abdominal muscles.

- Chapter 2, **Accurate, Relaxed, and Vibrant Vocal Tone**, provides exercises to guide and assess the functions of the glottis, vocal folds, and larynx, and to put shape to sound wave frequency and beats between frequencies for accurate intonation.

- Chapter 3, **Focused, Lifted, and Resonant Tone**, provides exercises to guide and assess the functions of the pharynx, palate, and nasal cavities and sinuses, and for enhancing vocal timbre and the overtones of the sound wave.

- Chapter 4, **Projection and Release of Sound**, provides exercises to guide and assess the sound leaving the body, the amplitude of the sound wave, and the acoustics of sound in a rehearsal or performance room.

- Chapter 5, **Freedom of Articulators from Other Functions**, provides exercises to guide and assess the movement of the teeth, tongue, lips, and jaw and to separate the functions of these articulators from breathing, tone production, resonance, and projection.

Notice in the progression of chapters the shift from sensing the body's supportive involvement *below and past the vocal cords*, to the areas in the body *around and including the vocal cords*, to the spaces and vibrations in the body *above and beyond the vocal cords*, to the spaces *away from the body*, then back to text articulations that tend to get in between the vocal cord tone and the resonance and projection of that tone (Figure 0.1). The issue of posture is addressed not separately but as it pertains in each chapter to different techniques of singing.

Though chapters are ordered in a logical topic-by-topic sequence, real live problem solving may require that topics be taken out of order to match present needs in singers. Though the book can be methodically studied in sequential order, there is total freedom

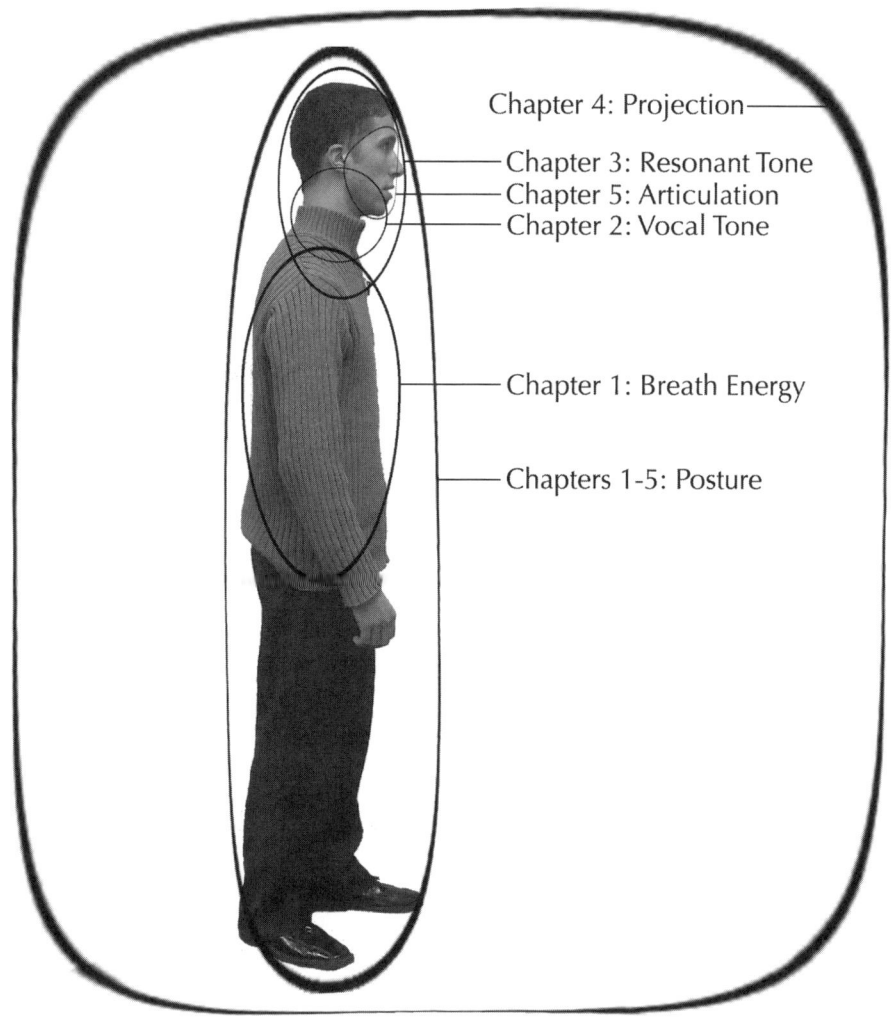

FIGURE 0.1 Chapters are organized to show how tone is supported, produced, resonated, projected, and kept separate from articulation.

to choose a direction of study that best fits a singer or choir. Gray highlights are marked on the side edge of the book to make it easier to find each chapter as problems arise in lessons and rehearsals. Use the quick-reference shadings to flip from one chapter to the next as problem solving leads to a search for specific solutions.

Because the book is written foremost to guide active learning experiences, an **Exercise Sequence** or a **Sensory Experience** starts sections of each chapter. The point of exercises is to guide singers to deliberately experience specific vocal techniques, whereas the point of sensory experiences is to have singers feel and sense things for themselves in free and open-ended exploration or to serve as a checkup or pre-test before direct exercises are prescribed. The main exercises are written to be self-guided if reading the book alone or to be used as instructions to students in voice classes, voice lessons, or choir rehearsals. Sequences are placed in alpha-numerical order when one step is to follow the next, but bullets are used for *critical thinking questions and reflections* that do not necessarily need to be experienced in the order listed. The intent of bulleted items is for singers to reflect upon the learning experience before a teacher provides feedback.

Background Information follows most every exercise in the book. These paragraph subsections are written to be easy to read and yet to provide sufficient technical language to understand the reasons behind each exercise. Though technical information may be familiar to experienced singers, voice teachers, and choir conductors, the multisensory approach may add new techniques and new insights into how different types of learners can be successful.

At times after the basic exercise sequence and background information is provided, additional steps are provided in paragraphs marked **Extended Exercise**. These added steps are provided as alternatives to the basic sequence or for deeper experiences beyond the basic sequence.

Placed in paragraphs marked **For the Voice Teacher**, **For the Choir Director**, or **For the Voice Teacher and Choir Director** are additional exercises and applications of exercises that require the teacher to be more directly involved in guiding the learning experience. These adaptations of exercises are written to maintain the focus on deep student learning even when the teacher takes over control.

Extending beyond the general principles described in the Introduction are specific principles embedded within each subsection, labeled **Important Principles for All Learning**. These principles provide further guidance to voice teachers and choir directors in developing a broader and deeper teaching style. Whereas exercises focus on *vocal* techniques, these principles focus on *learning* and *teaching* techniques.

CHAPTER 1

BREATH ENERGY THAT SUPPORTS VOCAL TONE

Breathing is the foundation, support system, engine, and source of energy of singing, which is the reason to start with this topic. In this chapter are exercises to assess and develop muscles and movements associated with breathing. Strong breathing techniques help solve problems in other areas; without strong breathing techniques, tension problems typically crop up in other areas of tone production, resonance, projection, and articulation. Exercises help move the singer beyond breathing itself to realize the purpose of breathing in singing, which is to support a vibrant vocal tone. Any exercise presented in this chapter can be used as a starting point for warm-ups in personal practice, voice lessons, or choir rehearsals.

Posture

Sensory Experience: Stand With Feet Together or Apart?

Exercise Sequence. A brief exploration of current habits and reactions can help a singer better appreciate new techniques about to be learned. Therefore, on occasion a new topic is introduced with this type of exploration. The following is to help the singer discover a balanced stance for singing.

1. Standing with feet together, have a teacher or trusted helper give the singer a slight unexpected push *forward* on the back.

   - Feel how one foot naturally wants to step forward to keep from falling over.

   - If a step forward is resisted or not taken, notice the off-balance tension required to keep the feet together and remain standing. It is this tension that must be released by finding a more balanced stance.

2. Standing again with feet together, allow one foot to step forward in response to being pushed forward gently against the back.

   - How far did the foot go forward?

- How far does it need to go forward to feel balanced?
- Find a comfortable distance for a balanced stance.

3. Standing again with feet together, have a teacher or helper give the singer a slight unexpected push *sideways* on one shoulder.

    - Feel how one foot naturally wants to step to the side to keep from falling sideways.
    - If a step sideways is resisted or not taken, notice the tension required in the stance. This tension must also be released by finding a more balanced stance.

4. Standing again with feet together, allow one foot to step to the side in response to being pushed gently on the shoulder.

    - How far did the foot go out?
    - How far does it need to go out to feel balanced forward and backward?
    - Find a comfortable distance for a balanced stance, usually about shoulder width apart.

5. Standing with one foot slightly forward and feet about shoulder-width apart, spring or bounce up and down by bending the knees and lifting the heels.

    - Notice the role of loose knees in maintaining balance—*keep the knees from locking back in place once a balanced stance is found*; keep this poised feeling of being ready to spring at any time in the stance.

6. Explore other common sensations where a balanced stance is required, even if extreme and exaggerated, and transfer these sensations to a stance for singing.

    - Act as if shooting a basketball free throw, with a springy balanced stance and light jumpy feeling in the legs.
    - Take the position of a wrestler in standing position ready for an opponent to attack and try to topple you to the ground, the feet apart with one foot forward, the knees bent to maintain balance against the force and weight of the opponent.

- Explore situations familiar to the singer in which a balanced stance has already been experienced—football, baseball, springboard diving, dance, ice skating, aiming at a target with a bow or gun, etc.

Background Information. Posture is a simple and common term that is not so simple to do and not so commonly understood in relation to singing. Three problems are that posture (a) is too often associated only with the issue of breathing, (b) is thought to be a position learned before breathing or singing occurs, and (c) is the wrong word to express the sensations involved in singing.

First, posture is most commonly associated with learning how to breathe. Instead, posture also impacts how we produce a vocal tone, resonate, project, and articulate. Therefore, instead of addressing posture only in this chapter about breathing, the topic is further addressed later in this chapter and in later chapters as different types of problems are considered.

Second, this is the typical place in the order of learning vocal techniques to find a section on posture, just before breathing. However, posture is not merely something to be done before singing takes place because an effective posture for singing cannot be learned outside the act of singing. Instead, posture is what results when finding how to breathe, turn breath into sound, resonate the sound, project the sound, and articulate words freely. Each issue in turn leads to a clearer understanding of the effects of flexible and balanced body alignment on singing. For this reason also, posture is further addressed beyond this section as related issues crop up in different chapters.

And third, the word "posture" can give the impression that the body is to be put into a single immovable position for singing, as in striking a fixed pose. The use of the word commonly leads to a position that is held through muscle tension that keeps the body from freely moving as needed for healthy singing. Alternate words such as stance, position, and alignment likewise suggest to stand or to sit in a fixed pose. Additional directions to use a "tall" posture or to "stand up straight" do not help because they can lead to locked knees and a tense, off-balance, inflexible, or military-like stance that chokes off efforts to sing. Instead, *posture is an experience of flexible and balanced movements that adjust and respond to the changing needs of singing.* So which term is "correct" to use? The suggestion is to first discover responsive flexibility and balance and give it the label that makes most sense to the singer—call it whatever you want in reference to the *experience* of it, even to call it "it" as in "that's *it*, you got *it*."

Extended Exercise. These added steps help in sensing how bending, tilting, and other off-balance postures affect breathing.

7. Get into a standing position.

8. Breathe air out relaxingly.

9. Keep the mouth and throat open as if ready to breathe in, but hold the body from breathing in air without using tension to stop the breathing process—like being frozen in the moment between exhalation and inhalation, muscles still poised to move but not moving.

10. Tilt the shoulders so one is raised and the other is lowered on one side and then the other back and forth, head staying upright and arms dangled at the sides, allowing the spine to curve side to side and the ribcage to bend and sway along with the motion.

11. With the throat kept open in an attitude of inhalation/exhalation, "breathing" noise may be heard as air moves in and out of the lungs, not due to actually breathing but due only to the change in shape of the space surrounding the lungs.

12. As air moves in and out of the lungs in this non-breathing process, breathe slowly in and out to sense the separate movement of air due to the normal breathing process.

13. Repeat this sequence to memorize the sensation of being open to the air contained in the lungs with no tension needed for airflow during breathing for singing.

Two outcomes are intended in this extended exercise experience. First is to sense how change in posture by itself alters the capacity and function of breathing. Poor posture places pressure on the lungs and adversely affects singing. Second is to sense that very little is required for air to move in and out of the lungs. With an open and relaxed throat, air is exchanged effortlessly from the outside air into and out of the lungs. This sensation is to be applied to breathing for singing to replace any tense, pressurized, air-grabbing habits of breathing. This relaxed throat sensation will be explored further in later exercises.

Abdominal Breathing

Sensory Experience: Do Abdominal Muscles Move In or Out?

Exercise Sequence. This exploration is of the direction the abdominal muscles move during exhalation. Do they draw in or extend out? Do the following exercise to find the answer.

1. Place the palm of one hand against the abdominal muscles.

2. Extend the other hand straight out with the index finger held up as a pretend candle (Figure 1.1).

3. Ready to sense the direction that the abdominal muscles move as you do this, blow strong bursts of air at a force that would blow out the candle held at arm's length.

4. Which direction did the muscles move, in or out?

Background Information. The aim of the exercises in this chapter are to *get abdominal muscles flexibly and strongly involved during singing*, and to coordinate with other strong muscles involved in breathing to sing. "Abdominal breathing" is a technical term that by itself does not tell what to do to breath during singing. Are the abdominal muscles supposed to tighten like a brick wall, relax and stay out of the way, or flex and move? If they move, then which direction and when?

Before the "correct" answer to the question is revealed, let me share that there are several approaches to abdominal breathing that are practiced in the field, ranging in direction of movement and area of muscles, high to low. Not to argue other practices, but the technique presented here exercises the upper two rows of abdominal muscles to move in different directions for a more flexible and controlled support of breathing. With this technique, both answers to the quiz can be correct, depending on which muscles were felt to move.

The answer "out" could be an indication that the ribcage is incorrectly held in, which keeps the abdominal muscles from being strongly involved and leaves them to expand out to make room for the expanding belly. The answer that the abdominal muscles move "in" could be an indication that either the entire abdominal area collapses in or that a portion of abdominal muscles move inward.

FIGURE 1.1 Blowing an imaginary candle at a distance helps in sensing abdominal movement.

Instead, in this exercise the middle abdominal muscles move inward in coordination with the strong outward flex of the top muscles.

Lower abdominal muscles are not so much the focus in these exercises. Their function is separate and different from the flexing top abdominal muscles and responsive middle abdominal muscles. Their function is to hold in firmly, and best serve as a durable shield that protects the lower back and organs, especially during lifting. As my physical therapist explained, we are to "breathe behind the shield" of these core protective muscles. As explained to a greater extent later, use of lower abdominal muscles triggers for breath to be held in by closing the throat, or more specifically by closing the glottis or vocal cords. For now, consider this—can you sing and lift a piano at the same time? There is a direct physiological conflict between the use of lower abdominal muscles and breathing for singing. To avoid this conflict, exercises for singing will focus on upper abdominal activity.

For the Voice Teacher. In a teaching situation, watch the singer's hand to verify which way it moves at the point of exhalation. Hold off on sharing what was observed, though, keeping the singer's own perceptions the more important point of the exercise. Check the singer's self-awareness of movement before sharing your perceptions of observed movement.

Important Principle for All Learning. Instead of focusing on the fact that a movement is incorrect, it is more helpful to find out how an incorrect action *correctly* indicates a *different* technique of singing than is aimed for. This follows a principle of the educational expert Jerome Bruner, that *students do not give wrong answers, but give correct answers to the wrong question*. To know the question that was answered correctly is more thorough, meaningful, affirming, and helpful than simply knowing that the singer answered the question incorrectly. In this case, a reply might be, "the answer 'out' is correct for one set of abdominal muscles or when abdominal muscles are allowed to get out of the way; let's go on to explore how else these muscles get involved in singing."

Double-Action Abdominal Movement

Exercise Sequence. This exercise is to replace old ineffective habits by finding and developing the strong double-action movement of the upper rows of abdominal muscles.

1. Blow out vigorously several times in a row, using the candle blow technique (as shown in Figure 1.1) or with a hissed [s] consonant.

2. As you blow repeatedly, use one hand to search for the *top abdominal muscles* that flex *out*.

    a. The muscles should feel like biceps pumping up larger as in a muscle-man pose.

b. If not felt, then extend the imaginary-candle finger further out and blow the air more quickly, focused, and forcefully on the point of the imaginary flame.

c. Check that the throat stays relaxed and open and allows air to flow freely.

3. With one hand touching the top row of muscles, take the fingertips of the second hand and find the *second row of abdominal muscles* that move *in* during exhalation. This row is about two inches below the first and may feel weaker, indented, or perhaps more ticklish to the touch.

4. Holding both hands in place, blow several bursts of air to feel the top row of abs flex out and the second row flex in and up (Figure 1.2). The upper-row flex assists the second row in drawing more strongly in and upward to help force air out of the lungs from below. Use this exercise as a regular warm up to emphasize and develop this dual-action abdominal movement.

5. To stimulate a stronger flexing action in the abdominal muscles, change the hands to fists that flex and churn in coordinated out-and-in efforts (Figure 1.3).

    a. Work to feel the same strong sensation of flexing in the abdominal muscles as felt in the fists.

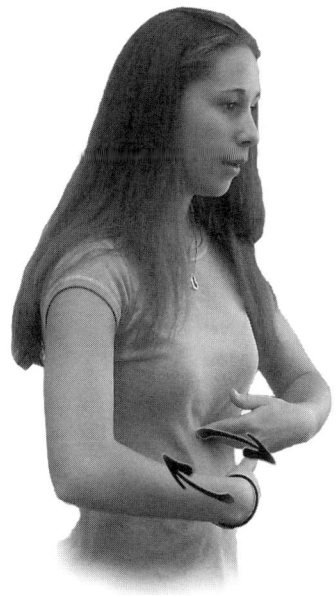

FIGURE 1.2 Hands used to indicate direction of abdominal muscle movement.

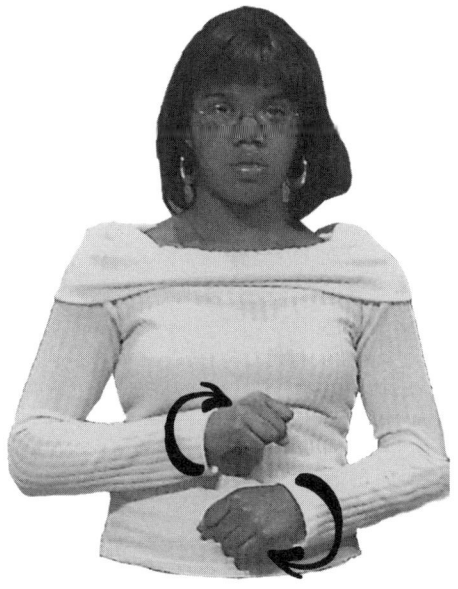

FIGURE 1.3 Fists used to accentuate abdominal flex.

b. Also work to match the outward motion of the upper muscles with an outward curl of the top hand and the in-and-up rotation of the middle muscles with an inward curl of the bottom hand.

c. Use this exercise until you feel an "aerobic burn" and repeat regularly to build stronger abdominal muscles for breathing.

Background Information. As world-class weight lifters, gymnasts, and athletes in other sports have discovered, touching or striking on and around a muscle that is not engaging properly helps activate that muscle, and a clench of one or both hands into a white-knuckled fist can increase by 20% the amount of weight lifted or power exerted (Tsatsouline 2003). Or in combining the two, they will strike a fist into the palm of the other hand. In this multisensory vocal techniques exercise, a touch of the hands is used to train the abdominal muscles how to be involved in breathing, and clenched fists are used to more fully engage those muscles for stronger abdominal support. Repeated use of this exercise helps build muscle and sensitivity to abdominal muscle movement, and helps internalize the sensation until the abdominal muscles remain strongly involved in singing without the external influence of the hands.

Applying the same principle, athletes are also trained to make firm contact with the floor and to squeeze together the gluteus, or buttock muscles. For example, weight lifters will strike down hard on the floor with their feet to excite the nervous system and prepare the muscles for extreme exertion. Less extreme applications can be used to heighten effort in the abdominal muscles indirectly and free the hands for other uses. The muscle activity that comes with gripping down on the floor with the feet or with squeezing the gluts together can be linked to abdominal muscle activity the same as in making a fist or touching the abdominal muscles, even though these activities are farther away in the body. Be careful in these lower-body efforts that the knees do not lock, which can cut off blood circulation and lead to fainting.

Muscle touch, fist clenching, glut tightening, floor gripping, and other possible solutions that follow the same principle serve another purpose in the coordinated efforts of singing. Besides helping to reinforce the function of breathing, they also serve to deflect tension away from the functions of vocal tone, resonant tone, projection and articulation. As the separate functions of singing are explored in later chapters, hold these four muscle-alerting solutions in mind and come back to them as general all-purpose solutions in serving to *focus effort where effort is needed* and *deflect tension from where tension is not needed*.

For the Voice Teacher. The visible techniques in this section replace some need to handle students in getting them to better sense movements of posture and breathing.

However, direct control of breathing is still necessary for some students. For these instances, the following cautious steps are added for consideration.

1. Inform the student ahead that to do this next exercise you need to touch the student's shoulder and hand, and that the student may freely say "no" if uncomfortable in any way, at any time, even after starting. Proceed unless told not to.

2. Ask the student to place a hand on his or her own abdominal muscles, place one of your hands on the singer's hand and the other on the singer's shoulder for balance (Figure 1.4).

3. Ask the student to slowly exhale.

4. During the exhalation, push in on the singer's hand at the spot of the second row of abdominal muscles.

    a. Listen for added air being exhaled.

    b. If no more air comes out, repeat with instructions to relax, open, and give control over to the push of the hand until more air is exhaled.

    c. Push at unexpected times to make sure the student is not anticipating, faking, or incorrectly controlling the exhalation of extra air.

5. With one hand still on the singer's hand and the other hand on the singer's shoulder to help with balance, have the singer sing a tone, then unexpectedly push the singer's abdominal area inward during singing.

    a. Listen for tone to burst freely through and out when the abdominal muscles are pushed in.

    b. If tone is not produced more freely, repeat with instructions to relax, open, and give control over to the push of the hand until tone comes out more freely.

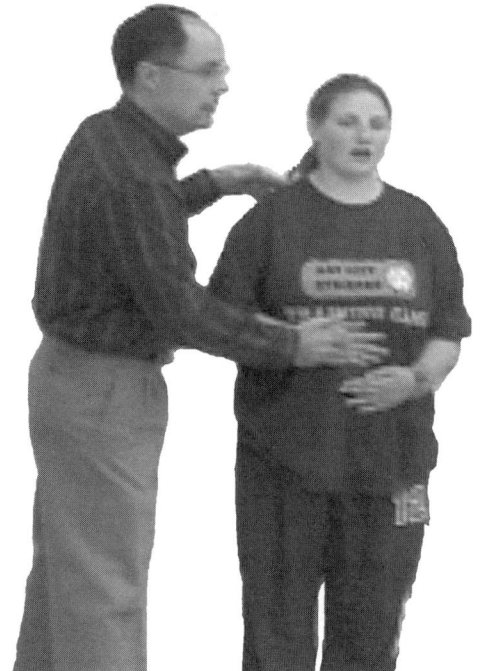

FIGURE 1.4 Voice teacher's abdominal push on top of the singer's own hand.

6. Have the student put his or her own two hands back in contact with the upper two rows of abdominal muscles and experience the same sensations of breathing and singing as when controlled by the teacher.

For the Choir Director. A demonstration of the Figure 1.4 exercise with one or two students in front of the choir may be convincing and accommodating enough for others to sense the same results. However, it may be embarrassing for some, so take care in choosing a brave and trusted subject until a trusting atmosphere is developed across the entire choir. The trick to curbing embarrassment is the success experienced by the demonstrator and observed by the rest of the choir. Obvious results lead singers to trust being chosen to demonstrate in front of the rest of the choir, and some want to experience results for themselves enough to volunteer. The problem with demonstrating is that there is no telling how others in the choir take a demonstration into practice. Therefore, follow the demonstrations by having the entire choir do the touch-abs movement as in Figure 1.2, and then circulate to observe each individual to verify correct breathing technique.

Deep and Relaxed Pant Breath

Exercise Sequence. This exercise compares the sensations and habits of ordinary breathing with breathing during singing. The goal is to use strong abdominal muscles with an open and relaxed throat and without a breathy sound.

1. Place the hands on the abdominal muscles as in Figure 1.2 to start with sharp awareness of upper abdominal muscle movement.

2. Breathe out and in on a steady and deliberate pulse, like a dog may pant slowly and deeply in hot weather.

    a. Feel the quick flex of muscles during exhalation.

    b. Work for abdominal muscles to play a more passive role during inhalation than exhalation as the lungs recoil and draw in air in an instant.

    c. Breathe at a slow enough pace that you experience a full expansion or return to an extended, relaxed position during inhalation.

3. Listen for the noise made during panting, placing the hands on either side of the face to point out the source of the noise, whether from the front of the mouth, back of the mouth, or the base of the throat (Figure 1.5).

4. Relaxingly open the throat until the breathy sound decreases and the source of the sound shifts to the back of the mouth and down to the base of the throat.

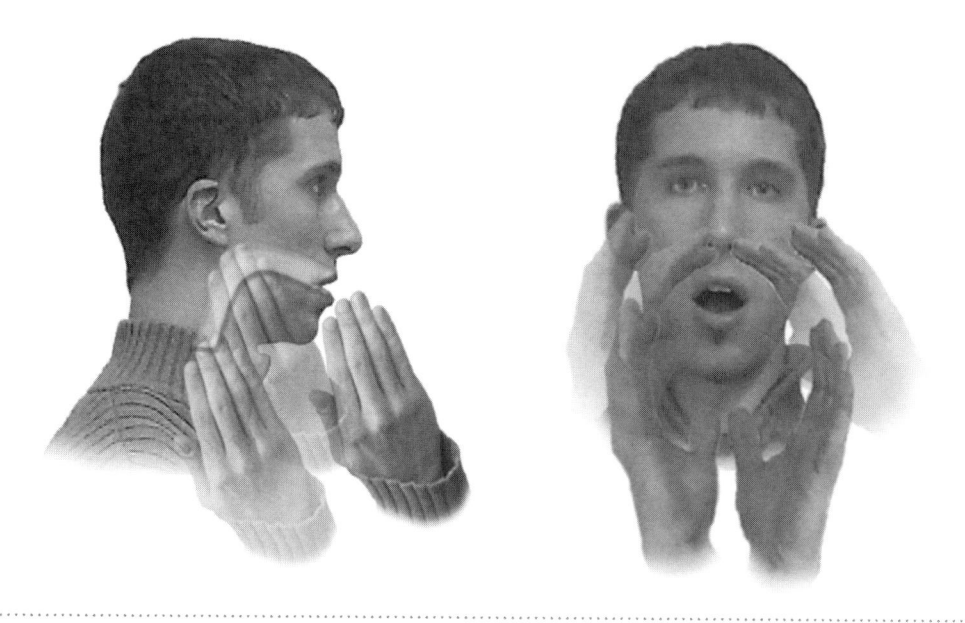

FIGURE 1.5   Hands used to indicate breath noise along the mouth and throat.

a. Move the hands along with the breath noise to sharpen attention and make it more externally obvious.

b. Avoid stretching and expanding the throat or jaw to make extra room; simply relax the throat, allowing the larynx to lower and the jaw to relax and lower.

c. The remaining breath noise should be barely audible and very low in the throat.

Background Information. Strong use of the abdominal muscles may trigger the body's reflex to close the throat, usually not all the way but partly closed as if unsure whether to open for singing or close off for lifting or protecting from being hit in the gut. *The reflex to close the throat is built in to the body to protect internal organs from damage.* When the abdominal muscles are used for lifting or tighten to take a punch in the gut, by reflex the throat seals to hold in air pressure, which further protects the organs. Protecting the internal organs by holding in air is much like how a toy inside a balloon or food in an inflated zip-lock bag stays protected. Under water, closing the throat also serves to hold in available oxygen to keep the brain alert; first priority is to stay conscious because if you go unconscious you will automatically breathe in water and drown.

The response to close the throat is so important to our survival that there is a nerve built in directly from the diaphragm to the larynx, called the phrenic nerve. The phrenic nerve bypasses the brain so no thought is needed for the reflex to happen instantly. The purpose of this exercise and others yet to come is to *get rid of any hints of this reflex in singing and instead send an "all is well" signal* for the larynx to relax and lower and the vocal cords to vibrate freely. For a more extensive study of this reflex phenomenon, see *Singing Technique* (Klein & Schjeide 1981).

You can tell when the throat is partly closed by the sound of noisy breathing or raspy, breathy singing tone. *Noisy breathing is the result of friction* of air molecules against the surfaces of the throat and mouth. The intent of this exercise is to eliminate air friction in breathing, not only because it is a noisy distraction. Like the friction of rubbing hands together dries and calluses the hands, noisy breathing makes the throat and mouth dry, and raspy singing over time can cause calluses to form on the vocal cords.

Extended Exercise. For singers who close off or tense tightly during panting, extend the exercise by mimicking other common breathing experiences. Draw upon familiar experiences for other examples of effective breathing. It is important to begin learning through past experiences so singers can draw upon something familiar as they replace ineffective habits of singing with more effective techniques.

5. Moving an arm forward and backward as if sawing a log, strongly and quickly pant out air as the arm moves with a strong and quick pull-back motion, and relaxingly inhale as the arm moves the imaginary saw quietly forward, ready for the next backward thrust.

    - This action parallels the direction of motion of the abdominal muscles.

6. Play or imagine the ha-ha or chuckle-belly game in which people lie down on the floor in a chain of one person's head on the next person's belly area, the point of which is for everybody to laugh uncontrollably as heads bob up and down, which makes them laugh more, which makes heads bob up and down more.

7. Pretend to be under water and blowing air out in short bursts without closing the throat between bursts.

In a chance meeting with one of my former voice students, he retold the story of the voice lesson in which I filled a work sink with water and actually had him blow air out with his face submerged under water. I had forgotten the extreme measures it took before he experienced open and relaxed exhalation. He claimed that this experience was the turning point in learning how to sing.

Sensory Experience: Is Breathing for Singing the Same as Panting?

Exercise Sequence. So far, breathing alone has been the focus of exercises. This exploration and the following pant-sing exercise take breathing a step beyond to find its purpose in singing—to support a vibrant singing tone. This exercise is intended to detect habits of tension used when producing a singing tone that are not present while panting deeply, openly, and relaxingly without singing.

1. Play a pitch on the piano or pitch pipe in a comfortable singing range, ready to check for what happens before and when the pitch is sung.

2. Breathe out four strong pants and on the fifth beat sing the pitch on an AH [a].

3. When taking the breath to sing the pitch, was breathing suddenly different than when panting? Repeat step 2 until breathing for singing matches the relaxed panting breaths.

   - Did the breathy sound come back in a sudden gasp for air?
   - Did the breath choke or catch in the throat?
   - Was the breath more labored?
   - Was the breath shallower?
   - Did the body stiffen or jerk in any way?

4. When the pitch was sung, did the throat close off or the vocal cords rasp, grind, or stop? Repeat step 2 until the pitch is sung with the same open and relaxed sensation as simpler pant breathing.

5. Was the pitch accurately produced? To sing the pitch accurately in between such strong panting breaths, repeat step 2 until old obstacles get out of the way.

Background Information. The word "support" is used to describe the purpose of breathing, which is to support vocal tone. However, the term can give the impression that breath is like a marble column rigidly holding the weight of a heavy building, or that sound is produced by bearing down or tightening up as when supporting, lifting, or pushing against a heavy object.

Imagine your reflex when being hit in the gut—the abdominal muscles tighten and the throat closes off. Imagine trying to pick up heavy furniture while singing—this kind of support tends to shut down breathing. Weight lifters learn to keep breathing as they lift because closing the throat and not breathing can lead to injury. But singing while lifting?

There are strong muscles involved in breathing, to be sure, but the aim in learning to support a vocal tone is to develop a flexible, flowing, and releasing experience of breathing. *Support in singing means to support a steady stream of vibrant tone*, so breathing for singing requires a release of any conflicting type of "support" that would shut down breathing.

Most often, the first effort to sing with such strong support causes the vocal cords to overshoot the target pitch and go sharp. The voice is accustomed to compensating for a lack of support by using tension to manipulate pitch. When tension is released due to newfound support, pitch aim needs to be readjusted, relearned, and newly stabilized.

For the Voice Teacher. Finding words to describe new sensations of singing can be difficult, and some singers will be flustered, but the point is not so much to find out if the singer is describing the correct sensation or using correct technical language. The point is to connect the parts of the brain that process verbal language with the parts of the brain that process movement and the other senses involved. The *attempt* to verbalize is the bigger purpose, and is the reason that students should talk and describe more than the voice instructor should talk and describe. Also, the movement experience is more important than talking about it, so keep episodes of verbalization brief.

Pant-Sing Exercise

Exercise Sequence. By adding only one sung note for every few pant breaths, singing can become as relaxed and natural as normal breathing.

1. Pant on a steady and even pulse, as in the earlier panting exercise.

2. Sing an AH [ɑ] every fourth pant (Figure 1.6).

3. At the moment a pitch is sung, check for added movements compared to panting. It could be that the head juts out, the neck stiffens, the throat tightens, the jaw grabs or forces open, the face tenses, the eye brows raise, breathing weakens, shoulders raise or jiggle, or the waist bends.

4. Vary between the pant-only exercise to sense the easier breathing pattern and the pant-sing exercise. Repeat until the sung notes are as relaxed and deeply supported as the panting breaths.

FIGURE 1.6 Basic pant-sing exercise.

5. Anticipating how breath supports tone (Chapter 2), resonance (Chapter 3), and projection (Chapter 4), add an arm movement on each sung note that outlines an arc from the larynx, past the eyes and forehead, and out (Figure 1.7).

   a. To compare this with incorrect tone production, motion with a clenched hand drawing out from the jaw and mouth as the *AH* is sung, hearing the harsher results (see Figure 3.7 on the topic of resonance).

   b. Be sure to go back to the upward-and-out motion to habituate the freer release of a deep-breath supported tone.

Background Information. Telling a singer to use "breath" in singing can be mistaken to mean that singing tone (a) is supposed to be breathy and therefore sound breathy, or (b) should follow the same path as breath takes, which is mostly through the mouth. Even some professional singers, voice teachers, and choir directors say too simply that singing tone comes out of the mouth. Without doubt, the mouth opens during singing, but singing tone does not come from the mouth the same as breath comes out.

Instead, *singing is a process of changing air into a vibrant tone*, sort of like water can change properties to steam, ice, or snow. Sound vibrations follow other internal spaces besides through the throat and out of the mouth. Further, sound can travel through skin and bone the same as sound travels through a wall into the next room or as the sound of a booming car stereo travels through closed car windows into another closed car.

The more breath escapes from the mouth during singing, the more breathy the tone, the less breath is transformed into sound vibrations, and the shorter the vocal line due to wasted breath. The Figure 1.7 arm motion draws attention to an upward-and-out release of sound instead of flat-and-compressed path straight from the mouth.

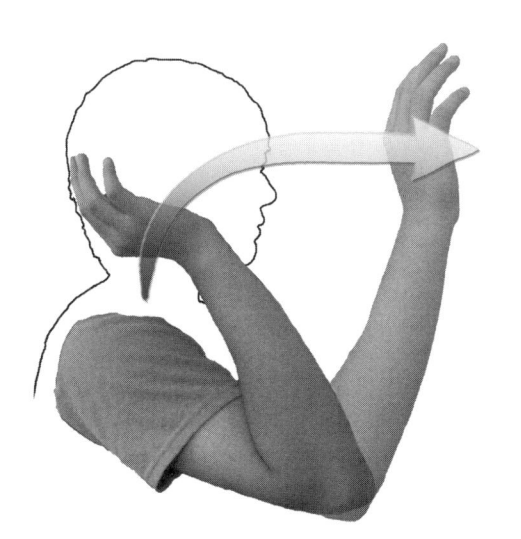

Compared to the first valiant efforts to make singing as relaxed as natural breathing, singers tend to become less careful and attentive when repeating an experience time after time. This exercise trains singers to stay alert every moment of singing. One indication of less alert singing is that the *AH* [ɑ] creeps

FIGURE 1.7 Path of singing tone.

into a muddy UH [ʌ], an issue solved by exercises related to a raised soft palate (Chapter 3) and vowel clarity (Chapter 4).

Extended Exercise. Vary the open-mouth panting exercise with options that add resistance against which the abdominal muscles can push more firmly. Placing resistance at the point that air exits the mouth can help the throat to open and the larynx to lower. This is an insightful experience of what is meant by support—instead of pushing/supporting pressure against partly closed vocal cords or squeezing/supporting tone through narrowed or closed off spaces, breathing muscles actually push against a point of resistance beyond the vocal cords, throat, and larynx. The experience focuses efforts from the source of energy down low to the release of energy out and beyond, leaving the throat and larynx in the middle to relax, stay out of the way, and do their separate work more freely and effectively.

6. Blow air into a curled-finger cupped hand, like a loosely held fist (Figure 1.8) that partly traps the escaping air.

7. Blow with a repeated hissed [s] consonant, as in /s s s s/, feeling the abdominal muscles flex and relax on each hiss and the throat and larynx relax in between.

8. Blow tone through loosely closed lips to make the lips flap and vibrate, like a small child making the sound of a car engine revving up—bbbbmm, bbbbbmm.

9. Blow with an initial voiced consonant such as [b], [d], or [m], feeling the abdominal muscles initially flex harder as they push against the resistance of a closed consonant.

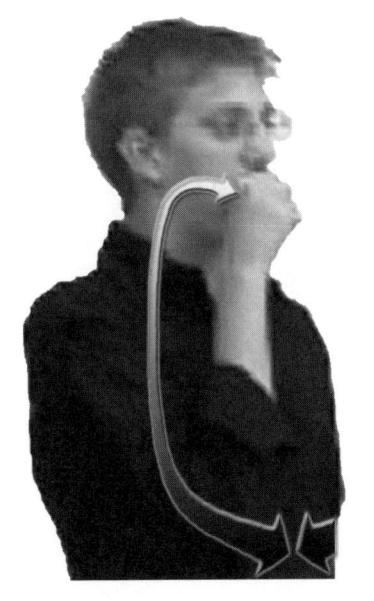

The pant-sing exercise is extended even further by two additional sequences in later chapters. The first is found in Chapter 2 in exploring how breath support helps maintain a vibrant tone as the voice changes pitch (see Pant-Sing on Scale Patterns section and Figure 2.4). The second is found in Chapter 4 in relation to articulation, and explores how breath support helps maintain resonant tone as vowel shapes change (see Pant-sing on Changing Vowels and Syllables

FIGURE 1.8 Blowing into a cupped hand replaces resistance in the vocal cords and throat.

section and Figure 5.2). To continue with the extended pant-sing sequence, go to these subsequent chapter sections; otherwise go on to other exercises in this chapter to continue to develop a sense of deeply involved breathing.

Important Principle for All Learning. It can take great effort to get something right the first time. However, after an initial sense of accomplishment it is common to let down effort as a new accomplishment is repeated. Repeated attempts are lazier versions of the first success.

By comparison, vocal techniques developed in this multisensory approach draw fuller attention to continued efforts to learn. They stack the deck, so to speak, to help maintain full effort until the best technique becomes habit. This becomes a principle of learning that *once is good effort but it takes continued good effort to make good habit*. Instead of being satisfied with discovering a new sensation of singing, work to build a habit of the new sensation through continued fresh and strong efforts.

This shift in thinking is similar to how the old saying "practice makes perfect" has come to be replaced with "only perfect practice makes perfect." However, there is further room for improvement in this saying with words of caution from Dr. Harriet Braiker, author of the bestseller *A Disease to Please* (2001). "Striving for excellence is motivating," but "striving for perfection is a demoralizing and guaranteed formula for failure" (pg. 26). Perfectionism brings tension and stress into the process, which are detrimental to singing efforts.

For the Voice Teacher. Use the following exercise to check that singers do not return to a panic-like breath or become less alert.

1. With your one hand on your own abdomen as in Figures 1.2 or 1.3, signal to the singer when and how slowly to pant-breathe.

2. Using the Figure 1.7 arm gesture with your other hand, signal when to sing the one AH [a] within the pattern of four exhaled pants.

3. Signal to sing on every other breath (pant-sing-pant-sing), in patterns of three (pant-pant-sing-pant-pant-sing), or again in patterns of four, shifting unexpectedly when the singer seems to anticipate the pattern.

4. Signal two or three sung notes in a row, then only signal to breath to allow a few silent pant-breaths in a row, switching back and forth unexpectedly.

5. Repeat the exercise until the singer is sharply alert and singing a tall vowel in a relaxed and unpanicked manner.

For the Choir Director. Use the sequence just described for voice teachers both to similarly direct a group of singers in staying alert and fully engaged in breathing, and to focus a choir on following conducting gestures accurately. Singers can come to see gestures as commonplace and grow unresponsive to conducting. This exercise counteracts that trend. Inattentive singers become obvious when a note is sung alone while other singers are only pant-breathing, and are motivated to stay more alert so to not stick out next time.

One of the classroom management benefits of this and other multisensory exercises is that when students' bodies and perceptions are so involved, they are fully occupied and less able to talk or move otherwise. Learning is therefore more interesting and engaging. Another advantage is that the conductor or a student leader can begin this exercise without any verbal instructions by placing hands on his or her own abdominal muscles to start the pant, signaling when to sing a pitch, and then visually reinforcing student involvement with purposeful eye contact and a nod of the head as singers follow the exercise. Such nonverbal communication further establishes that students are not to add their own out-of-turn talking during music learning. Talk provokes others to talk; action provokes others to action.

Using gestures to guide breathing and singing points out that all gestures used by a conductor have a potential affect on the singing mechanism. This is how choirs come to sound like what the conductor looks like, and why conductors should stand and gesture in ways that support good posture, breathing, and singing tone. Try this as an exercise with the choir.

1. Conduct the pant-sing exercise—or any exercise or passage of music—with a downward-slap motion, with clenched fist tension, with slumped shoulders, with wet-noodle floppy motions, and other exaggerated motions.

2. With each new gesture, look for changes in the singers' visual appearance and listen for changes in vocal tone; some will be very subtle but very telling of how singers respond to gestures.

3. Now use gestures that are abdominal lifting, rib expanding, and breath releasing—those used in the breathing exercises of this chapter or anything similar.

Diaphragmatic Breathing

This series of exercise sequences uses the hand as an extension of the diaphragm so that singers can externally observe and contemplate its internal movement and so a teacher or conductor can observe and verify the student's understanding and awareness of its movement.

Sensory Experience: Does the Diaphragm Move Up or Down?

Exercise Sequence. Before teaching new sensations, explore a singer's current understanding of the function and sensation of the diaphragm. Do this before revealing the correct answer to detect current understanding, awareness, and sense of movement.

1. Place one hand palm down at the base of the ribs, horizontal and about even with the diaphragm (Figure 1.9), ready to move the hand either up or down to match the direction of the diaphragm during inhalation.

2. Take a slow, deep breath and move the hand up or down to show which direction you feel or think the diaphragm is moving as you inhale.

3. Which way did it feel to move or did you think it moved as you took breath in, up or down?

Background Information. "Diaphragmatic breathing" is a technical term that is used in describing correct breathing. However, the diaphragm is always involved in breathing, so simply telling someone to use diaphragmatic breathing or to breath from the diaphragm adds no new intention or function to the process of singing. The diaphragm is not a powerful muscle that demands a singer's attention and effort, so it is not a meaningful direction for guiding physical efforts of breathing for singing. Instead, the aim of the exercises in this chapter is to *have the diaphragm respond to the workings of strong muscles below and around the diaphragm.*

The correct motion for the internal diaphragm is that it actively expands *down* to allow more room for air capacity in the lungs. Many budding singers will move the hand *up*, which indicates either (a) chest breathing, (b) that the singer is sensing the upward movement of the lower ribs that are connected to the diaphragm, or (c) that the singer was guessing due to uncertainty or an inability to sense the movement of the diaphragm.

First, if the singer is using chest breathing you will see a rise in the shoulders, upper chest, collarbone, and possibly also the head

FIGURE 1.9 Diaphragm-hand position.

during inhalation. Chest breathing is shallow and only takes air into the smaller upper lobes of the lungs. This upper chest breathing is the easiest and quickest, yet takes in less air and is the type used in panic or distress.

Second, an upward motion during inhalation could be an indication that the singer may be breathing more deeply yet is sensing the upward movement of the expanding ribs (see the next two exercises), instead of the lowering of the diaphragm. The action of the diaphragm is most supported when the ribs expand at the same time that the diaphragm moves down. *An outward movement of the rib cage and downward movement of the diaphragm together provide the most expansive breath capacity and most vigorous support for singing.* Therefore, use this incorrect answer to transition from the diaphragm-hand exercise to one of the ribcage exercises in the next section to learn the mutual effect of the two areas.

Third, for those who have not yet sensed the movement of the diaphragm, sniff quickly in as if trying to get a quick smell of something. Otherwise, it may take some learners time to grow in awareness of internal movement—do not rush the process; give it time.

For the Voice Teacher. Avoid advising how to breathe "correctly" until the singer has first explored the motion of the diaphragm alone. It builds confidence, receptivity, and motivation to affirm the student's current understanding and helps the student discover improved breathing through personal experience.

For the Choir Director. Used in a choir situation, the diaphragm-hand exercise allows the conductor to assess an entire group on their understanding of diaphragmatic breathing. It is easy to see how many hands went up and how many went down, whom to point out as good examples to others, and to whom to give additional assistance.

Diaphragm Hand Movement

Exercise Sequence. Use this exercise to develop a sharper sense of diaphragmatic movement. The exercise also helps maintain consistent attention to deep breathing.

1. Place a hand parallel to the diaphragm at the base of the ribcage, as shown in Figure 1.9.

2. Move the hand down during inhalation and up during exhalation. Start with slow relaxed breathing either through the nose or mouth.

3. To get a deeper sense of expansion, extend the motion down into the abdominal area, beyond the limited space of the diaphragm's actually movement.

4. Keep the wrist flexible with a curve of the wrist down on inhalation and an arch of the wrist up at the peak of inhalation.

5. Are there any changes in the sensation of breathing? Answers often are that there is more breath capacity, less labored breathing, more expansive breathing, a deeper sensation of breathing, more relaxed and calming breathing, or longer length of breathing.

6. Switch from slow relaxed breathing to a steady-beat pant or hiss; increase the quickness of panting while continuing the diaphragm-hand motion.

    - What must happen for the diaphragm to move quickly and deeply at the same time?

    - Can you stay relaxed, keep from grabbing at the chest-breathing area, and keep the throat open while breathing quickly and deeply?

    - Notice how quickly you are able to fill the lungs deeply with air.

7. Coordinating the diaphragm-hand movement with the Figure 1.7 pant-sing hand gesture, sing an AH [a] on each exhalation. As the diaphragm hand moves up, the pant-sing hand moves up and out. As a result, sense more of a vibrantly flowing "honk" or surge of sound through the path of the sinuses rather than lazily singing from the mouth.

    - Is the tone rich and vibrant?

    - Does it seem to vibrate out many places in the face?

    - Is it easier to produce?

    - Does it require little effort beyond the deep-felt breathing?

    - Rather than "honk," how would you describe this sensation in your own choice of words?

8. Sing a longer tone, moving the diaphragm hand steadily up and beyond the actual diaphragm position. Just keep moving up and up through the length of the singing tone.

    - Can you stay open and vibrant?

9. Even after a correct motion is accomplished, repeat this exercise on a regular basis to maintain an external awareness of the deep sense of breathing.

Background Information. The diaphragm is the shape of a deep dome or parachute, which makes breathing more dynamic than if it were flat. In the diaphragm-hand exercise, the upward arch of the hand, wrist, and arm on exhalation imitates this dome shape. The picture on the right in Figure 1.10 shows that the top of the dome shape is at a level above the base of the sternum, or breast bone, where the ribs rise to meet in front, and that the diaphragm follows the descending contour of the lower ribs. The diaphragm is attached all the way around to the back, where it also attaches to the spine. These attachments make it important to expand the ribcage, which is the focus of the next section.

Extending the hand downward in front of the abdominal area during inhalation focuses attention to what happens below the lowering diaphragm/hand. If the diaphragm expands down, the organs below must move out of the way!

Therefore, consider what must happen during inhalation for the organs to get out of the way. A possible answer is that the belly area must expand out, but this motion

FIGURE 1.10 The dome of the diaphragm follows the curve of the ribs.

conflicts with the strong role of the abdominal muscles. For the diaphragm to move down and yet keep the belly from protruding, the rib cage must expand. As the diaphragm expands down, there may also be a sensation of the organs being pressed down at the base of the belly area, down into the pelvic area. This is the location of a second diaphragm, the pelvic diaphragm, which forms the floor under the internal organs. This diaphragm, too, can learn to expand and lower in deeper breathing, potentially increasing the "all is well" response for the throat the relax open and the larynx to drop relaxingly low. By continuing the effort to relaxingly drop the pelvic diaphragm while singing, the low larynx leads to a consistently warm and full-voiced tone. Work to feel this connection between the flexible movement down into the pelvis and the relaxation of the throat and larynx.

Extended Exercise: Pelvic Diaphragm. Add a motion with the other hand that represents the pelvic diaphragm at the base of the abdomen.

10. With one hand in position parallel to the upper diaphragm, position the second hand at the level of the hips.

11. Move both hands down during inhalation, with the mind connecting the hand movements with the sensation of each diaphragm.

12. During exhalation, delay the rise of the lower diaphragm/hand.

    - What new is sensed?

    - Can you sense the connection between the lowered pelvic diaphragm and a low, relaxed larynx?

    - Does a lower pelvic diaphragm counteract previous sensations of full upward pressure?

Some may actually feel the effects internally, some may not, but everybody can use the movement and imagery to physically guide and mentally understand this process of deep breathing.

Double Hand Push and Resist

Exercise Sequence. This exercise works to develop a balanced resistance to strong efforts to exhale air, leading to a more efficient and economical use of breath for singing.

1. Place one hand palm down in the diaphragm-hand position, as in the previous exercise, and the second hand palm up, below and touching the first in the opposite

direction, fingers pointing to wrists (Figure 1.11). Hold both hands lightly together for the entire exercise.

2. Move both hands down as you inhale deeply.

3. Singing a relaxed-jaw AH [ɑ] on exhalation, push up slowly with the lower hand in the direction the diaphragm is moving, yet resist the upward motion slightly with a downward push with the upper hand, connecting the sensation to a low and relaxed larynx and sense of air and tone flow.

4. Inhale and sing again, exaggerating the upward movement across the first half of breath capacity and downward resistance across the second half of breath capacity.

   - Allow the upward movement to influence breathiness in the tone and the downward push to influence a decrease in sound and airflow.

   - Feel the effects of these exaggerated opposing efforts so you know the difference compared to producing tone with balanced resistance.

5. Experiment with the range of sensations between too much push and too much resistance to find the "sweet spot," the point at which tone is warm, vibrant, and most freely produced.

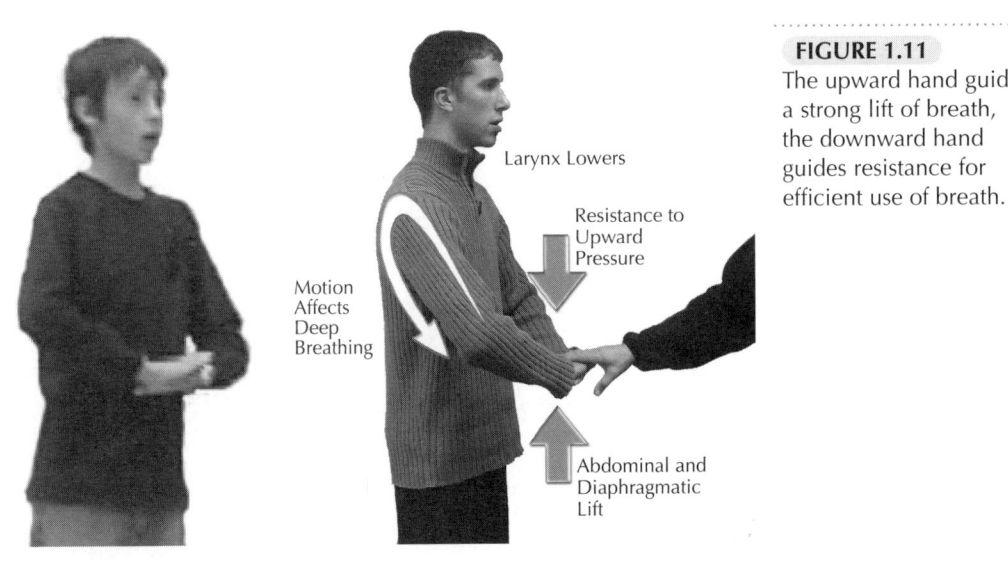

FIGURE 1.11
The upward hand guides a strong lift of breath, the downward hand guides resistance for efficient use of breath.

6. Jiggle or shake the two hands as you sing until the shake affects singing—the arms freely shake the ribs, the ribs freely shake the diaphragm, and the diaphragm freely affects the amount of breath energy. You know this is working when the sound grows louder and softer with each shake.

7. Repeat this sequence until done without tension, with the throat open, the larynx low, and the vocal cords vibrating throughout.

Background Information. Breathing for singing is not all about moving a lot of breath and sound up and out. As experienced in step 4, if too much air comes flooding out then vocal tone is breathy. Breathing to sing should include a sense of resistance to strong exhalation, not like pushing back or closing off, but simply having breathing muscles resist full-throttle movement. The difference is between turning on a hose full blast, water gushing out with great force, and using the hose *as a siphon, letting gravity and flow do the work in a relaxed manner*. Somewhere between a strong blast and a small trickle of breath is a point at which singing tone comes into vibrant and shimmering focus. Tone comes to vibrate freely in and all around with a perfect balance of energy release and flow, a wonderful sensation of singing.

Important Principle for All Learning. It is important at this point to explain the difference between (a) developing awareness of effective breathing techniques, (b) developing stronger breathing techniques, and (c) drawing upon effective breathing techniques for singing.

First, exaggerated effort is often needed to point out or make someone aware of a new technique. In a manner of speaking, sometimes you must magnify a picture in order to see the slight details, or make a very big commotion to get someone's attention. That does not mean that such a large picture or big commotion is needed once the new technique is discovered.

Second, hard and repetitive exercise can build muscle and develop coordination. Borrowing from the language of physical fitness, the suggestion is to repeat exercises regularly and to work up an "aerobic burn," and then to periodically increase the level of activity as new plateaus are reached.

However, this does not mean that every time you sing you must exercise to the full extent. There must come a point that singing does not require full-strength effort. Besides, full-strength effort can lead to tension problems related to lifting, pushing, getting hit in the gut, and drowning—and other overexertion problems in areas explored later in the book. Therefore, the third distinction is to draw from developed techniques only the effort needed to produce a vibrant, artistic tone. Maybe full effort is needed to produce full sound in an early learning stage or when singing habits need to be revived, but at some point full effort starts to overload the system. At this point you must start to work more efficiently rather than more strongly. Do strong workouts and warm-ups, yes, but then ease back for a smooth and efficient experience.

For the Voice Teacher. While a singer is holding the double hand position and doing the breathing exercise, you can influence the effect of resistance by pushing down unexpectedly on the singer's hands (Figure 1.11, right). Pushing on the hands is less disturbing and offensive than pushing directly on the abdomen, though you may still want to warn the student and allow the singer to decline to be touched. The push down on the hands directly influences breathing and singing tone. It carries to the shoulders and into the ribs and diaphragm, causing involuntary bursts of rich singing tone. The singer's reflexive response is to rebalance posture, and in so doing it frees up tension. Have the singer exercise with the teacher pushing down at random until the same tone can be produced under the singer's own control. To exaggerate the maneuver, lock the singer's two hands together in a grasp and pull out, push down, and move side to side until the student balances and lets go of tension, and consequently connects the ribcage and diaphragm to the breath and the breath to the singing tone.

Ribcage Expansion and Costal Breathing

Sensory Experience: Do the Ribs Move During Breathing?

Exercise Sequence. The point of this exploration is to detect current habits of ribcage movement during breathing.

1. Touch the front points of the lowest ribs on either side with the fingertips to sense the movement of the ribcage during breathing, with no pushing or pulling by the hands to influence rib movement.

2. Inhale slowly and deeply.

    - Did the hands reveal any noticeable movement of the ribs?

3. Hang your arms down with your hands held in front, in a "fig leaf" position. How does this restrict the movement of the ribcage and abdominal muscles during breathing?

4. Hang your arms down with your hands meeting behind you at the rear.

    - How does this restrict the movement of the ribcage and abdominal muscles during breathing?

Background Information. The lower ribs should expand during breathing. If they currently do not, it is easy enough to find out how in the next exercise. If they do, perhaps you notice that ribcage movement is restricted when you hold your arms with the hands meeting behind or in front of the body. Beginning singers especially find that they do not know what to do with the hands during singing, and so hold the hands in front, in back, on the hips, in pockets, or perhaps even folded at the chest. These postures can get in the way of singing because they keep the ribcage from moving and stretch the abdominal muscles into a weaker position.

In this book, the hands and arms have an important role in learning to sing—to help sense other movements involved in singing. After exercises are over and done, the hands still have an important role in posture—to stay actively out of the way, hanging at the sides, allowing the ribs and abdominal muscles to assist in breathing. However, even in a neutral position the hands and arms can continue sending signals for other parts of the body to relax, expand, and move to their full potential. Therefore, arms and hands can continue to move, but more slightly and inconspicuously until these guiding movements are internalized into an active and responsive posture for singing. Keep this in mind as you work through the different exercises throughout this book and then move the arms to the side for performance.

Rib Touch Movement

Exercise Sequence. This exercise serves to guide and develop the expansion of the ribcage during inhalation and its contraction during exhalation. The motion of the ribcage complements the motion of the diaphragm to provide a fuller capacity of air in the lungs and a more systematic approach to controlled exhalation during singing.

1. Place the fingertips of each hand to the outermost point of the lowest rib on either side.

2. Breathing in, allow the lower ribs to expand out as a result of increased air, and use the hands only to follow and make the movement more obvious (Figure 1.12).

3. Maintain an extended position of the ribs without breathing out, keeping the throat open; hold in the breath simply by sensing the outward flex of the muscles across the ribcage.

    a. How is breath being held in during this expanded position?

    b. Is the path of the air still open as if air could move in or out at will?

4. Let breath out slowly, either keeping the ribs expanded throughout or waiting until late in the exhalation to allow the ribs to move inwardly.

FIGURE 1.12 Rib-touch hand positions before and after inhalation.

5. Breathe slowly in and out, capturing the full expansion of the ribs during inhalation and maintaining expansion either throughout exhalation or until late in exhalation, repeating until the process seems natural.

Background Information. As previously described, the diaphragm is attached partly to the lowest ribs. Therefore, lifting and expanding the ribs helps the diaphragm to function more dynamically. Muscles around the ribs other than the diaphragm, called the intercostals, are used to raise and expand the ribcage.

"Costal breathing" is a technical term not as common to everyday language. Costal refers to something that is ribbed or ridged, and in the case of singing is associated with the use of the ribs for breathing. Costal cartilages connect most ribs to the sternum (breast bone) or to each other. The space between each pair of ribs is an intercostal space. And different types of costal muscles fill the spaces, run inside (internal intercostals) and outside (external intercostals) across the spaces, both parallel and at an angle to the ribs. The intercostal muscles are the ones that most assist the movement of the ribs during breathing. To keep things simple, most of the discussion will focus on the movement of the ribs and rib cage.

In step 3 of this exercise, the muscular expansion of the ribcage to hold in air replaces a common response to contain and block the air by closing off the throat. Taking the place of closing the throat, the costal muscles hold the ribs out and consequently hold the diaphragm from moving. Air stays in the lungs simply by holding the extended position. The expansion of the ribcage helps bring the diaphragm into a stretched position that on exhalation, like a springy trampoline, gives a more dynamic lift to breathing.

Two options are provided in this exercise during exhalation, either to hold the ribs fully extended at all times with inhalation serving to refresh the sensation of full extension, or to delay the movement of the ribs inwardly. The first option, to maintain full extension at all times, has the advantage of keeping the diaphragm in its most dynamic position and focusing efforts on the upward lift of the abdominal muscles the entire time that singing tone is produced. The second option, to maintain full extension of the ribcage but include the ribcage late in the process, keeps the abdominal muscles in charge to the extent of their range of movement and then allows the ribcage to provide a refreshing late-stage sense of strength and support. Teachers of singers vary on their choice of these options, so the primary point here is to explore which makes most sense and functions best for the individual singer.

For the Voice Teacher and Choir Director. In a voice lesson or choir situation, this exercise allows the teacher to more clearly assess the small motions of the singer's rib cage during breathing. Even in a large choir situation, these movements are noticeable in each singer. An important byproduct is improved monitoring skills, which shifts the underlying focus of teaching *from covering material to uncovering deeper understanding*, and *from giving directions to getting results*.

Finger-hinged Arms Exercise

Exercise Sequence. This exercise leads to a greater awareness of the expansion and contraction along the full height of the ribcage.

1. Place the tips of the extended fingers together, slightly overlapping the fingers like a loose hinge at the top end of the arms (Figure 1.13).

2. Bring the elbows out and up as breath is taken in, and then bring the elbows down and in as breath is exhaled out.

3. Explore answers to the following questions and any questions that crop up in response to the experience of ribcage expansion.

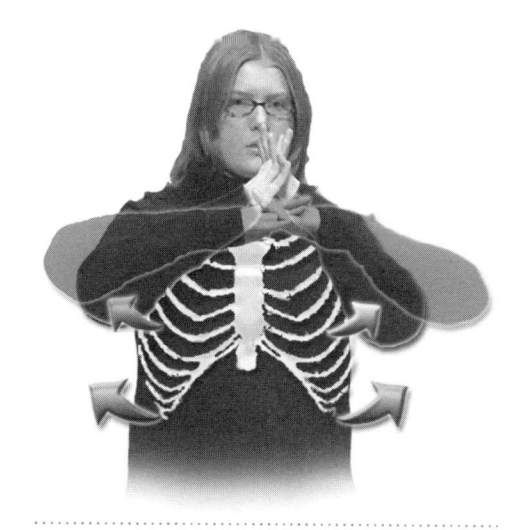

FIGURE 1.13 Rib expansion arm movement.

- What improvements or new sensations are felt in guiding ribcage expansion with the finger-hinged arm motion?

- Where do you feel expansion of the ribs, only at the bottom or also in the middle?

- How does this affect abdominal muscle involvement?

- How is breathing made easier?

- What is the affect of this movement on posture?

Background Information. This full arm motion draws attention away from chest breathing. Hand movement, which corresponds to chest breathing in the area of the upper lobes of the lungs, is restricted. Lower arm movement, which corresponds to the lower rib cage and larger lobes of the lungs, is enhanced. Air may be felt to fill the areas of the ribcage and lungs that correspond with wrist, forearm, and elbow movements.

Thumb-hinged Hand Expansion Exercise

Exercise Sequence. There is another movement involved in using the rib cage for breathing that also needs attention—the ribcage hinge at the spine. The ribcage is not only able to move up and out, it also expands sideways, hinged at the back.

1. Touch the thumbs together to represent the "hinge" movement at the spine.

2. Hold the hands as if holding a large cup, the fingers representing the ribs curving round front (Figure 1.14).

3. Move the fingers away from each other during inhalation and closer together during exhalation, hinging at the thumbs/spine.

FIGURE 1.14 Thumbs represent the hinge at the spine; fingers represent ribs expanding out.

4. At least five related questions can be asked. Explore these and other questions that may arise.

   - What must happen for the ribcage to hinge at the spine and expand sideways?

   - What do the back muscles feel like during expansion?

   - How does his sideways expansion improve and otherwise affect posture?

   - What can now let go of tension and control given this type of expansion?

   - How does this add to the awareness and sensation of the diaphragm inside and the abdominal area below?

5. Using the thumbs to represent the back muscles on either side of the spine "hinge," wiggle the thumbs a bit to stimulate a sharper sense of involvement of the back muscles.

Background Information. This sideways movement helps inflate the lower lobes of the lungs, which of course have the greater air capacity and control than the upper lobes. Because the diaphragm is also attached partly to the spine, this sideways motion may also aid in gaining a fuller awareness of diaphragmatic function.

Notice that the back muscles become much more involved in breathing with this sideways movement. Wiggling the thumbs can feel like a mental muscle massage if the connection is successfully made between the thumbs and back muscles. In first experiences with this motion, the back muscles may cramp or spasm, so be careful to mentally guide with the thumbs to relax and soothe the muscles.

This sideways-expansion exercise changes the notion of posture as a fixed position into a more dynamic sensation of posture. Effort to maintain a fixed posture is reduced as the ribs and spine become more actively involved in defining a flexible stance. The body is aligned in a way that serves breathing most effectively, which is a flexible and moving posture that helps enliven the diaphragmatic function, expands air capacity, and allows interfering muscle tension to relax. The shoulders no longer need to hold a static position, but instead respond with the sideways expansion of the ribcage with a sensation of going along for the ride.

Developing Breath Capacity at Both Ends

Exercise Sequence. In this exercise, breath capacity is increased both in the amount of air that is taken into the lungs and the amount of air that is used.

1. Inhale steadily and slowly to the farthest comfortable extent that the ribs can go—out, up, and sideways—until the back muscles are involved and the back area also expands. Quickly switch between the rib touch, prayer hands, and thumb-hinged hand movements to involve each ribcage movement in the inhalation.

2. Holding the ribs either in place or with the sense that they are still expanding, begin exhaling on a hissed [s] or into a cupped fist with a quick-snap flex of the abdominal muscles. The top row of abdominal muscles will jut quickly out then steadily continue their coordinated movement with the second row of abs.

3. Only after the abdominal muscles are well into their motion, allow the ribcage to move inward. Use the later ribcage movement to increase the quantity of air used, send a fresh signal for the larynx to relax and throat to stay open, and to lengthen exhalation.

   - Did the throat want to squeeze shut toward the end of exhalation? Ignore the body's signal to close the throat and keep moving the abdominal muscles up and the ribcage in beyond the point of this sensation.

4. Repeat to expand breath capacity more fully in the inhalation and to use up more of the breath capacity on the exhalation. Whether each sensation is felt or not in this first experience, this sequence of movements can be exercised for strength and endurance like an athlete.

5. Repeat this exercise sequence with singing until a vibrant tone is achieved for longer periods with no reduction in tone quality.

Background Information. Starting inhalation with a quick flex of abdominal muscles sends a firm and early "all is well" signal for the larynx to lower and the glottis to open. In singing, this quick flex should occur slightly before the vocal cords start turning air into vibration, as if putting a car into gear before applying the accelerator.

At the end of typical exhalation, 20 to 40 percent of the useable or vital breath capacity remains unused in the lungs. By using a combination of upward abdominal muscle movement, inward costal muscle pull, and contracting ribcage movement, breath capacity can be used more to its fullest.

When air is used to this extent, the body sends a warning signal to save the last bit of air, the same as felt when in danger of drowning. Like the low-fuel light on a car that warns the driver to stop and fill up soon, the body warns that the lungs are running out of air and that you need to stop and breathe soon. And just like you can continue to drive the car 50 or so miles further, you can train the body to keep utilizing the lung's air without panic. By continuing abdominal and costal muscle activity, the body's "danger" signal can be replaced by the "all is well" signal. Ignore the danger signal; you are not about to die. Be assured that you are not drowning, you are doing something healthy—you are singing. Therefore, feel safe to dip further into the reserves of your air capacity. When air is out, there is simply no more air to come out, so movement and air stop. There is no need for panic, for the throat to close, for the shoulders to hunch over, or for the chest to collapse. Posture stays open and tall and the throat stays open and relaxed. And breathing is left free to support a vibrant and, literally, a full-bodied tone.

Breathing is the topic of only one of the chapters in this book. However, because breath supports the entire process of singing, this is probably the issue to come back to when problems in other chapters are not readily solved. Improper breathing causes tension that intrudes on tone production by the vocal cords (Chapter 2), closes off sound from going into the resonators (Chapter 3), limits the release and projection of sound (Chapter 4), and tightens the movement of the jaw, tongue, and other articulators (Chapter 5). When abdominal, costal, and diaphragmatic muscles are not involved in singing, muscles farther up come in to help take the place of a lack of breath support. For this reason, when working in other chapters in the book, continuously check posture and breathing as potential causes of problems elsewhere. It could save you time and effort to always keep this most important issue in mind.

Now, extend this chapter by adding a related posture or breathing exercise of your own. Give it a name, describe its benefits and purpose, write it out step by step, and provide some background to how it works and why.

Name of Exercise

Exercise Purpose:

Exercise Sequence:

Background Information:

CHAPTER 2

ACCURATE, RELAXED, AND VIBRANT VOCAL TONE

As defined in Chapter 1 in reference to breathing, *singing is a process of changing air into a vibrant tone*. In this chapter the focus is on the point at which a vibrant tone is produced, a process also called tone production or phonation. Phonation uses the same root word as the words "telephone," "Euphonium," and "phonics," which all have to do with producing sound.

Exercises in this chapter not only help to produce a vibrant tone, but also to produce accurate pitch and remove tension that conflicts with singing. We begin with the most basic property of pitch, which is frequency.

Acoustics: Frequency

Slow and Fast Pitch

Exercise Sequence. Pitch is associated in this exercise with the velocity or speed of sound, using the common experiences of throwing a ball and speaking familiar expressions. The exercise requires a teacher or other musical person to check the accuracy of pitch and make decisions for improvement. The teacher may demonstrate each step for the singer to repeat and match.

1. Hold a soft sponge ball in the dominant hand, or hold an imaginary ball if no ball is available.

2. Say a name or word in a relaxed speaking range with an underhanded throw of the ball that matches the energy released by the voice (Figure 2.1).

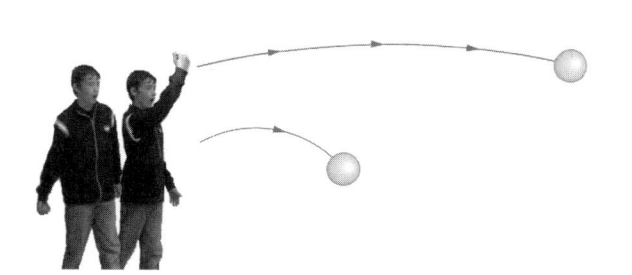

FIGURE 2.1 Ball throws: fast for a high-pitched tone, slow for a low-pitched tone.

3. Using the same throw of the ball, match a pitch in the same range as the speaking voice that is played on the piano or sung by the teacher. Feel and watch the speed of the ball to achieve an accurately sung pitch.

    a. Release the tone at the moment the ball is released, not before or after; fully sense the ball throw in connection with the sensation of singing.

    b. Check that the sung pitch is the same as the one provided and that the ball is thrown at the same energy level as the pitch, slow for a low pitch.

    c. If not accurate, then throw the ball for the singer at a matching distance and speed to the pitch actually sung, as in "that pitch would be correct for this speed and distance from you."

4. Say a bewildered "Whoa!?!" with a loose throw of the ball.

    a. Check that the ball is thrown with moderate energy.

    b. Check that the pitch rises and falls appropriately in a medium range.

    c. If not, demonstrate the throw that would match the singer's incorrect pitch and reinstruct.

5. Match pitches in the same range with the same ball throw speed and energy release.

6. Say a high-pitched and excited "Yippee!" or a cowboy "Yee-haw!" with an overhand throw of the ball that matches the energy released.

    a. Check that the throw is faster and more energetic and that the pitch is higher.

    b. If not, throw the ball harder, matching the voice's energy to its velocity and energy until the voice pops up higher.

7. Match pitches in a high range with the same speed and freedom as felt in the fast ball throw.

    a. If the voice does not respond with an easy high pitched tone, go into a full fast-pitch wind up, body sideways, one leg lifted and curled, the body's weight shifting back on one foot, and release an energetic high pitched tone at the moment the body uncoils with a forward-moving fast ball release.

Background Information. The ability to match pitch is commonly thought to be something that a person either has or will never have. Sadly, many adults report that during childhood they were told by a parent, relative, or music teacher that they were tone deaf, an out-of-tune singer, a monotone, that they had a tin ear or could not keep a tune in a bucket, and told not to sing or to only mouth the words. The belief is also out there that it is too late to learn to sing once adulthood is reached.

This exercise can prove these beliefs wrong, that the ability to match pitch indeed can be learned at any age. In my own experience I have had success with singers of all ages, weeks old to the elderly. Individual successes have varied in degrees up to careers in singing and vocal competition winners, with everybody at least able to successfully match pitch with a pleasant tone.

The sound of pitch is commonly thought to be of greatest importance in learning to match pitch. I have watched music teachers bang the piano harder and louder and tell students to listen harder, just to stop trying and conclude that the person lacks the ability. Attempts to help students match pitch only from the standpoint of hearing pitch are well meaning but incomplete. Research does not support that the auditory mode of learning has any advantage musically and instead that visual and kinesthetic information helps pitch memory and vocal accuracy (Apfelstadt 1986, Sanders 1991, Zikmund 1988). Therefore, singers can more easily sense accurate singing through a variety of modes of learning and recall the sensation by what it sounds like, feels like, and looks like to be in tune.

Pitch matching solutions are found in the body, not in the ear or memory. Solutions are found in everyday experiences in which the person already easily changes pitch. As implied in the first paragraph of the book, anyone who can laugh, cry, raise the voice in excitement, and speak in lower tones of a sad or tired voice should be able to translate these pitch changes into controlled singing. Each of these expressions relates to a condition of the entire body, not something drawn from the ear or pitch memory. A crucial part of the solution is to *stop thinking of pitch as high or low but instead as fast or slow, as high speed or low speed, or as speeding up and slowing down*. A first grade music class early in my career revealed this to me when I asked them to sing higher and pointed up, and the entire class looked up at the ceiling to see what I want pointing at. Instead, people successfully sense pitch as *velocity*, which is acoustically correct because pitch corresponds to the *frequency* or *speed* that a sound wave waves (Figure 2.2). The faster the frequency, the higher the pitch; the slower the frequency, the lower the pitch. Whereas the word "high" often leads to stretch-neck singing, a tight and *high* larynx, and eyebrows stretched *high* to indirectly yank up the pitch, the *speed of a pitch* very easily transfers into appropriate sensations in the body.

"High" Fast Pitch 〰〰〰〰

"Low" Slow Pitch 〰〰〰

FIGURE 2.2 Higher pitches have frequencies that are faster and closer together; lower pitches are slower and farther apart.

Extended Exercise. Compare other sensations that vary in speed. Find the sensation that fits the background of the singer until the sensation is transferred to an accurate release of pitch at different ranges.

8. In baseball, compare the sense of swinging a bat to hit a low grounder, a hit to center field, and a home run.

9. In basketball, compare the sense of shooting a lay up, a free throw, or a long shot from half court.

10. In fishing, compare the sense of dropping a line into the water, casting out to a spot a ways off the boat with a loose flick of the wrist, and a long cast out over the lake.

For the Voice Teacher and Choral Director. In addition to playing a pitch on the piano to indicate a pitch for singers to match, use the piano as a tool to verify the accuracy of solo and choral singing. The task is to match the frequency of a single piano string to assess and guide solo and unison intonation. The feedback to the singers is immediate—when the string vibrates, singers are matching the pitch of the string.

1. Open the lid of the piano fully, and position the singer(s) in a way that singing tone enters the open piano.

2. Play a single pitch on the piano to give the choir the pitch to sing.

3. Release the piano key to silence the string.

4. Hold the same key down gently to silently bring the hammer off the one string.

5. Have the singer or choir sing the pitch and then inhale silently on cue to abruptly stop sound.

6. Listen to whether the one string is ringing clearly, faintly, or not at all.

7. Repeat until the string rings clearly and strongly, which means singing is in tune with the string.

Sound Wave Hand Wave

Exercise Sequence. The purpose of this exercise is to trace the speed at which air is converted into vibration, and to change pitch without adding tension.

1. Singing a pitch in a low range, wave the hand up and down slowly (Figure 2.3).

    a. Move with relaxed and flowing fingers and wrist, as if floating on top of a wave in the water or on a current of air like a kid playing the wind with an arm out the window of a fast moving car.

    b. Synchronize the speed of the hand with a speed that approximates how the sound is felt to wave.

2. Singing the same pitch an octave higher, move the hand twice as fast as before. Transfer a relaxed and loose wave of the hand into a relaxed and free release of tone as high speed.

3. Singing a variety of pitches in a scale or melody, speed up and slow down the hand wave along with the body's sense of pitch speed.

FIGURE 2.3 Matching the speed and shape of a sound wave with the hand.

Background Information. A hand wave is an appropriate motion for learning the sensation of pitch in singing. A sound wave does not tense up to go faster, it simply waves faster in the air with the same ease. Similarly, the hand must relax and free up tension in order to wave faster, and it is this free and fast sensation that is the point of this exercise. Did you notice that the hand cannot go fast when the hand, wrist, or arm are tight? The same goes for the vocal cords that they cannot wave fast when tight, and when relaxed and left to vibrate freely the voice can extend to surprisingly high speeds.

Like a wind band instrument, singing is the process of changing breath into sound vibrations. Contrast this with a piano, which is a percussion instrument with a hammer hitting a string. Like a percussion instrument, singers can mistakenly start tone with a strike of the vocal cords against each other—called a glottal stop because the glottis pushes closed to stop sound. Also contrast this with how a violin or other stringed instrument works, whether by stretching the string to tune it higher, dividing the string by pinching it against the fingerboard, or plucking or scraping across the string to produce a vibration. As in tuning a stringed instrument, singers mistakenly try to stretch the vocal cords tighter by raising the larynx to a higher position. And as in bowing a stringed instrument, singers mistakenly apply pressure against the vocal cords to rasp the sound out. Instead, sound waves are most successfully produced by keeping the larynx low and relaxed so that the vocal cords can freely vibrate faster. This free-flowing vibration is the target sensation of this exercise, the exaggerated arm movements not only guiding this sensation but also serving to override mistaken conceptions of singing.

For the Voice Teacher. For singers who have greater difficulty matching pitch, there are always more solutions to be found that take advantage of different senses to different degrees. Here are a few.

1. If the speed of the singer's own hand movement makes no sense or fails to get results, have the singer watch you demonstrate at an appropriate speed the free-flowing movement of a sound wave as the singer attempts to match pitch.

2. As the singer continues unsuccessfully to match pitch, demonstrate with a sound-wave hand wave the speed at which the incorrect pitches would move, varying the speed along with the pitch sung by the singer to show visually the result of efforts to sing. The singer will sing a more stable pitch at the instant the movement is realized to correspond with the sensation of pitch singing.

3. Ask to take hold of the hand of the singer, either in a handshake or a light grasp along the full length of the fingers. Sing a pitch for the singer to match, and just as the singer attempts to sing, move the singer's hand in a wave at a speed appropriate for the pitch being matched.

a. Often the singer is surprised at the sudden movement and lets out a high-voice expression of surprise that frees up tension and almost by accident matches the target pitch.

b. For added affect on balance and breath energy into the tone, pull the singer's arm to a more extended position as you move it in a wave until the body connects more supportively under the tone.

4. Have the singer do three things: attempt to match the teacher's singing pitch, listen for a third pitch or irritating buzz heard in the ear during these attempts, and watch as the teacher demonstrates the movement of both singers' pitches in two side-by-side hand waves.

a. When the student stays on the same pitch as the target pitch, the teacher waves hands together, side by side at the same speed and with the same relaxed motion in parallel motion.

b. When the singer's pitch is incorrect, wave the hands at different speeds, allowing the sides of the hands to collide with a soft whisking noise to represent the sound made in the air or ear when two pitches collide.

c. Have the singer match repeatedly, working not to "sing the same pitch" but to *eliminate the noise produced by two colliding pitches*.

The third pitch or noise that is the focus of step 4 is produced by the *beats* that occur when two close pitches collide in acoustical space. This is how anybody, not only trained musicians, knows when somebody is not singing the correct pitch. Beats are heard as an irritating noise in the ear. Matching pitch in this process is a matter of getting rid of the beats that occur between two unmatched pitches. When beats go away, the pitches are the same—otherwise said to be matched, in tune, or accurate.

Because most anybody can hear or feel the irritation of beats, most anybody can learn to match pitch by getting rid of the irritation. Some may not even have the sense that the pitches are the same, but they know the beats are gone, which gives the same results of accurate intonation. Another advantage is the smoother and easier tone that singers seem to find when learning to match pitch in this way.

For the Choir Director. Having several singers in one place is the perfect situation for a singer to learn to match pitch—together. Even the most selective choirs can benefit from a clearer understanding of how sound waves function in matching pitch within a section or entire choir. Let us continue the hand-wave sequence in a choral situation.

1. Have a trusted choir member sing a pitch repeatedly as needed in this sequence.

2. Follow step 4 in the previous sequence for voice teachers, with the choir director the one to sing out of tune as the difference between parallel pitches and colliding beats is demonstrated.

    a. Assure the choir that it was you and not the choir member who sang out of tune.

3. Ask the entire choir to show thumbs up when beats are not present and the pitches match, and to show thumbs down when beats are heard and the pitches do not match.

    a. Join the one choir member again in singing, and alternate between perfectly matched singing and slight off-pitch singing.

    b. Watch to evaluate that everybody in the choir is personally sensing the presence and absence of beats correctly, and plan to work individually with those who may need further assistance in this task.

4. Ask the choir to join in and match pitch when pointed to. Point for one individual to sing a pitch, then point for other singers to join in turn, one at a time, until the entire choir is singing without the presence of beats.

    a. Add singers slowly at first to hone your own senses in evaluating each choir member's added sound and so the choir can practice sensing beats.

    b. Feel for subtle sensations of irritation in the ear, watch the air above the singer to focus your senses, and listen for the static of beats in the air.

    c. Every so often ask for the choir to show thumbs up or down to confirm that they are mentally involved in judging the evolving pitch accuracy of the choir.

    d. To not interrupt concentration on the sound of singing, use few words, such as "show me thumbs up or down, beats or no beats," or nonverbally gesture with a quick up-down thumb movement and a look of questioning on the face.

5. At any moment during rehearsal or warm-up singing, call singers to sharper attention to beats by signaling with a sound-wave hand motion or thumbs up or down gesture. For that matter, a quick gesture during a concert can remind singers to use their refined sense of ensemble pitch accuracy to solve and avoid problems in live performance.

There is a special way for choir directors to listen to choral intonation that is based on the presence and absence of beats between pitches. Instead of listening for singers on wrong pitches, listen for static in the air above and around the choir. Intonation problems can be localized and identified by where beats are heard *and felt*. Likewise, when two pitches are not in agreement, there is an absence of clear pitch and tone, as if a dent or hole is in the overall tone of the choir. The sound is weaker because fewer people in that localized area are on the same pitch. At this point the topic of intonation turns into an issue of choral dynamics and sound projection, so this topic will be picked up again in Chapter 4 on the topic of projection. Pitch accuracy, beats, and other technical and musical sources of choral dynamics are discussed in my article in the *Choral Journal* (Gumm 2003b). For a more extensive study of how we perceive pitch, beats, and other acoustical attributes, see *Music Cognition* (Dowling & Harwood 1986) or other source on acoustics and music perception.

Intonation is also affected by whether tone color and vowel color match between singers. Just as more than one pitch collides in air to create irritating beats, more than one tone color or vowel color in a choir collide and affect perception of accurate pitch. This is why some choir directors prefer to call being in tune "being in tone," which is closer to the word "intonation." To develop a clearer unified tone color, work through the techniques of Chapter 3; to develop uniform vowel color, work through Chapter 5.

Pitch Accuracy

Pant-Sing on Scale Patterns

Exercise Sequence. In sequence with the pant-sing exercises in Chapter 1 and the pitch frequency exercises previous in this chapter, next is to maintain breath energy and pitch accuracy as pitch moves around.

1. Exhale on steady pant breaths.

2. Without interruption between breaths, switch to singing a rising and falling scale of pitches, as in the top five-note scale pattern (Figure 2.4, no. 1).

    a. Sing at a pace slow enough that a full inhalation is achieved with the abdominal muscles fully lowering before flexing again on the next tone.

    b. Target the same sensation of support and relaxed phonation up to the highest pitch as felt on the lowest pitch at the start and the end of the pattern.

    c. Memorize the unpanicked sensation of the low pitch as a model for higher pitches.

3. Reflect on the experience by answering these and other questions that arise.

   - Did the quality of tone stay consistent across the entire pattern of pitches?

   - Did breath support stay strong and relaxed and send the same "all is well" signal on each pitch?

4. Keep the same sensation of deeply supported tone into the extended range in a more challenging pitch pattern of alternating thirds (Figure 2.4, no. 2).

5. Pant-sing a melody by producing a fresh tone each beat or twice a beat, keeping each tone steady and supported. For instance, pant-sing on an eighth note pulse—with two staccato tones for each quarter note, four for each half note, and so on. Choose a vowel that seems to match the character of the melody, for instance an OO [u] for a smooth and flowing melody, an AH [a] for a robust or majestic melody, or an OH [o] for a broad and jolly melody.

6. Again, answer questions to reflect on the experience.

   - Did you sense the same relaxed phonation regardless of the range of the pitch?

   - Was the quality of tone more consistent with an absence of panicked tension, whether on a fast rhythm or long held-out pitch in the melody?

Background Information. Even after learning abdominal and costal breathing, there is something about singing scales or a melody that slips a singer back into previous bad habits of tension. The very thought of "singing" conjures up well-worn habits. This is

FIGURE 2.4   Pant sing scale exercise. 1. Five-note rise and fall. 2. Extended-range thirds. Note that commas and rests indicate to breathe after each pitched tone.

why I tell students to never "sing" again for the rest of their lives—from now on only "phonate," only produce a healthy sound with healthy sensations, never to use the old tense "singing" voice again. Remember, once is good effort, but it takes many repetitions without going backwards to make a good habit.

Taking the sensation of pant singing into a melody, an effective approach is to separate pitch from both the rhythm of the melody and the text. By using a neutral vowel, the singer can learn to support a vibrant pitch across the vocal range without having at the same time to address tension problems due to articulation of text. The sensation of tone production on a neutral vowel can be memorized and maintained as text is added, and allows problems of articulation to be detected and solved separately. Getting the sensation of a melody into the body while singing on a neutral vowel also may help solve problems in articulation of text before they ever appear, which is a systematic and proactive approach to learning to sing a melody with a beautiful tone.

Important Principle for All Learning. Notice the pattern of problem solving in vocal techniques: sing on a single note, add an easy rise and fall scale pattern on a neutral vowel, move to more complex scalar or arpeggiated chord patterns, sing a melody or choral part on a neutral vowel, add syllables with different combinations of vowels and consonants, and then sing a melody or choral part with text. It is more effective to isolate sources of problems and solve them separately. It can also happen that a solution to one problem may benefit in solving problems in other areas before they arise. The need to separate problems and the ability to solve problems in one system by solving a problem in another is all due to the strong communication between different areas of the body.

Solfége Syllables and Hand Signs

Exercise Sequence. Solfège syllables (*do, re, mi, fa, so, la, ti, do*) and hand signs are used to distinguish between different pitches. Hand signs are already multisensory in nature, which may explain the effectiveness of the method. Two suggestions to take full advantage of this method are:

1. Sing simple scales and interval patterns, such the example shown in Figure 2.5, using appropriate solfége syllable and hand sign for each pitch.

2. Link the sensations in the arm and hand to the physical sensation of singing and to the sound of the pitch, feeling the effects of the shape of each hand sign on pitch accuracy (Figure 2.5).

    a. The *do* fist lays a firm foundation for the first pitch of the scale, the home pitch.

FIGURE 2.5 A simple interval pattern to practice multisensory solfége syllables and hand signs.

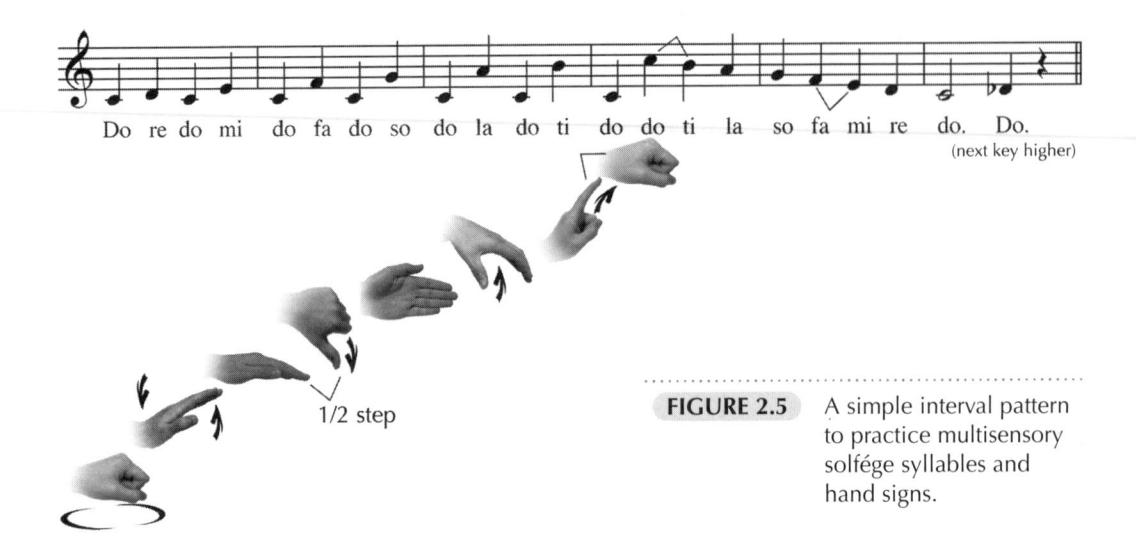

Do re do mi do fa do so do la do ti do do ti la so fa mi re do. Do.
(next key higher)

1/2 step

b. The rising *re* fingertips can vocally lift the voice an accurate whole step from *do*, and the down-turned wrist can be emphasized when the pitch pushes sharp.

c. The *mi* gesture can either float upward buoyantly or rest downward to tune the whole step above *re*.

d. The thumb-down *fa* gestures the close half-step relationship with the pitch *mi* and keeps it from overshooting the interval.

e. The open-handed *so* opens the voice to sing an accurate whole step up from *fa*, which can be under pitch after the previous half step.

f. The lifting hand shape on *la* could not come at a better place in the scale to help the tone to flow and lift at a higher pitch range; the shape can be associated with a raised and arched soft palate.

g. The upward-pointing *ti* gesture likewise helps lift tone, but instead of simply pointing lifelessly up, an active upward move helps draw the pitch up to a half step below *do*.

Background Information. The most effective approach to pitch is to use more of your senses in distinguishing one pitch from another. It is important to realize that the sensation of pitch is already multisensory without the use of verbalized syllables and hand signs. Not only is the sound of pitch heard, but a kinesthetic sense of touch is involved as well. Each pitch has its own intensity of vibration and physical sense of effort that can be felt and memorized. These connections are how singers develop an ability to see a pitch in the written music and sing it correctly with no outside help simply by remembering the feeling in the body at that pitch. This type of "pitch memory" is not about hearing the pitch in the head, though this ability is also possible. Work to connect sight, sound, and feeling to develop a whole-body sensation of pitch that builds upon your natural strengths and newly developed habits.

Solfége syllables and hand signs enhance the multisensory experience of pitch with added verbal, visual, and kinesthetic modes of learning. Because the reason for syllables is to make a clear distinction between different pitches, it makes no sense to *talk* about "do, re, mi, fa" etc. without putting pitch to the syllables. It is most meaningful and consistent to always sing the syllables, even when merely referring to them and especially when teaching somebody what the syllables mean. Syllables designate pitch and *talking is pitched*, so talking *about* the syllables on arbitrary pitches of the speaking voice confuses their purpose and meaning. In this book, when you read the italicized syllables *do-re-mi-fa-so-la-ti-do*, the intention is not for you to hear your voice speak; instead it is intended that you sing them or hear them in your head. If you do not already link pitch to the typed syllables, do so as you reread the last sentence, and then work back through the exercise with pitch associated with each pattern of syllables. Avoid the habit of lazily reading about pitches without committing to singing the pitches out loud or in the mind.

Hand motions assist in pitch accuracy by connecting movement sensations to the distance between pitches and to physical sensations of singing. Because of the problems in thinking of pitch as high and low, explained at an earlier point in the book, it is more important to gesture with lifting, flowing, and floating gestures rather than focus on the fact that the next hand sign is held in a higher position. Holding a static and stiff hand position at each higher level can send the signal to sing with tension, leaving teachers to doubt the effectiveness of hand signals in helping singers' pitch accuracy.

A lot of work can go into learning scale patterns and into singing accurate pitch. Using multisensory techniques can reduce a lot of work to two things—the sensation of a half step and the sensation of a whole step. To help the visual task of reading music, half steps can be marked in a music score with a ^ caret mark between notes (see Figure 2.5) and otherwise assume whole steps, though whole steps can be marked with a sideways]-bracket linking two notes. There are only two half steps in the major scale, between *ti* and *do*, and between *mi* and *fa*; in natural minor the half steps are in the same place if you start the scale on *la* (*la-ti-do-re-mi-fa-so-la*) but fall between *re-me* and *so-le* if you start on *do* (*do-re-me-fa-so-le-te-do*). The rest are whole steps. By feeling the distance within a half step and the difference between a half step and whole step, singing becomes an accurate physical sensation as well as a more accurate hearing and reading sensation.

For the Choir Director. Following is a way to turn the interval pattern in Figure 2.5 into a harmonic exercise.

1. Sing unison on the rising intervals in the first half of Figure 2.5, still using syllables and hand signs if preferred.

2. Across the descending-scale portion in the second half of Figure 2.5, signal to each choir section—SATB, SSA, or whatever section are in the choir—in turn to hold assigned pitches until signaled to resolve to the tonic chord.

    a. For a IV-I cadence, signal for the pitches *do-la-fa-do* to each be held out by a different choir section as the pitches are descended upon, with the middle two pitches resolving to *so* and *mi* on your final signal.

    b. For a V7-I cadence, signal for the pitches *ti-so-fa-re* each to be held out by a different choir section as the pitches are descended upon, with the chord resolving to *do-so-mi-do*, *so* staying the same and other voices resolving to the nearest tonic-chord pitch.

3. Expand the harmonic exercise to pitches outside of the major and diatonic scale.

    a. To assign a cluster chord, divide into eight groups by rows or subsections with each singing one of the pitches in the descending scale *do-ti-la-so-fa-mi-re-do*.

    b. As the choir sings a sustained chord, signal with an upward or downward point of an index finger for specific sections to sing a half step sharp or flat, choosing different pitches out of the chromatic scale *do-ti-te/li-la-le/si-so-sa/fi-fa-mi-me/ri-re-ra/di-do* (the slashes indicate the same pitch as related to neighboring diatonic syllables).

Divided Half Steps

Exercise Sequence. This exercise, adapted from a tuning exercise used by the late Robert Shaw, develops a wide sense of distance between half steps.

1. Hold one hand out front with fingers spread, use the other hand to point to the thumb, and sing *do*; then point to the little finger and sing *ti* a half step lower (Figure 2.6).

2. Move back and forth between *do*-thumb and *ti*-finger several times to get a solid sense of the distance of a half step.

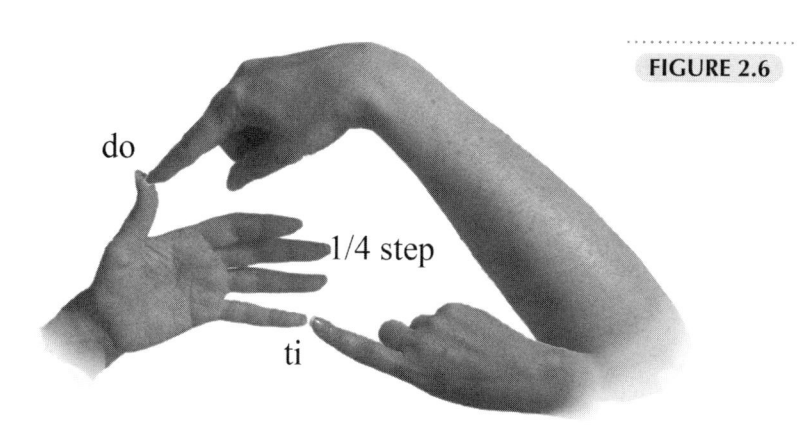

FIGURE 2.6 Signal the division of the half step between *ti* and *do* into 1/4 steps and smaller; do the same for other half step intervals.

3. Divide the half step in half as two quarter steps. Point to the thumb while singing *do*, point to the middle finger while singing *do* on a pitch half the distance between *ti* and *do*, then sing *ti* while pointing to the thumb.

    a. Check with a piano or with pitch memory that the starting and ending pitches are still *do* and *ti*.

    b. Sing back up from *ti*, to the quarter step in between while still singing *ti*, and then to *do*.

    c. Check the piano or memory for accurate starting and ending pitches, that the pitch in the middle did not push the interval beyond an accurate half step.

4. Divide the half step into four steps, pointing to little-ring-index finger and thumb and not singing the next syllable until accurately arriving on the destination pitch.

5. Repeat steps 1-4 for the other half step in the scale, *mi-fa*, and for other half steps outside of the major scale such as *do-di*, *re-ri*, *fa-fi*, *so-si*, and *la-li*, and descending half steps *ti-te*, *la-le*, *so-se*, *mi-me*, *re-ra*.

6. Sing a quarter tone scale, hand signing and singing the next solfége syllable only when accurately on the next scale pitch, as in *do-o, di-i, re-e, ri-i, mi-i, fa-a, fi-i, so-o, si-i, la-a, li-i, ti-i, do; do-o, ti-i, te-e, la-a, le-e, so-o, se-e, fa-a, mi-i, me-e, re-e, ra-a, do*. Verify the accuracy of scale pitches with a piano or relative pitch memory along the way and at the end.

Background Information. Singing accurate pitch takes more than matching someone else or finding the distance between whole- and half-step scale degrees. It also requires a keener sense that there is an entire range of pitches to avoid between scale step degrees. The best way to avoid singing slightly out of tune is to identify and sing the notes to be avoided, then to choose the correct pitches with great certainty. This sensitivity to pitch allows singers to choose from the one pitch that is most in tune with another singer or instrument, or within the key and scale.

Even the *attempt* to sing micro pitches between the half step improves sensitivity to pitch accuracy. Singers do not have to be drilled until micro tones are executed accurately to gain the benefit of pitch sensitivity. The mind is thrown out of the context of a familiar and lazy diatonic scale, so when returning to sing diatonic melodies and harmony parts, singing will be more perceptive to precise intervals and pitches. Therefore, this sequence can be used as a brief warm-up exercise simply to sharpen perception of pitch; otherwise, it can be used to its full extent to develop a stable sense of micro pitch in singing.

Though used as a typical pitch reference, the piano is not a good tool for learning to sing in tune. As discussed more at length in *Lies My Music Teacher Told Me* (Eskelin 2005), the piano is not tuned well for singing in tune. The piano is tuned to divide the *do* to *do* octave into twelve equally-spaced tones, *do-di-re-ri-mi-fa-fi-so-si-la-li-ti-do*, which ends up with pitches that are wrong within keys or scales starting on different pitches A, A#/Bb, C, C#/Db, D, etc. Different intervals are out of tune in different keys and scales because of the attempt to make all half steps equal. Therefore, it is best to learn to sing in tune with little aid from the piano except to get an initial reference pitch or to check that singing has not strayed from a reference pitch. This micro-pitch exercise helps singers adjust the tuning of intervals within scales starting on different pitches, something the piano cannot do.

Lower Larynx

Sensory Experience: Does the Larynx Stay Low or Move High?

Exercise Sequence. The role of the larynx is to stay relaxed and low to allow free and flexible vibrations of the vocal cords. Try this exercise to check its current movement.

1. Touch the front of the larynx.

2. Singing in a rising pitch from low to high, feel the movement of the larynx, or voice box. Avoid pushing or pulling the larynx; only use the hand to sense the movements.

3. Does the larynx move up with the rising pitch, stay low by pushing and tensing, or stay low in a relaxed manner?

Background Information. It can be a frustrating experience to want to keep the larynx low and yet have it raise and lower as if it has a will of its own. The causes of the upward movement of the larynx range from lack of breath support to misconceptions about how pitches are produced, as discussed in the first section of Chapter 2 on the topic of frequency.

If the larynx moves higher when singing higher-speed pitches, it may help to use the other hand in a throwing action as shown in Figure 2.1, a hand wave action as shown in Figure 2.3, or trace the path of tone up and out as shown in Figure 1.7. The relaxed but energetic action of the hand may help release the tension of the larynx and allow it to stay in a low relaxed position. Using strong and active abdominal and costal breathing helps keep the larynx low and relaxed by triggering the "all is well" signal from the diaphragm to the larynx.

The lowering of the larynx is a vocal technique with a long history. The famous tenor, Enrico Caruso, who set the standard for operatic tenors across the twentieth century, worked diligently to lower his larynx to extend his range and regulate his tone quality across the range. The caution in working to lower the larynx is to not push excessively low, but to rather let it stay in a natural buoyant position, and maintain the low buoyancy as pitch rises. The sensation aimed for in the next exercises is not to exaggerate the larynx position but simply to maintain a relaxed and open sensation consistently at any pitch level.

Singing High With a Low-Pitch Sensation

Exercise Sequence. Here is an option that also keeps the larynx low and provides a sense of relaxed singing as higher pitches are sung—memorize what it feels like on a comfortable low pitch.

1. Singing an AH [a] on a pitch that falls from mid to low vocal range, follow the descending pitch with the hand in a downward falling gesture (Figure 2.7), stirring the hand loosely at the bottom to capture the open and comfortable feeling of the lowest pitch. Keep the focus of tone moving up and out as in Figure 1.7 in the last chapter—don't lose what is gained!

2. Repeat several times until the open and relaxed sensation on the bottom pitch and at the bottom of the hand gesture is well memorized.

3. Still moving the hand down and focusing on the sensation of downward singing, choose a moment to sing an upward, rising pitch instead of down. Focus the main attention to the physical sensation of falling notes and hand, and "sneak" the rising pitch in without distracting from the downward sensation.

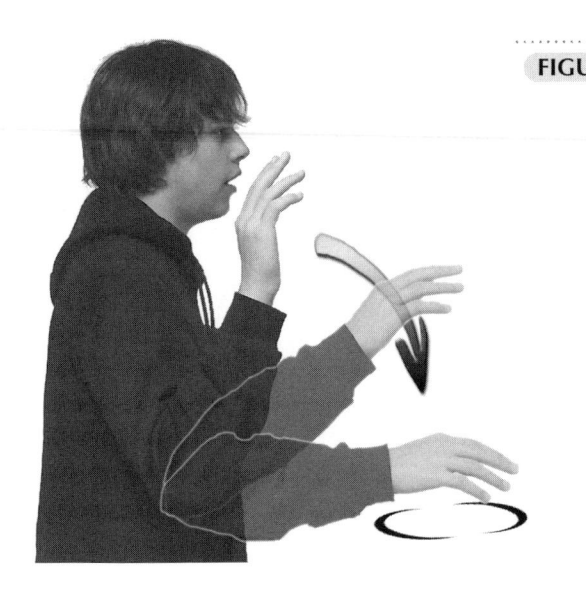

FIGURE 2.7 A falling gesture down to a low, comfortable pitch is used to guide the same comfortable sensation on high notes.

4. Were you able to trick your voice into feeling low when you sang higher? Concentrate and repeat as needed.

Background Information. In this exercise, one simple understanding is all that is needed to sing more correctly in any range, that high singing can be as free and relaxed as low singing. By feeling and habituating the sensation of singing a comfortable note, the body can be convinced to produce tones in any range just as comfortably. The one sense of comfortable singing can overrule all of the many bad habits and misconceptions about how to sing in one habit-changing experience.

Important Principle for All Learning. This type of upside-down experience was the inspiration for the book *A Soprano on Her Head*, which contains similar life lessons so beautifully told by Eloise Ristad (1982). Instead of studying so many technical details and facts about a subject, sometimes a simple, holistic solution is most effective. Every so often, stop digging for details and look at the big picture. Find where learning is simple and successful, and make learning that simple in other situations. This is the principle applied in the next exercise as well.

Open and Relaxed Throat and Glottis

Sword Swallower

Exercise Sequence. The intent of this exercise is to release pressure on the vocal cords and open the glottis and trachea. The exercise also helps keep the larynx in a low position for relaxed phonation.

1. Hold an imaginary sword at shoulder's width, by the handle in one hand and by the blade in the other hand.

2. Like a sword swallower at a circus or carnival, raise the handle up above the head and the tip of the blade going in the mouth, the sword in line to go down the throat (Figure 2.8).

3. Releasing the hand from the tip of the imaginary sword, move the blade smoothly down as if entering into the throat and past the vocal cords. Straighten everything out as the sword comes through—be careful and don't get cut (pretend that hard!).

4. Feel the vocal cords opening to allow the blade to pass. Feel the larynx lower. As the blade continues, feel something drop open at the very base on the neck, between the two collarbones, down into the chest.

5. Perform the sword swallower act all over again, this time singing a tone as the sword passes into the mouth, down the throat, and so on into the chest area.

Background Information. If you are a good play actor, this exercise can bring about new sensations of relaxation and openness like little else can. At the base of the neck is the trachea, which when it opens can open up the potential for vibrations in the hollows of the chest area. Though this experience is related to the topic of resonance, which is to let sound vibrate in more areas, why wait for the next chapter when the sword-swallower experience can get you to experience such openness and deep vibrations that far down in the body.

For the Voice Teacher. In a teacher-student situation, start the exercise by presenting the singer the

FIGURE 2.8 Pretending to be a sword swallower to open the glottis and lower the larynx.

imaginary sword as if a valuable gift. Hand it over in a way that without verbal explanation sets the distance of the arms and length of the sword, and establishes that the object has weight if mimed that way as the sword is handed over. Master the change in tone in this exercise yourself and demonstrate the difference for the singer to observe, which adds to the singer's multisensory experience.

Floppy-throat Hands

Exercise Sequence. As in previous exercises in which sensations of the hands guide sensations in the body, this exercise further develops the sensations of an open glottis and trachea, and a lower larynx position.

1. Holding the elbows up and out in line with the shoulders, relax the wrists so that the hands hang down in front of the throat, at about the width of the throat (Figure 2.9).

2. Sing a single pitch, rising scales, and then any melodic material while relaxing and stirring the hands, flopping the hands down slightly on each new pitch to send a fresh signal of relaxation and openness.

   - Is the throat able to stay open and relaxed on every note, low to high?

   - Does breath feel more accessible for singing?

FIGURE 2.9 Floppy hands to guide an open, relaxed position for singing.

- Is sound vibrating down into the chest area and more easily up into the head? (This will be discussed further in Chapter 4.)

- Is the jaw relaxingly opening as part of the experience? (This will be discussed further in Chapter 5.)

Background Information. Each chapter topic is so interconnected with the others that solving one issue often solves another. In this exercise, a low relaxed larynx and an open throat allow breath to be drawn more directly, the vocal cords to vibrate efficiently, and tone to travel more freely out and into the room. This is why in practice this book should not necessarily be followed in the order it is written, but instead be guided from section to section and from chapter to chapter in response to new problems as they become obvious and need sorting out.

Upside-Down Funnel

Exercise Sequence. The purpose of this exercise is to help move the sense of openness and relaxation of an open glottis and low larynx into the upper throat (pharynx) and sinuses. The hand gesture starts by "conducting" the glottis open on an initial low pitch and moves this open sensation higher as pitch rises.

1. Hold the hands out with the fingertips close and the palms of the hands farther apart, in the shape of a pyramid or upside-down funnel (Figure 2.10).

FIGURE 2.10 Upside-down funnel hand gestures open on top as pitch rises to open the pharynx and sinuses to sound.

2. Starting on a low note and ascending higher on rising patterns (e.g. *do-re-mi-fa-so*) or rising and falling patterns (e.g. *do-re-mi-fa-so-fa-mi-re-do*), move the fingers farther apart as you sing higher until the hands are like a wide right-side-up funnel on the top note.

   a. Use the movement to help carry the relaxed and open feel of the low note up to the highest note.

   b. If first attempts are stiff or otherwise unsuccessful, exaggerate the hand movement with a grander outward flop (like the man in Figure 2.10 is doing) until a more open and relaxed sensation is achieved.

3. Verify the results of the experience.

   - Did the tone quality and sensation on the top better match that of the lower note?

   - What stayed open where you typically want to close off?

4. Pay no attention to how high you are singing—only pay attention to maintaining the sensation of low singing in every note—as you sing scales a half step higher each time (D, E-flat, E, F, etc.), going back to a lower range as soon as tension creeps back in, until an open and deeply relaxed sensation is achieved in a high vocal range.

5. Having paid no attention to how high you sang, go back now and check.

   a. Were you able to sing higher than you typically sing or ever have before?

   b. Did the voice make a smooth transition into a lighter and higher head voice with little change in tone quality?

6. Sing other scale or melody patterns, maintaining a relaxed sensation and free release of tone on high notes by flopping the hands out to the side on high pitches.

Background Information. A common habit especially in novice singers is to close off space as pitch goes higher, as if trying to ram the sound through a smaller space. The acoustics of sound partly explain this. Because frequency gets faster and closer together as pitch goes higher (compare again the top and bottom pictures in Figure 2.2), in any given space there are more waves and more intense sensations than with low pitches. Intensity can be mistaken for tension and pressure, to which muscles respond by trying to help out with a squeeze and a push. Instead of trying to push sound through a tighter space, this exercise works to open up to let sound out. Instead of ramming down the door, it opens up a window and welcomes sound to come through.

You may have heard the saying, "mind over matter." In this exercise it is the mind that must stay out of the picture and allow physical matters to take over. By concentrating on the multiple sensations of seeing and feeling, the ear is shut off from hearing—and the mind from judging—the sound. This takes us back to the principle to *sing by how it feels rather than how it sounds*. By ignoring the pitch that is sung, the voice responds with relaxed phonation on notes typically produced with tension. Sometimes it takes very large gestures to get the mind to let go of control. The larger the movement, the stronger the signal through the nervous system, and the less room there is for attention to sway back to worrying about how high you are singing.

Important Principle for All Learning. As soon as the mind starts thinking about what you are doing, it puts limits on the possibility to do better, not only physical limits but mental beliefs that keep the body from responding in new ways. If you have not done something before, the mind keeps you from doing something new on the belief that you cannot. It is a self-fulfilling prophecy to think you cannot do something and therefore never do what it takes to accomplish it. Instead, focus on fully experiencing the actions and senses involved in the new task. You will go beyond old notions of your limitations and instead be convinced to change your mind about your learning potential. The same goes with a teacher's attitude toward singers, that *judgments of a singer's potential or lack of potential can become a self-fulfilling prophecy*. Avoid predicting a singer's potential and help the singer avoid self-predicting, and with effort in the right direction the singer may go farther than ever expected. Believe in human potential, our bodies are built for singing!

For the Voice Teacher. Tension in singing will be obvious in tense hand motions in this exercise. Most often, singer's hand movements will look like the singer sounds, so work on getting the hand movement to be relaxed and floppy. It may take a demonstration or require taking hold of an arm, by permission, to get the singer to sense a relaxed outward flop on the top note.

Vocal Fold Pressure

"Uh-huh" Glottis Press and Release

Exercise Sequence. A typical habit in novice singers is to start singing with the vocal folds touching, as when someone replies no by saying "uh-uh," indicates trouble by saying "uh-oh," or responds yes by saying "uh-huh." The intent of this exercise is to learn to keep the vocal folds from unintentionally touching or tensing toward a closed glottis position during phonation. Instead, singing starts smoothly and comfortably, with no initial tension. The fingers represent the vocal cords.

1. Push the fingertips tensely together in a V-shape pointing away from the body, say "Uh-uh," and at the same time move the fingers open (Figure 2.11), repeating the move twice, once for each of the two "uh"s.

2. Check for correct sensations.

   - Feel the closure of the glottis as the vocal cords come together; connect this feeling to the tensely closed fingertips.

   - Feel the release of pressure as the glottis opens and the sound comes through; connect this feeling to the opening of the fingers and release of tension.

3. Saying "Uh-huh," start with the same fingers-together and fingers-release movement for "Uh," but follow up by keeping the fingers apart as you say "huh."

   a. Repeat the "Uh-huh" expression and movement to feel the difference between starting with vocal cords pressed together on "Uh" and starting with vocal cords apart on "huh."

FIGURE 2.11 Closed and open glottis hand movements train attention to starting sound on a stream of air rather than with tension and pressure around the vocal cords.

4. Keeping the fingers apart to guide the vocal cords to stay apart, sing a tone that starts with a smooth vibration without the glitch of a glottal stop and without an airy "h".

5. Hold the fingers apart as you sing a scale or melody, concentrating on a sensation of relaxation and warm vibration around the vocal cords.

6. Check for signs of success.

    a. How much more vibrant was the tone?

    b. How much easier or comfortable was it to sing?

    c. Where did tension go away?

    d. Did tone rise up higher and more freely than usual?

Background Information. A glottal stop is when the vocal cords are touching, which traps breath and causes pressure to build up underneath. The sudden release of pressure causes a strong flood of tone, but not before the vocal cords clash and wear a bit.

People use this type of tension as part of their image. Young teen boys put this tension in their voice to sound low and mature before their voices actually drop—a reflection of the image crisis of adolescence. Some keep tension on the vocal cords as a part of a sassy, sly, emotional, or hip style of singing—a trademark of the Britney Spears and Jessica Simpson generation of singers and the cause of cancelled concerts due to vocal fatigue. Country star Kenny Rogers' characteristic grinding quality, used selectively in the music to add an emotional edge, was undoubtedly the cause of a loss of vocal range across his career and something he spoke about in media interviews. Actors and actresses speak with such tension on the vocal cords to express harsh emotions, to sound very old, to express exhaustion, or come across as tough or sultry—think Demi Moore or Betty Davis. Bill Clinton has a raspy, hoarse quality that helps him come across as rather folksy, a habit that caused severe vocal fatigue during his presidential campaigns. Such pressure on the vocal cords is also the cause, I suspect, of permanent vocal damage experienced by *The Sound of Music* star Julie Andrews after she added a masculine gruffness to her voice to play a woman impersonating a man who impersonates a woman in *Victor/Victoria* on Broadway.

This type of pressure on the vocal cords is also due to a lack of breath support. Problems solved by this exercise are also solved by using the series of pant-singing exercises that extends across several chapters in this book. The all-is-well signal sent from healthy diaphragmatic movement can work to reduce vocal pressure from below, and the exercises in this section work to reduce vocal pressure through direct attention to the vocal cords.

Constant repetition of harsh pressure on the vocal cords can lead to temporary or permanent loss of voice due to calluses and blisters, called vocal nodes or nodules. Sing with a healthy habit and the voice can stay vibrant and youthful well into old age. Controlled use of the glottal stop or glottal pressure is safe enough if a more vibrant technique is otherwise used to maintain the healthy function of the vocal cords.

Aim for the Back of the Vocal Cords

Exercise Sequence. This exercise focuses on releasing pressure around the vocal cords.

1. Hold the fingertips together in a V shape pointed away from the body as shown in Figure 2.12.

2. Watching the front tip of the V shaped hands, aim air pressure forward as if singing at the front tip of the vocal cords (Figure 2.12, left).

3. Notice any stress accompanied by this incorrect technique.

   - Did air escape through the vocal cords, producing an airy quality to the tone?

   - Did air feel trapped toward the front of the larynx or under the vocal cords?

4. Watching the more open end at the back of the V shape, put a sense in the heel of the hand and in the arms as if the V is spreading open (Figure 2.12, right), and sing into this more open space at the back.

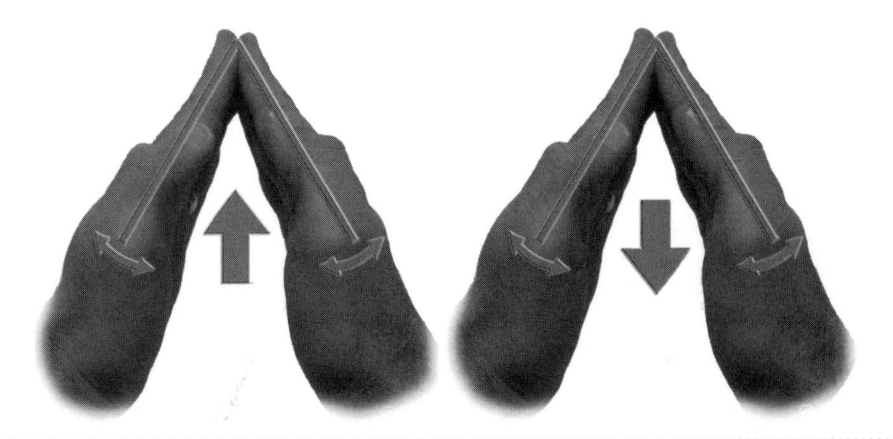

FIGURE 2.12 Hands in a V, on the left the direction of effort aims toward the narrower opening at the front of the vocal cords; and on the right the direction of effort is toward the back, which swings wider and narrower in forming a sound wave.

a. If open too much, air will escape, so find the right balance where the tone is most vibrant.

b. Work between too much push and too much openness until the experience would match the meaning of the word "equilibration," equal pressure above and below with the most air turned into vibrant tone.

Background Information. Let us take a closer look at the definition of singing that has been carried throughout this book so far, that *singing is a process of changing air into a vibrant tone*. There are two other possibilities for the air that are considered in this exercise: that air escapes without being turned into a vibration, and that air is trapped and not allowed to come out. In the first case, part of the vocal cords do not fold together properly, remaining an excessive distance apart and letting air escape. In the second case, tension on the vocal cords keeps them held tighter than they need to be for phonation, which traps air under the vocal cords and builds up air pressure. So let us enhance this definition by saying that *singing is an efficient process of changing the most air into a vibrant tone*, without either letting air escape as noisy air or holding air in, causing raspy tone.

A vibrant tone is the result of little air escaping and little air being held in. This allows an *equilibration* of air pressure above and below the vocal cords. This is the sensation aimed for throughout this chapter, and the particular focus of this exercise. With the hands as an external model of the vocal cords, efforts can more directly focus on pulling pressure off of the front of the vocal cords where air is pressurized, and instead aiming visually and kinesthetically for the vibration to occur farther back along the fuller length and opening of the vocal cords. In this way, more air is turned into sound, less air escapes out of tense vocal cords, and less air is trapped in the smaller frontal portion of the vocal cords.

Arm Push Game

Exercise Sequence. A kid's game is the source of this exercise, which works to develop a sense of released tone rather than pushed.

1. Stand in a narrow door opening and push the arms out to the side against the doorframe, or have a teacher or trusted helper hold the arms firmly down at the side (Figure 2.13).

2. Hold for at least 30 seconds, a minute if you can, pushing out strong and steady the entire time.

3. When time is up, relax the arms down to the side, not trying to move anything, and sing a tone in a way that connects with the sensation being experienced. The experience is of the arms rising with no conscious effort. Let the tone radiate out of you with no effort, just as the arms raise simply from the muscle memory of the previous efforts to push. Do not push, just let the sound pour out on its own.

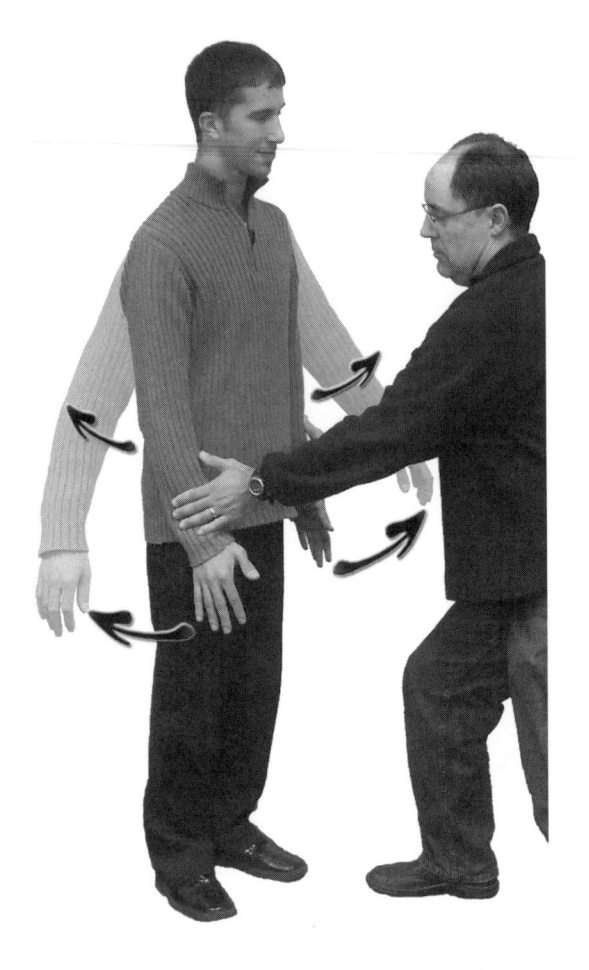

FIGURE 2.13 Arms trapped to the sides, pushing out, then let go to raise with no added effort.

Background Information. This little party game is one of those experiences in which a new revelation about singing can occur. Sound can be produced with little effort at all, it simply rises out of you from somewhere beyond your control. As the arms lift themselves after fighting against being trapped and held down for so long, vibrations just as easily find their way up and out of the body, producing a richer tone than when you try hard to sing. The result—more sound; less effort.

In my senior year of college, I sang for up to five or six hours a day, two to three in choirs, one in voice lessons two days a week, and three or so hours in the practice room getting ready for recital. I worked long and hard on making any last improvements I could manage in order to sing the most difficult music I had sung to that point. One day, worn out after fighting against tension I had not yet conquered, at the very moment I had no more strength left, something mind boggling happened. With the tension gone simply due of fatigue, this effortless and vibrant tone started to rise out of me. Up it went to the peak of the highest notes and richly down to the bottom of my range. This is the point of this exercise, the same point made in the last chapter when learning to siphon the sound out instead of heaving out breath to force sound out. There is a time to work to build strong technique, and then there is the time to let go and simply draw upon the technique that has been built.

Paper in Front of the Mouth

Exercise Sequence. This simple but effective technique is thanks to Carol McAmis, Feldenkrais practitioner, who I believe borrowed it from someone else down from one colleague to the next. The object is to keep phonation moving at all times.

1. Take a piece of paper, a 3 × 5 note card works well, hold it vertical, and place it upright against the lips (Figure 2.14), avoiding pressure or movement that would cause a paper cut.

2. Blow air across the paper in a way that causes a whistley rush of air against the paper.

3. Sometime as you are blowing air, add vocal tone on an OO [u] without interrupting the air stream. Start the phonation of vibrant tone seamlessly, smoothly turning air into sound vibrations.

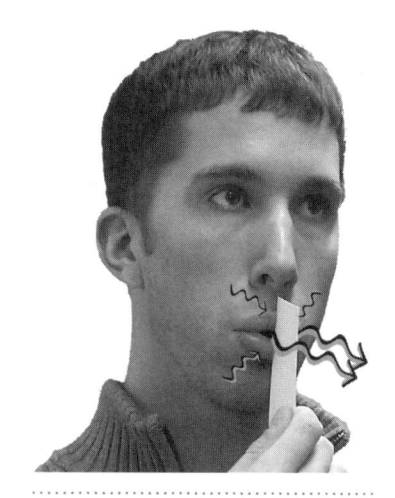

FIGURE 2.14 Developing consistent tone by buzzing across paper.

   - The proof that air is still moving is the whistley rustle of air against the paper.

   - Is the vibration felt on the lips?

   - Do you notice the throat staying wide open yet relaxed?

4. Sing up and down like a siren, extending to the upper range of the voice down to the lowest range.

   - Can you maintain a consistent tone and buzzing noise on the paper?

   - Where does sound travel as you sing higher?

Vocal Registers

Chest Voice and Falsetto Hand Movement

Exercise Sequence. In this exercise, the transition from the chest-voice to falsetto or head-voice register is guided using a sensible hand gesture. The thick thumb is used to represent the use of the full thickness of the vocal folds for chest voice register and the thinner index finger to represent the wave motion of the thinner edge of the vocal cords.

1. Hold the hands out, palms toward each other, with the thumbs on top and the thumb tips touching (Figure 2.15, left).

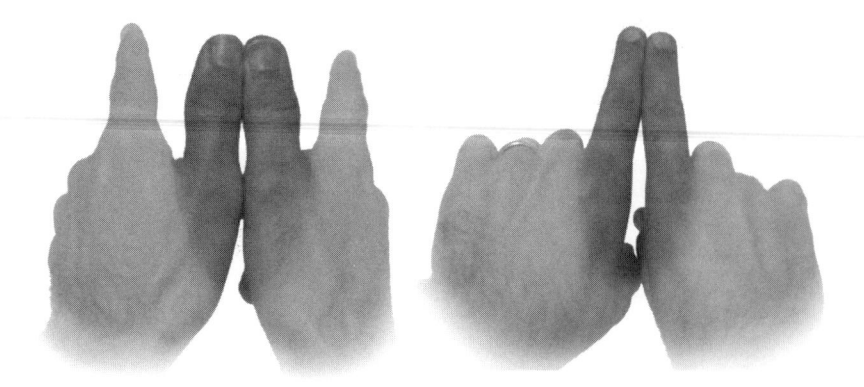

FIGURE 2.15 Thumbs represent the use of the thicker portion of the vocal folds in chest voice; index fingers represent the thinner surface of the vocal folds that vibrate more quickly in falsetto register.

2. Sing a low tone in speaking range guided by the sight and feel of the thumbs moving slightly in waves closer and farther apart.

    a. Relate the thickness and movement of the thumbs with a thick tone and slow vibration.

    b. Relax the arms and hands to signal a buoyant position of the larynx around the vocal cords.

3. Maintaining the same sensation and staying in speaking-range quality of the chest voice, sing a rising scale or melody.

4. Rotate the index finger over the thumb (Figure 2.15, right).

5. Perform a lightly sung high pitch in falsetto register.

    a. Sense the thinner width of the finger to signal a quicker and livelier vibration on the thin edge of the vocal folds.

    b. As with chest-voice singing, feel the same low and relaxed position of the larynx, the only different being the thinner and livelier vocal fold edge.

6. Switch between thumbs on top with a slow, low-pitched, chest voice and fingers on top with a fast, high-pitched, falsetto voice.

    a. Maintain the same buoyancy, relaxation, and position of the structures around the vocal cords.

    b. Guide a smooth and effortless transition between chest and head voice registers with a smooth rotation of the hands to put thumbs or fingers on top.

7. Aiming for a consistent sensation between registers and hand movements, sing the *same pitch* in middle range in chest and head voice, repeating at various pitch levels.

Background Information. Previously, the difference between low and high pitch was redefined as the difference between slower and faster frequencies. Another difference is how the fuller thickness and thinner edge of the vocal folds help produce slower and faster pitch. Compare the difference in thickness in strings on a guitar, piano, violin, or other stringed instrument—the thicker the string, the lower the pitch it can produce. However, the fuller thickness of the vocal folds can still vibrate very quickly to produce high pitches if relaxed and supported enough to allow it.

A common distinction between the two vocal registers is that one is used for speaking and the other is used for high emotional expressions such as an excited "yippee," an attention-getting "yoo-hoo," or a victorious "woo-hoo." In singing, the chest-voice register is also called *modal voice*. Falsetto produces a weak and airy quality, as in a fake or artificial version of the chest voice. Because falsetto tends to ring in the head, an alternate term used by some voice teachers is *head voice*. However, head voice is also used to distinguish the false quality of falsetto from a richer quality that is possible by borrowing the thicker resonance from chest voice. The goal in this current exercise and the exercise that follows is to borrow the easy production of high pitches from falsetto and the resonant quality of chest voice for a consistent tone quality from low pitch to high and back down.

The transition between falsetto and chest voice is often tense in novice singers, and during the adolescent maturation process the voice flips erratically between the two registers. This flip between registers, whether tense or smooth, is commonly called the "break." A tense break between vocal registers is used with emotional purpose in popular and folk singing styles, and is the key feature of yodeling. Transition, switch, and shift are common words that avoid the connotation that something is broken when switching from one register to the other.

Singers can have such difficulty and make a great deal of switching between registers. Though the transition is but a slight switch between two parts of relatively small surfaces, there are changes in air pressure and sound intensity that can be difficult to manage. Tension in the surrounding structures of the voice can lead to discomfort and even pain. Much of the work in learning to switch registers with ease involves unlearning the needless efforts that result from singing with tension.

Four approaches to managing registers are to (a) keep registers separate but work for a smooth transition at the break point, (b) overlap the registers across an extended *passagio* to camouflage where the break occurs, (c) blend the best qualities of both registers for a uniform timbre across the entire range, and (d) ignore manipulating the registers altogether and instead allow the transition to occur on its own within an overall healthy tone production. This exercise focuses on the first approach listed, making a smooth transition between registers by consciously watching and sensing the switch on the external hands. However, if phonation is as relaxed and supported as intended in previous exercises in Chapters 1 and 2, the vocal cords will make an unnoticeable transition when they need to switch, as noted in the fourth option, without thinking about it or trying to "help" the process. In other words, by focusing exclusively on consistent and vibrant phonation, you can ignore registers and relaxingly allow them to do what they need to do without conscious effort to make them switch. As previous exercises have been attempted, perhaps a smooth transition has already been experienced. Check out this possibility and consider not putting so much attention on register break unless it becomes a particularly stressful problem.

Using One Register to Guide the Other

Exercise Sequence. In this exercise, the (b) and (c) approaches of overlapping and blending the registers are presented. Registers "learn" each other's sensation and tone quality.

1. On a focused OO [u], sing descending pitches like a siren from a high pitch in head-voice register down to a low pitch in chest-voice register.

    a. Maintain the focused tone quality of the head voice and OO [u] vowel into the chest register.

    b. Keep the transition smooth and effortless without a tense break between the registers, using the previous hand motion exercise if needed.

2. On a resonant AH [a], sing ascending pitches from low chest-voice quality up into head-voice in higher range.

    a. Maintain the open and resonant vibration of the chest register into the head voice register.

3. Staying on the same vowel of your choice, switch between the two registers while singing the same pitch, while moving between two pitches close to each other, and while moving between two pitches farther apart such as a fifth and an octave.

a. Find the common relaxed and resonant tone that stays consistent between pitches and registers.

b. Retain the best qualities of both the relaxed, open, and resonant tone of the chest voice and the focused and easy tone of the head voice.

Background Information. Voice teachers have long used the principle of motor learning to borrow the sensation of one register and pitch range to guide the sensation in another register and pitch range. Some use the lighter head voice quality to guide the chest voice to be lighter as well; some use the chest voice to maintain a thicker resonance up into head voice. Rather than choose one quality over the other as the model, several approaches are presented in this exercise. The intended outcomes are to release excess effort and tension in the transition, to learn how to overlap or blend the registers, and to keep the best qualities of the two registers.

The caution with these approaches is that too much attention to overlapping and blending the registers can lead to a fusing of the two, one not able to work separately from the other. Although one goal is to find the tone quality that stays consistent between the two registers, and therefore sing with one sound throughout the singer's range, the ability to separate the two registers should be maintained. An inability to sing in one register or the other is an indication of tension, much the same as the mixed signals in the breathing muscles that close down the vocal cords instead of allowing them to freely vibrate. Work for an even tone quality, but avoid fusing the functions of both registers to the point that chest singing sounds false or head register sounds stressfully chesty.

Effects of Posture on Phonation

Back, Up, and Out Direction of Singing

Exercise Sequence. Poor posture affects the ability of the vocal cords to turn air into sound vibrations. The purpose of this exercise is to find a more direct path for air to travel past the vocal cords as it is turned into tone.

1. Reach a hand around and place a finger or two on the middle of the back of the head.

2. With the neck, shoulders, ribcage, and hips following along in their separate movements, allow the head to elevate up and back above the shoulders, using peripheral vision to see that the *chest rises in front* and the *shoulders come into view on either side*.

a. From the point where the fingers touch, rotate the head back and up (Figure 2.16, arrow a), comfortably and not strained or over stretched.

b. Release neck tension to allow separate movement of the head.

c. Release shoulder tension to allow the shoulders to find their own separate, relaxed, lower position and the neck and head to move separately.

d. Lengthen the distance between the base of the neck and the point on the head that is being touched (arrow b), feeling the extension down into the back muscles and spine.

e. Rotate the chin and forehead down slightly in a rocking motion, like nodding yes (arrow c).

f. Lengthen the distance between the hip and front points of the ribcage (arrow d), which rotates the entire ribcage and elevates the chest into a relaxed but athletic position.

3. Singing a single note at length, start with the head in an incorrect head-forward and bent-neck position (Figure 2.16, left) then move into an improved posture for singing (right). This brings the vocal cords in line with the path of breath and the vocal cord tone in line with the resonators.

FIGURE 2.16 Moving from a forward-leaning posture (left) to an up-and-out posture (right).

a. Explore the movement until you find the path of least resistance for tone to go directly up and out as vibrations traveling through the head instead of out of the mouth.

4. Consider the change of tone while moving from incorrect to correct posture.

   - Did tension release around the vocal cords as the head moved back, up, and more in line?

   - Did the tone start out in the throat or mouth and suddenly get richer and more vibrant as posture came more in line?

5. With a well-aligned posture, sing scale or melodic patterns that rise and fall.

   - Was the transition between registers easier and smoother?

Background Information. In so many instances in this book, problems of singing are solved by aiming efforts in more beneficial directions, for example to expand the ribs out and the diaphragm down during inhalation, to flex the top abs out and the middle abs in, and to keep the larynx low. A general direction that causes problems in singing is the *tendency to sing forward.*

Singing in a forward direction is understandable given that the eyes, ears, nose, and mouth aim most of our senses forward, which focuses our attention forward, which focuses thinking forward, and thereby focuses singing efforts forward. Forward effort is encouraged in voice lessons by students always facing the teacher, in performance by aiming efforts out to an audience or into a microphone, or in a choir when singers are elevated on risers and look straight out and down at the conductor. The solution is to look forward but focus singing efforts and our other perceptions in more beneficial directions.

Forward singing is most obvious in a singer's posture, especially looking from the side to see how much a singer reaches forward with the head or leans forward at the waist. This posture throws the body off balance, which causes tension in muscles that interfere with singing. It causes air to take a detour right at the point that it is supposed to turn into sound, as if taking a trombone or flute and hammering severe dents in it then attempting to play a beautiful tone through the bent up thing. Forward-leaning postures place the vocal cords more above the floor than above muscles that support singing tone.

More than a change of motion or posture is at issue in this exercise; it also involves a drastic change in perception. In finding the right posture for singing, the solution is to face out to the audience but focus on maintaining healthy posture for singing. Instead of reaching out to the audience, invite the audience in to a poised and expressively vibrant performance. Besides, maintaining a healthy posture for singing happens to look visually more engaging from the audience point of view than leaning toward the audience.

I wonder as I write this how many readers noticed in Chapter 1, Figure 1.1 that the singer's attention to blowing out an imaginary candle caused her forward-bent neck and head, and that this is the same photo used to demonstrate a before-and-after movement in Figure 2.16. This back-up-and-out posture exercise should serve as a follow up to any exercise that focuses attention forward and in so doing juts the head forward and the body off balance. More generally than using this specific exercise, regularly switch to an overall view of the singer as narrower problems and exercises are tackled—take the blinders off, so to speak, to *see how little things are affecting the bigger picture.*

The strength of this exercise is that these posture changes can be seen externally. The weakness is that this exercise may lead singers and teachers to simply focus on external changes and ignore the deeper sensations that are the more important goal. The issue of jutting the jaw forward is that air pressure gets trapped below the vocal cords, something that cannot be seen but must be felt and heard. The head can be moved back and up to put the vocal cords visibly in line with the diaphragm and lungs, but the intended outcome is a release of air pressure in the form of a luscious, vibrant sound that is felt and heard. This exploration of the effects of posture on the release of tone will continue in the next chapter on the subject of resonance.

For the Voice Teacher. Without explanation, but perhaps with warning and permission, do this exercise with the teacher's hand on the back of the singer's head (Figure 2.17). Push the head forward unexpectedly to cause the reaction to let go of neck tension and rotate the head into a more effective position for singing. Tone suddenly floods the resonators and releases freely out, instead of being grabbed and held in by a bent and tense posture. With every push the singer senses anew how less effort leads to more sound and a more vibrant quality of sound.

Beyond the exercises provided, write down an exercise related to Chapter 2 that you have collected, been taught, or developed yourself.

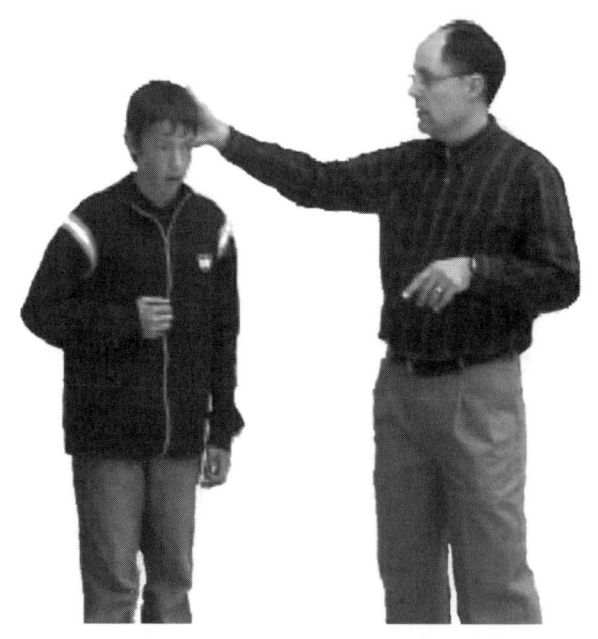

FIGURE 2.17 The head aligns with the vocal cords with a push back and up against a teacher's hand; a slight push forward by the teacher triggers a release of vibrant tone.

Name of Exercise

Exercise Purpose:

Exercise Sequence:

Background Information:

CHAPTER 3

FOCUSED, LIFTED, AND RESONANT TONE

The exercises in this chapter help to bring out the natural color, character, timbre, and resonance of the voice. Resonance shares the same root word as "sonar," "sonic," "sonorous," and "sonogram," which all have to do with sensing the echo of sound within a particular space, literally a *resounding* tone. By echoing sound into different spaces and vibrating sound through different structures of the head and chest, the intensity, vibrancy, richness, and power of the voice are increased. Exercises also help the singer perceive sound vibrations and structures in the head and chest.

Acoustics: Timbre and Harmonics

Sensory Experience: Where Do Sound Waves Concentrate?

Exercise Sequence. The purpose of this exercise is to find out where sound vibrations are centrally focused.

1. Place one hand in front of the face with fingers together and pointed up, palm facing in, and curved like a radar or sonar dish; cup the other hand behind the ear to catch the tone that is bounced off the first hand as you sing (Figure 3.1).

FIGURE 3.1 Sonar hands help detect the primary source of sound coming out of the body.

2. Sing an AH [ɑ] in a medium range, positioning the "sonar" hand in front of each bulleted item to bounce the sound to the other hand and directly into the ear. In the search for the central tone, *feel* where sound vibrations are most intense, *hear* where sound comes out the most, *watch* the front hand and surrounding space to focus attention, and mentally image sound and space. Is sound more intensely focused in:

   - The chest?
   - The throat?
   - The jaw, low in the mouth?
   - The mouth, straight out the throat?
   - The top teeth, high in the mouth?
   - The nose?
   - The eyes and cheekbones and across the bridge of the nose?
   - Someplace else? Where?

3. Sing on different vowels, AE [æ], EH [ɛ], EE [i], OH [o], OO [u], UH [ʌ] and IH [ɪ] on the same pitch as before. Searching down the list with your sonar-hand positions, does the center of sound vibration change with each vowel? Are answers different than found in step 2 on an AH [ɑ] vowel?

4. Sing a rising scale or melody on a choice of one vowel. Does the center of sound vibration change with change in pitch?

5. Sing a melody on a neutral vowel and then with the text to find how much the central focus of tone shifts during singing.

Background Information. The character, color, or timbre of a singer's voice is determined to a large extent by the spaces and structures in which sound concentrates. Sound can be focused in the chest, the throat, the mouth, the nasal cavity and sinuses, and the nasal passages of the nose (Figure 3.2).

The mouth and throat areas, on the whole called the pharynx, are divided into the oropharynx associated with the oral cavity or mouth, and the nasopharynx associated with

ACOUSTICS: TIMBRE AND HARMONICS 91

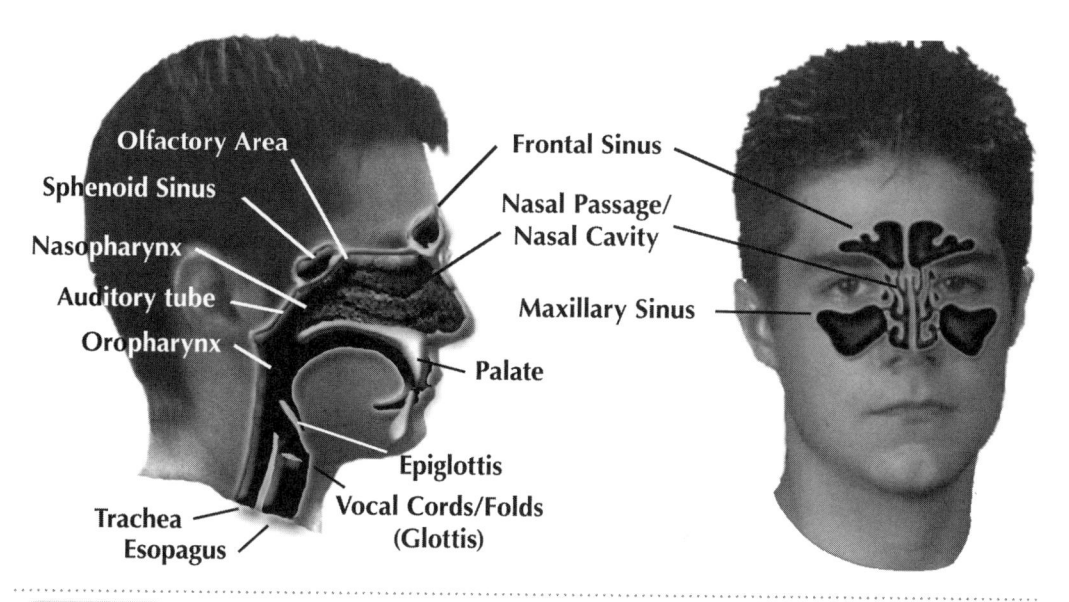

FIGURE 3.2 Resonant spaces.

the nasal cavity. Note how the nasal cavity is multisensory in that it contains the olfactory area that is involved in smelling and one end of the auditory tube that is involved in hearing. The auditory tube, also called the Eustachian tube, is at the crucial point in the path from the oropharynx to the nasopharynx, which is why resonance affects the singer's ability to hear the voice.

Dividing the spaces of the head is the palate, made up of the hard palate in front and the soft palate that curves down at the back of the mouth. The most difficult lesson with resonance is in getting sound to make the transition from below the palate to above it, as will be experienced in the exercises later in the chapter.

A goal in learning to sing is to find a singer's natural resonance. However, two notions about natural resonance come into conflict in learning to sing. The first is the selective resonance that is already "natural" to the singer, *the tone the singer is in the habit of hearing and producing*. Health, physical fitness, habits of posture, and other conditions that arise through heredity and experience all help shape this tone. The problem is that tension is so often used to produce this tone. For instance, those who have had dental braces often have a tight-jawed tone that comes from hiding the braces or keeping them from scraping the inside lips and cheeks. Another example is when tall people hunch over to be down at the level of shorter people, which also shapes the character of their tone. Vocal tone also reflects a singer's self image, which is shaped by regional, ethnic, social class, personality, or family characteristic or copied from a favorite person, singer, social group, or musical style. For example, based on personality:

RESONANT TONE

- A shy, gentle person may place an unresonant, gentle, whispery quality into the voice.

- An extrovert may put a boisterous, all-around-resonant quality into the voice.

- A perfectionist may tensely control tone with a tight-jawed and tense-tongued vocal quality.

- A sarcastic person may use a harsh abrasive quality that comes directly through the hard palate.

- A humble, folksy person may put an unrefined coarseness into the voice.

Also consider the stereotypical tones of a southern belle's vocal lilt, a Texan's nasal drawl, or the hollow-throated tone of a California surfer "dude." These tones may come through conscious effort to carve out a particular character or the singer may be unaware that self-image is shaping the way they sound. Either way, the tension used to produce this "natural" resonance makes it not so natural after all.

Second is the tone that is natural to the unique shape and size of the singer's vocal instrument. *This tone takes fuller advantage of the spaces and structures in the head and chest* beyond current limited use of the resonators. In this approach, options are increased as to which spaces and structures create a suitable tone for the singer and for the musical style being sung.

In the search for the natural tone that a voice is able to produce, the results can sound ugly and unnatural to the singer. This is because the auditory tube connects to the nasopharynx and interferes with the singer's sense of hearing. There are three options in managing this potential barrier to learning. First, an outside listener such as a voice teacher is needed to confirm that a resonant tone is more beautiful. Second, the singer must learn to stop judging the voice by its sound and instead to sing by how resonant vibrations feel—to trust other sensations than hearing when developing new resonance. Third, listen with fresh ears to what resonant tone sounds like—if it sounds ugly when the voice is resonant, then aim for a sound that is ugly to the outer ear. The ugly, muffled sound is a clue that the inside of the ear is being vibrated and that tone is on its way through the resonators.

Resonant spaces not only determine the timbre of the voice, the structures and surfaces that sound hits and travels through also determine vocal timbre. For instance, resonating through the hard palate or hard bone adds a hard quality to the tone; resonating into soft tissues results in a soft quality to the tone; resonating through hard and soft surfaces results in a more complex vocal timbre. Each singer has a unique shape and size of resonators, some with blocked or narrow nasal passages that keep sound from flowing into the sinuses, some with large open sinuses, some with larger tongues that trap sound in the mouth, some with high cheekbones that give lift to tone, and so on. When considering nose surgery for a more attractive appearance, Barbara Streisand infamously passed up the chance in favor of preserving the source of her resonant tone, her long and spacious nasal passages. When Michael Jackson had his nose narrowed, it constricted and reduced the timbre of his voice.

What we cannot readily see is the size and shape of the spaces and structures inside. The exercises in this chapter allow for the size and shape to be heard and felt, which allows the singer to develop something like a sonogram image in the mind. Work to develop this image to make better sense of how to sing.

For the Voice Teacher. It helps to make the two notions of natural tone clear when working on the psychologically sensitive issue of resonance, especially considering that a singer may shy away when voice lessons lead to a sound that is unfamiliar or ugly to the singer's own ear. It also helps to point out whether voice lessons are aimed at a particular style of singing, especially operatic singing, or simply intended to give the singer more options and more freedom than before.

For the Choir Director. Two options for managing the variety of resonance types in a choir are to develop a common vocal technique and to place the existing voice types in an advantageous order. First is to work for all singers to channel tone through the same resonant spaces. However, if a choir director does not take the time and effort to identify each singer's resonance, the director ends up making decisions for all voices based only on the overall tone produced by combined voices. What the director hears is an average tone with singers working in a range on either side of the average. Directions to adjust the overall tone can cause one singer to exaggerate in one direction to compensate for another singer on the other side of the balance of tone. It is important in working for the same resonance to check each singer. Aside from outside voice auditions or lessons, here are some options for identifying individual voice types. If desired, take notes on individuals' efforts and progress for later problem solving or even to track progress over time for grading purposes.

1. Circulate down each row as the choir sings to detect individual voice type, and make quick adjustments and suggestions with individual students as you hear them.

2. Have the choir use sonar hands (Figure 3.1) to visually see the center of tone they detected, and provide individualized tips to help them match the unified vocal technique suggested for the entire choir by the director.

3. Have singers pair up, face each other, and take turns singing and listening to identify where sound is focused, and to apply what they have learned in choir to make suggestions for matching the prescribed choral tone.

4. Detect voice types either personally (step 1), independently (step 2), or collaboratively (step 3), then group similar voice types together and provide particular solutions for those of the same type.

The second approach is to assess where singers' tones are currently centered and then arrange them within their sections in a sensible order by similar voice types.

1. Work with one section at a time, asking singers in other sections to observe, verify, visually affirm with a nod or thumbs up, or even help conductor decisions.

2. Listen to the whole section, pairs of singers, and individual singers as they sing a phrase from music in their voice range they have learned.

3. Sort the voices by resonance from dark to light, thick to thin, throaty to nasal.

4. Put the singers in a standing order that centralizes the singers with the conductor's desired tone and wraps other voices around the center; or use other orders that draw the singers into a unified tone.

5. An added step is to check that neighbors hear each other well and sing in tune with each other, either due to the strength of their hearing in one ear or the other or due to being by a singer whose timbre helps them match.

This preliminary exploration can be followed by solutions that follow in this chapter or other solutions already favored by the director. Additional choral applications are found in Chapter 4 as they pertain to hearing a choir in a rehearsal or performance space.

Different Harmonics for Different Spaces

Exercise Sequence. Beyond finding out where sound is centrally focused, the question turns to how ably the singer can adapt and change resonance. This exercise helps focus sound in different places along what Royal Stanton called the Tonal Continuum in his books *Steps for Singing for Voice Class* (Stanton 2000) and *The Dynamic Choral Director* (Stanton 1979). The remaining sections of the chapter are intended to solve specific problems of resonance that are identified in this exercise.

1. Singing on a comfortable pitch and vowel, relax and open each area in turn across the following continuum. Use the hands to follow and point out where efforts to resonate are focused, using either sonar hands (Figure 3.1) or as in tracking

breath noise (Figure 1.5). Visually track the internal spaces by watching the path of resonant spaces in Figure 3.2.

  a. from a hollow tone low in the chest and throat,

  b. into the oropharynx at the back of the mouth,

  c. up into the oropharynx, and

  d. curving around the nasal passages into the nose.

2. Open the lid of a piano, play an A as the target pitch to sing, depress the sustain pedal to allow all strings to vibrate during singing, and listen for which piano strings vibrate as the A is sung with tone centered in the following:

  a. in the throat,

  b. in the mouth,

  c. in the nose, and

  d. across the width and height of the pharynx and nasal cavity.

Background Information. Timbre is a more complex issue of sound than simple pitch frequency as presented in Chapter 2. Rather than a simple wave, timbre is determined by sound wave frequencies that occur above and sometimes below the actual pitch that is sung. The frequencies that vibrate other than the actual target pitch are called *overtones* and the underlying frequency is called the *fundamental* pitch (Figure 3.3). Each frequency represented in the tone, from the fundamental on up, is called a harmonic. Notice that the second harmonic is the first overtone, or the first frequency tone "over" the fundamental, and that the pattern continues for each harmonic and overtone.

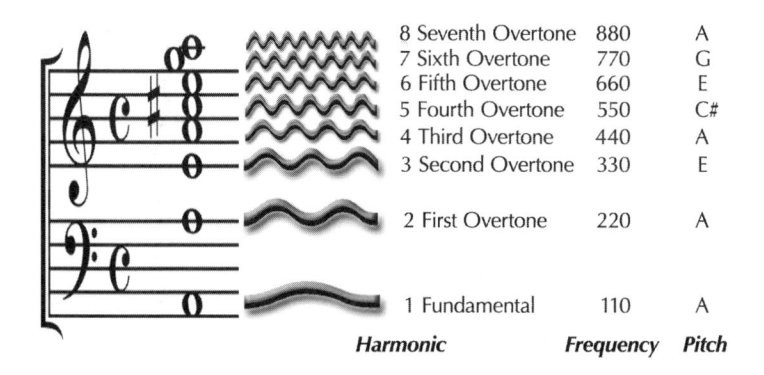

Harmonic		Frequency	Pitch
8	Seventh Overtone	880	A
7	Sixth Overtone	770	G
6	Fifth Overtone	660	E
5	Fourth Overtone	550	C#
4	Third Overtone	440	A
3	Second Overtone	330	E
2	First Overtone	220	A
1	Fundamental	110	A

FIGURE 3.3   Harmonic series: the fundamental pitch and overtones.

The complexity of timbre is determined by the spaces and structures open to resonance, and by closed off places that trap or block resonance. Described the other way around, resonance determines the harmonics that are included in timbre and which pitch in the harmonic series is highlighted the strongest. Chest and throat resonance primarily accentuate the lower harmonics, mouth resonance accentuates the lower middle overtones, nasal resonance thinly rings many overtones, and deeply supported and open resonance enhances several overtones (Figure 3.4).

For the Choir Director. A choir can learn a lot about choral timbre by singing into piano strings with the lid in full open position. The strings that ring after the choir has sung represent the frequencies in the harmonic series that are part of the choir's timbre. It works best when on risers with voices arranged wide and tall at somewhat equal distance from the piano.

1. Remove the piano lid or bring it to full open position; a grand piano works best because of it's large opening and exposed strings, but an upright is adequate.

2. Hold down the sustain pedal on the piano to lift the hammers off all strings and allow the entire spectrum of sound produced by the choir to be revealed.

3. Have the choir sing with a nasal tone and hear the upper strings ring in a steely timbre.

4. Have the choir sing in the throat and hear the lower strings ring with a hollow timbre.

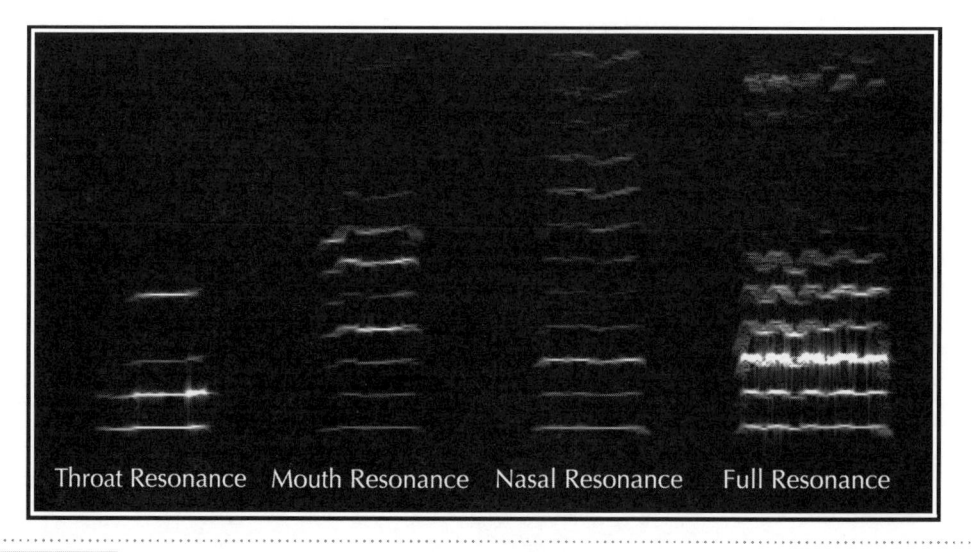

FIGURE 3.4 Frequencies in the harmonic series change by singing in and through different resonant spaces, which changes the timbre of the voice.

5. Have the choir sing a number of different "choral" tones to hear how many overtones ring and which vibrates loudest within the harmonic series.

The feedback to the choir is immediate. To make a sound at all, the choir must sing with enough resonant power to vibrate the strings and direct the tone into the piano strings, which itself is a good lesson in choral tone. When singing *in tune with blended tone* they will hear a sonorous sound of select strings vibrating pitches in the harmonic series; when *out of tune* or with an *unrefined tone* they will hear a mesh of strings vibrating on clashing pitches. Clashing pitches are the inharmonic or partial overtones that do not mathematically relate to the fundamental and therefore are "out of tune."

Unrefined tones—yelled mouth-oriented tone, strident hard-palate tone, throaty tone, or a tone with no uniform direction at all that allows each singer to produce whatever tone happens to come out—will ring out a fuzzy mess of strings that reveals the need to work more diligently on refining the tone. An *overly refined choral tone*—one that focuses primarily on the central ringing quality of the voice—rings a limited set of strings with fewer overtones. This may explain why many choir directors prefer a very refined tone, because there are fewer overtones to affect tuning and less resonance to tame across the choir. A *highly resonant tone* will vibrate many strings in the harmonic series. The trick with this mature-sounding choral tone is to maintain uniform balance, timbre, vowel color, and tuning across the numerous overtones.

A related phenomenon, called *octave illusion*, occurs with the boys changing voice. When the male voice begins to mutate in adolescence, the tone quality of the voice becomes husky before pitch actually drops. Even music teachers have been foiled by the illusion that a boy is suddenly singing an octave lower with a husky quality, when the pitch is actually high but the quality gives the illusion of a low pitch. This is how resonance and timbre affect the perception of pitch, especially in a choir. For more on the topic of working with voice change, see John Cooksey's (1999) *Working With the Adolescent Voice*. To test out the phenomenon of octave illusion for yourself, try this next sensory experience.

Sensory Experience: Is the Pitch Higher, Lower, or the Same?

Exercise Sequence. This exercise is a puzzle for one person to try on another. One person sings as the other listens and answers whether two pitches stay the same, if the second pitch is lower, or the second pitch is higher than the first. The singer performs the following options in an unexpected order.

1. Sing the first tone focused in upper resonant space, such as high in the nose or at the top of the nasal cavity by the olfactory area, and a second tone on the *same* pitch but focused low in the chest.

- The illusion is that the second pitch is lower, yet the pitch is the same.

- Did the person listening to the singer answer correctly or did the illusion lead to a misjudgment?

2. Sing a low pitch with resonance focused in upper resonant space, and a second tone an octave higher with round resonance focused low in the chest.

   - The illusion is that the pitches are the same, yet they are an octave apart.

   - Did the person listening answer correctly or did the illusion work?

3. Sing a high pitch with resonance focused in upper resonant space, and the second tone on octave higher with round resonance focused low in the chest.

   - There is no illusion and few mistakes on this final choice.

Background Information. High pitches are best perceived when resonance is placed high and low pitches are best perceived when resonance is placed low in the body. When high pitch is sung with low resonance and low pitch is sung with high resonance, judgments of pitch range can be thrown off.

Quite apart from perception, however, this inconsistency of resonance is the problem we are trying to *solve* in this chapter. When a single voice changes to a thin sound up high and a thick sound down low, the voice sounds unrefined and amateurish. This high-low-same pitch sensory experience is simply to drive home the point that resonance confuses pitch perception. Individual voices should develop a character, color, resonance, and timbre that is consistent throughout the vocal range, across different vowel colors, and across words and syllables with different consonant/vowel combinations. Likewise, a choir should develop a consistent concept of choral tone, whether as described in this book or one preferred and understood by the choir director. The remainder of this chapter presents specific areas to explore in developing a consistent approach to resonance.

Raised and Open Soft Palate

Sensory experience: Does the Soft Palate Stay Raised for Singing?

Exercise Sequence. Singers are commonly told to raise the soft palate, but not commonly given a way to find out what a raised soft palate feels like. A simple yawn is one way to sense it. This exercise shows that a wide-open-yawn mouth is not necessary to raise the soft palate.

1. Open your mouth and place an upright index finger behind the top front teeth (Figure 3.5). The top teeth move forward like buckteeth and the lower teeth and jaw shift down and back to make room.

2. Check for the sensation of a raised soft palate in response to this finger position.

    a. Does the roof of the mouth feel stretched and raised?

    b. If not, move the finger farther behind the top teeth to touch the inside gums, and push gently back on the lower teeth to move the jaw further back until the back of the roof of the mouth responds by raising.

3. While keeping the finger in this position, sing a tall AH [a].

4. Check for successful results during singing.

    a. Did the stretched and raised sensation of the soft palate stay during singing?

    b. Did sound vibrate through the nasal cavity and sinuses, above the soft palate?

Background Information. The roof of the mouth, called the palate, is divided between a hard and a soft palate (look back to Figure 3.2). The hard palate starts behind the front teeth; the soft palate extends behind the hard palate and terminates with the uvula, which hangs down visibly in the middle of the back of the throat. In most people, the buckteeth finger position triggers a reflex for the soft palate to raise, much the same as when a doctor says to open wide and sticks a wooden tongue depressor on the back of the tongue to see the back of the throat. Should this reflex not occur, go on to the next exercise for an even more concrete experience of the soft palate.

FIGURE 3.5 Buckteeth finger position to trigger a raised soft palate.

Thumb Print

Exercise Sequence. This exercise uses both the sense of touch and the sense of taste to help track the movement of the soft palate.

1. Make sure hands are clean.

2. Extend your thumb out in a hitchhiker gesture, open your mouth wide, and lightly but fully touch your soft palate with the rounded pad of the thumb (Figure 3.6).

3. Moving the hand back out of the mouth, feel the sensation of touch and possibly taste a slight acidic flavor that remain after the thumbprint is made.

4. Yawn to feel the thumbprint move up.

5. Using the thumbprint sensation as a target, intentionally move the soft palate higher and lower, if you can.

6. Singing on an open AH [a], feel if the thumb print sensation raises or lowers; sing other vowels to sense if the soft palate responds the same as the AH [a].

7. Go back and forth between yawning and singing until the raised soft palate can stay raised during singing.

Background Information. Compared to raising, perhaps the more important function of the soft palate is as a gate to the oropharynx, nasal cavity, and sinuses. The soft palate can (a) move away from the back of the throat to allow breath and tone into upper spaces and passageways, or (b) touch the back of the throat to close off, trap, and channel tone out through the mouth. The soft palate closes off, for instance, when breathing through a snorkeling tube to stop water from coming in through the nose, or when coughing to channel air and debris out through the mouth. In singing, the final proof that the soft palate is raised is a rich vibrant tone coming out above the palate. The next section concentrates on the resonant tone that results once the soft palate has opened the path to spaces above the palate.

FIGURE 3.6 Placing a thumbprint on the soft palate.

Beyond the Palate

Sensory experience: Are Sound Vibrations Getting Above the Palate?

Exercise Sequence. So much attention is put on raising the soft palate, but the more important issue is that sound is allowed to enter and pass through the upper resonators. This exercise checks that the singer can get sound to vibrate above the palate.

1. To experience the problem to be solved, hold the hand out in a clutched, claw position (Figure 3.7, left) to guide the exploration of different mouth-oriented tones.

    a. Say "yeah" in an irritable or sarcastic voice out through the mouth.

    b. Say "hey" as if scolding someone near you.

    c. Sing a pitch or melodic pattern straight out through the mouth with a harsh tone.

2. By comparison, hold your nose closed with a light pinch of the finger and thumb (Figure 3.7, right) and resonate sound from above the palate and out the sinuses and nasal cavity.

3. Explore different uses of the voice until sound vibrates in the sinuses around the nose and into the nasal passages to the fingers at the tip of the nose. *The sound will not easily vibrate in your nose if trapped in your mouth, so relax and open the path behind the soft palate to the nose.*

FIGURE 3.7 Resonating sound out through the mouth (left); resonating sound through the sinuses and nasal cavity (right).

a. Say your name.

b. Say "hey!" as if enthusiastically calling for a friend's attention from a distance.

c. Say "icky" as if something actually tastes nasty and disgusting.

d. Make a resonant, high-pitched "kaw" bird call.

e. Say the first [ae] of an "a-choo" sneeze or a wailing "waaa" baby cry—do the sound as if actually getting ready to sneeze or imitating a baby.

f. Sing short "beep" sounds in a comfortable middle range and feel for sound to still be vibrating in and around the nasal passages into your nose.

4. Verify the accuracy of the experience.

a. Check that a fake nasal sound is not being produced in the throat by squeezing it tight—this sound will come out into the palm of the hand that is pinching the nose.

b. Do the fingers vibrate slightly as you beep?

c. Check that the vibrant sound *includes* the nose and is not merely a small sound stuck *in* the nose.

5. Sing up and down a scale of four notes (*do-re-mi-fa*) or five (*do-re-mi-fa-so*) on different vowels, BEE-BAY-BAH-BOH-BOO /bi be bɑ bo bu/, keeping the vibration flowing into your nose.

6. Let go of your nose and keep the vibration flowing into, around, and through the nasal cavity, again not *in* the nose but *including* the nasal passages and the surrounding sinuses.

Background Information. Singing from the mouth creates a vocal timbre that involves fewer overtones in the harmonic series. Notice in Figure 3.7 that there are fewer rows of sound waves shown coming out of the figure on the left and more overtones shown on the right. This is a stylized version of the type of graph shown in Figure 3.4, positioned to show that the number of overtones match the amount of space involved in resonance. Open up the nasal cavity and sinuses and the timbre is fuller and richer, both in overtones and in the beautiful and lush sensation in those who hear the tone. Also notice the taller sound wave on the right, showing that opening the resonators more fully creates a natural amplification of the sound. The tone is louder—with a taller amplitude—with less effort than when pushing sound out through the mouth. More sound with less effort.

To help in this exercise, develop a mental picture of what is going on inside the head by comparing Figure 3.7 with Figure 3.2. Notice how the path of the wave-filled arrows of Figure 3.7 approximately follows a path starting at the vocal cords where air is turned into sound. Picture the sound wave traveling past the oropharynx, behind and over the soft palate, past the nasopharynx, through the nasal cavity, and finally into the nasal passages to the fingers pinching the nostrils. Develop a mental picture of sound waves coming out of the head at different levels, based on where resonators are opened. In your mental image of sound waves, give the sound waves and overtones thickness, height, and color.

Important Principle for All Learning. Take advantage of imagery in learning. Developing visual images in the mind enhances the multisensory experience of singing by providing a mental target to guide physical efforts. Use the pictures in the book to learn to watch efforts of singing in the "mind's eye." As you physically work to sing, mentally picture what is to occur inside the body and in the sound waves in the air.

There are people who are born with synesthesia, as in different sense perceptions involuntarily in sync with one another. Synesthetes experience one sensation that is not actually present in relation to sensing something that is actually present, such as seeing colors when music is played, tasting or smelling a color or sound, or hearing music when they see colors. The goal of this book is not to develop true synesthesia, because it seems to be genetic and not learned. However, you can practice imagining sound waves or internal structures in the body to the point that your visual image makes learning more effective. The idea of seeing what you hear and feel will continue to be developed along with other multisensory connections, in the name of developing your full ability to learn or teach singing.

Palate Hands

Exercise Sequence. The purpose of this exercise is to further guide vocal tone into the spaces above the palate. The task is to resonate sound out through the upper head instead of from the mouth.

1. Extending the elbows out to the sides, bring the inside curve of the hands up against the face, with the tips of the fingers touching or overlapping just below the nose and the thumbs extending back under the ears (Figure 3.8).

    a. Make sure the side of the hands is sealed against the skin all the way around to block sound from traveling directly from the mouth to the ears.

    b. Hold this position for the extent of this sequence.

FIGURE 3.8 Palate-hand position.

2. Say your name and listen how sound coming from the mouth is trapped under the hands, distant as if coming from somewhere or someone else.

3. With the mouth only slightly open, sing a pitch on a neutral vowel, and at the same time lift and draw sound into the spaces of the head above the hands.

    a. Sense that sound is not coming so much from below the hands, but instead is coming directly from out of the head above the hands.

4. Sing up and down a scale, still keeping sound coming out through the head and not from the mouth.

    a. Sense that when pitch rises, the central focus of vibration climbs, like a ticklish vibration rising up the back wall of the pharynx and into the nasal cavity.

    b. Sense that sound keeps resonating out above the head regardless of the rising vibration.

5. Sing a song and identify trouble spots where sound no longer resonates fully. Work through this sequence or previous exercise sequences to identify whether the problem is a mouth-oriented tone, a particular vowel, syllable, or pitch range at each spot until solved. Repeat until the song is sung with consistently full resonance.

Background Information. For a singer to personally judge the quality of his or her own voice, tone is commonly channeled out through the mouth so the outer ear can hear it. This is the difficulty in learning to sing alone without a voice teacher. A singer cannot hear the quality of tone that others hear. Instead, singers typically reduce the depth of quality until it sounds sweet to the outside ear. Singers avoid a full resonant tone on their own because it vibrates the inner parts of the ear and sounds hollow, muffled, and ugly. For this reason, aim for a sound that vibrates the inside of the ear and sounds ugly to the outer ear—*sing by vibration and not by the prettiness of the sound*!

The rising sensation in the open space of the pharynx and nasal cavity, mentioned in step 4 of this exercise sequence, is due to the increasingly higher overtones and to the increasing pitch speed finding their natural place in acoustical space. For low pitches, the intensity of vibration naturally centers lower in the available resonant space; for high pitches, the intensity of vibration centers higher in the space. This is an acoustical reason for defining pitch as higher or lower. As pitch rises, sound vibrations speed up, become faster in frequency, increase the number of waves in the same space, enliven higher overtones, and rise until space is no longer available to rise into.

But resonant space needs to be open for sound vibrations to rise and find a way out. Sound vibrations can no longer rise when sound pressure gets trapped, which is the reason that high pitches are more difficult to sing. There are three spots where sound pressure commonly gets trapped: (a) at the top of the throat, which is unblocked by lowering the larynx, relaxing the tongue out of the way, and relaxing the throat open; (b) against the roof of the mouth, which is unblocked by raising the soft palate away from the back of the throat to allow sound into the nasal cavity; and (c) in the back of the sinuses, which is unblocked by opening the front sinuses and nasal passages. The arc through which sound is released in singing is the reason for all the rounded arrows in this book, from Figures 1.7 to 3.7 and yet to be found in later graphics. In the end, the main pressure release is in the front through the frontal sinuses, maxillary sinuses, and nasal passages, which is where sound is heard to come out as a result of this palate-hands exercise.

From the Oropharynx to the Nasopharynx

Hands in Front of Ears

Exercise Sequence. This exercise solves the problem of singers pushing sound up through the hard palate as a short cut to the front sinuses and nose. The task is to get sound to travel up before it goes forward.

1. To experience the problem to be solved in this exercise, place a thumb behind and pulling lightly forward on the top teeth, and sing with a tone that is trapped behind the thumb and against the hard palate.

    - Do you hear air or other raw vocal cord noise escaping from the mouth?

    - Where does it feel like sound pressure is building up?

2. Place the inside edges of the hands against the side of the face on either side, in front of the ears (Figure 3.9) and in line with the internal back wall of the pharynx.

3. Sing with a tone that first travels up behind the hands before turning forward into the nasal cavity. Attempt to have sound waves come out directly to the ears from behind the hands.

   - Do you hear less vocal cord flack escaping from the mouth?

   - Do you feel less pressure in the sensation of singing?

Background Information. A natural human response in learning a new task is to work hard, knuckle down, and put some elbow grease into it. In singing, such hard effort has the detrimental effect of trapping, stopping, and pressurizing sound. When sound pressure gets trapped in the mouth or oropharynx, a natural response is to push harder to shove sound through the hard palate—which is another aspect of the forward-singing problem discussed at the end of Chapter 2. While the effort to get sound above the palate is correct, the path is too direct. This type of effort results in a harsh, piercing tone that carries the quality of the hard palate with it. Instead, a full resonant tone should carry the quality of both soft and hard tissues, and first travel beyond the oropharynx into the nasopharynx before falling forward on its way out. In my own learning experience, I came to call this upward path "singing up the back stair case," and called the natural and effortless forward release of tone a "forward flop."

Another way to perceive the difference between a mouth-oriented tone and a lifting, resonant tone is to compare the amount of flack noise of the vocal cords when switching from one to the other. When tone comes from the mouth, escaping air and other vocal cord noises are easily heard because the raw tone is directly exposed. By contrast, when tone goes up before going forward, a complex timbre comes out that has traveled through spaces and surfaces,

FIGURE 3.9 Aim sound behind and above the palate before turning the corner forward.

that carries the colors of the several spaces and surfaces, and that leaves excess vocal cord noise trapped inside and unable to escape.

The technique in step 1 of putting a thumb behind the top teeth happens to be a strategy that can help in developing a *belting tone*. However, the difference between forcing tone through the hard palate and belting and is that belting traps sound behind the teeth just enough to echo the tone against the hard surface of the palate and amplify it, giving it a hard edgy quality. Belting otherwise involves proper breath support, relaxed phonation, and resonant tone with little tension elsewhere.

Important Principle for All Learning. Like my own phrases "singing up the back staircase" and "forward flop" were important insights in my learning to sing, such made-up phrases are important in any singer's learning experience. As new sensations of singing are successfully experienced and learned, hold on to any descriptions or terms that come to mind. Technical terms such as oropharynx and timbre are only as meaningful as the experience that comes from their use, and often the terminology and descriptions that come from the one doing the learning is more effective than unfamiliar terminology from a textbook or terminology that comes from the teacher's experience. The singer's own terminology helps simplify and personalize learning experiences and makes it more likely to remember and repeat at a later time. Moreover, personal terminology can make technical terminology more memorable by association.

Extended Exercise. Beyond blocking the direct mouth-to-ear path of sound with the hands, steps can be added to this exercise that draw on other senses.

4. To get a better sense of the incorrect tone produced in step 1:

    a. Look at the resonant spaces in Figure 3.2 that are in a direct line from the vocal cords to the bridge of the nose, and aim singing efforts straight through the mouth and hard palate.

    b. Knock on a hard table with the knuckles to hear sound from a hard surface, and sing through the hard palate in a way that carries the same hardness of tone.

5. To get a better sense of correct tone production:

    a. Look at the resonant spaces in Figure 3.2 that are traced by the position of the hands in this exercise, moving from the oropharynx behind the soft palate and into the nasopharynx, and aim efforts to sing along this same path.

b. Shake a cloth or dangling shirtsleeve or shirttail to make a flapping noise, and sing again with an aim to add the softer quality of timbres coming from the soft palate and similarly soft tissues of the pharynx, sinuses, and nasal passages.

Deeper and Wider Sinus Resonance

Smell a Rose

Exercise Sequence. This exercise is perhaps the most extreme multisensory technique in this book, primarily because it directly focuses on the least used sense in formal education—the sense of smell.

1. Use imagination to the fullest extent possible that you are holding a wonderfully fragrant rose in the palm of the hand (or something else as enjoyably fragrant like bread baking, a good coffee, or rich chocolate dessert).

2. Lift the rose up to the nose and smell the fragrance slowly, deeply, and lingeringly (Figure 3.10).

    - Do not sniff briskly in a way that forces in air and pulls in the nostrils for lack of air flow; flair the nostrils if necessary and open the nasal passages wide.

3. Verify the correct sensation.

    - Do you feel the sinuses open to their fullest to deeply take in the scent?

FIGURE 3.10 Smelling an imaginary rose opens the resonators up to the olfactory area.

- Do you feel air travel in spaces between the eyebrows and into the frontal sinuses?

- Do you feel air filling the maxillary sinuses below the eyes on either side of the nose?

- Is it a relaxingly open experience to open up this much?

4. Inhale the scent until the full sensation is memorized.

5. At the end of a successful smelling sensation, open the mouth slightly with a gentle release of the jaw, and sing a slow vibrant tone while maintaining the same sensation of smelling the full fragrance of the rose.

   a. Have the mind imagine the sense of inward smelling to trigger the sinuses to open, overruling any conflicting sensation that may come with the outward flow of singing tone.

6. Practice repeatedly until it is a habit to stay open while singing in any situation.

7. Add to the sensation by visualizing the arrows shown on the right of Figure 3.10 and by tracing the path in Figure 3.2 through the nose and up to the olfactory area.

Background Information. Using the sense of smell luxuriously relaxes and opens the resonators clear up to the olfactory area, which is as far up into the nasal cavity as you can go. It also may relax the jaw and involve the space in the mouth to excite the taste buds along with it. Better than a yawn, which is commonly used to open the resonant spaces of the voice, the sense of smell is far deeper of an experience of open and vibrant resonant space.

For the Voice Teacher. To get a student to be fully involved in the sensory experience, mime that you are enjoying the fragrance of your own rose and then hand it to the student to do the same. The more believable you are, the more apt the student is to fully imagine the experience and open up the resonant spaces. The demonstration also provides a visual and auditory model for students to follow.

Draw the Tone Wide

Exercise Sequence. So far, exercises have focused on moving sound farther up. This exercise aims efforts in outward directions across the width of the sinuses.

1. Bring the hands in front of the face, palms in and fingertips together.

2. As you sing a single pitch, draw the hands out from the center (Figure 3.11), repeating the movement as needed. Reduce other movements, especially the jaw, that may pull tone down and out of this wide area.

3. Explore the sensations surrounding this movement of tone out and across the face.

    a. Watch the hands move to each side and watch the space open up in between.

    b. Feel for vibrations tingling the surface of the skin under the eyes.

    c. Does the vibration on the skin extend down and across the cheeks?

    d. Do the cheekbones vibrate more intensely?

    e. Do you hear a more complex vocal timbre?

    f. Do you notice anything relaxing to stay out of the way of producing this vibration?

4. Sing a scale pattern of rising and falling pitches on a variety of vowels.

    a. Identify which vowels, and related movements, tend to pull tone out of this wide resonant area.

FIGURE 3.11   Hand motion to draw tone across the width of the sinuses.

b. Continue the hand motion to draw tone across the face for consistent resonance on each vowel.

5. Sing a song you have learned.

    a. Identify melodic intervals, vowels, and other situations that tend to pull tone out of this wide resonant area.

    b. Continue the hand motion to draw tone across the face for consistent resonance in every instant of the song.

    c. To heighten the sensation, picture the sinuses in the right image of Figure 3.2 on your own face as you sing.

Background Information. This exercise helps tone take full advantage of the maxillary sinuses, which reach across under the eyes. It can be a soothing and meditative experience to explore the rich vibrations of the front sinuses. Singers with allergies or colds have reported that their stuffed-up and congested sinuses suddenly release pressure; some have reached for a tissue fast! Some report that a headache is suddenly gone, or that they are more calm, relaxed, and peaceful. These are all signs of a deeply relaxing experience of resonance. It is this type of relaxation that allows resonance to occur more fully.

Hold and Release Movement

Exercise Sequence. The hold-and-release movement in this exercise is similar to the Chapter 2 arm-push game (Figure 2.13) in which tone is produced effortlessly in response to a slow rising motion of the arms after being held down. This exercise expands tone in a similarly free manner up into the resonators, but occurs with a fast upward motion the instant the arm is released. As with the earlier exercise, this requires a trusted helper.

1. Holding the hand out front, push up as a teacher or other helper pushes down on the hand with equal resistance to hold the arm in place (Figure 3.12).

2. Inhale a breath to sing, and on the release of singing tone the person holding the arm lets go suddenly to let the arm rise unexpectedly or uncontrollably for a moment.

3. Questions focus on what happens in the instant after the arm is released.

    - What happened to the tone as the arm flew up?

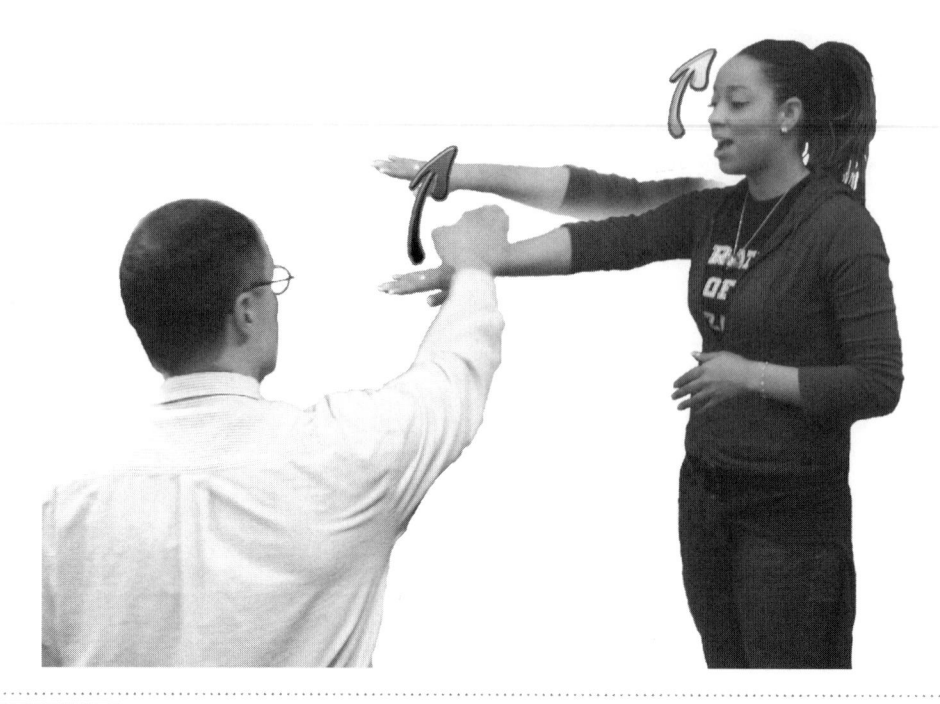

FIGURE 3.12 Hold the arm down and sing on the release for a surprisingly tension-free tone.

- Was it unexpectedly louder as more sound was easily released?

- Did sound vibrations take a new path and come out higher in the head?

- How was the movement of the diaphragm affected?

- Which resonators were newly opened and included?

- Most important, can you repeat the experience without the arm being released?

4. An alternative to an arm being held down and releasing tone up is for the singer's two hands, palms together, to be held in place by the overlaid hands of a teacher or helper as the singer pushes outwardly, and sensing a release of tone wider as the hands are released at the onset of singing tone.

Background Information. To the surprise of many singers, it takes little effort to achieve a resonant tone. It is the intended experience in this exercise for a more resonant tone to occur when efforts of pushing and tensing let go. For sound to travel freely, any weight or barrier to sound must get out of the way. In the instant the arm is released and flies up, the tone is released and allowed to flow more freely than many have ever experienced. Capture this experience the first time, because it may be difficult to repeat once a singer starts to anticipate the sensation. Repeat it nonetheless to see if the easy resonance can be experienced and memorized. Otherwise, go on to other exercises to continue to explore a free release of resonant tone.

Vowel and Register Resonance

EE into an AH and AH into an EE

Exercise Sequence. Borrowing an external sensation to guide an internal sensation of singing has been the most common multisensory vocal technique in this book. In this next series of exercises, the internal sensation of one vowel is borrowed and placed into another vowel with little external movement involved.

1. Sing the scale pattern in Figure 3.13 on different combinations of vowels, moving the scale up or down by half steps as the pattern is repeated.

    a. Sense the forward sinus resonance of an initial EE [i] and retain this sensation into an AH [ɑ].

    b. Sense the tall height of the AH [ɑ] and retain this sensation into the EE [i].

    c. Sense the roundness of OH [o] and retain this sensation into the OO [u].

    d. Sense the forward mouth-oriented resonance of OO [u] and retain this sensation into the OH [o].

    e. Retain the sinus-oriented EE [i] sensation into the mouth-oriented OO [u] sensation.

    f. Retain the roundness of the OH [o] into the tall AH [ɑ].

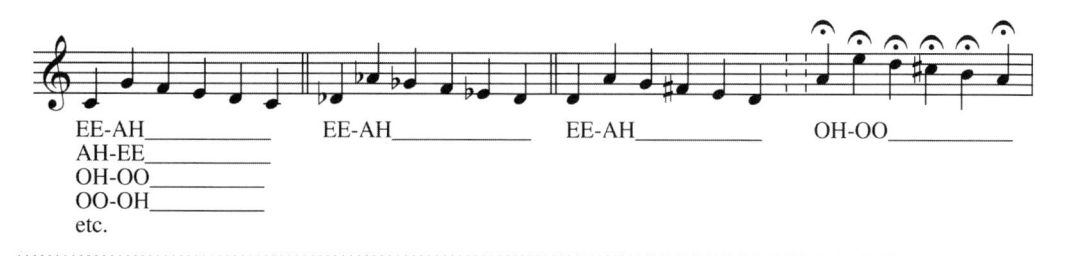

EE-AH_____   EE-AH_____   EE-AH_____   OH-OO_____
AH-EE_____
OH-OO_____
OO-OH_____
etc.

FIGURE 3.13   Borrow the first vowel sensation to sing a more resonant second vowel.

Background Information. This borrowing of sensations from one vowel to the next helps shape the full resonance of the voice. Each vowel has its own natural space in which it resonates, a tendency that is further explained in Chapter 5. Here the focus is to use the natural placement of different vowels to coax other vowels to resonate more fully.

Different vowel combinations can serve different purposes in developing fuller resonance. EE [i] helps to keep front resonators open in other vowels, AH [ɑ] to maintain the full height of resonance, OH [o] for roundness, and OO [u] for forward focus.

For the Voice Teacher and Choir Director. Whether realized or not, many of the warm-up exercises and vocalises in common use with singers and choirs are successful because they apply a principle of multisensory learning. They start with a desired sensation in one vowel or consonant and place it into a subsequent vowel, especially in using vibrant consonants to excite resonance into ensuing vowels. Go through your file of warm-ups to identify combinations that are beneficial to resonance, such as in the following samples, and then use them to their fullest effect on resonance.

- EE-AY-AH-OH-OO /i e ɑ o u/

- AH-AY-EE-OH-OO /ɑ e i o u/

- MEE-MAY-MAH-MOH-MOO /mi me mɑ mo mu/

- MAH-MAY-MEE-MOH-MOO /mɑ me mi mo mu/

- MOO-MOH-MAH-MAY-MEE /mu mo mɑ me mi/.

- ZEE-ZAY-ZAH-ZOH-ZOO /zi ze zɑ zo zu/

- ZING-UH-ZEE /zɪŋʌ zi/

- Aluminum Linoleum /əlumɪnʌm lɪnoliʌm/

- My Mommy Made Me Mash My M&Ms /maɪ mami meɪd mi mæʃ maɪ ɛmʌnɛmz/

What makes these combinations successful, which again is to borrow from a desired sensation to improve another sensation, should be applied as a general rule for all situations of learning to sing. This rule also happens to define the difference between effective and ineffective voice teachers. To have singers dryly repeat old warm-up patterns leads to little positive effect, bores singers, and perpetuates bland singing. To plan exercises and warm-ups with purpose, to pay sharp attention to improvements in resonance as the result of vowel and consonant combinations, to let singers know when improvements occur, and to go back to repeat exercises and warm-ups until full resonance is achieved—that is an effective teacher.

Important Principle for All Learning. Notice the cyclical pattern just used to describe an effective teacher. Effective teaching means literally to have an effect, to present new layers of experience and information to initial efforts, and to not move on until results are achieved. This requires three basic steps found in common to effective moments of teaching.

1. Task Presentation: Present a learning task that is active, observable, and musical in its intend—each exercise in this book presents just such tasks.

2. Monitor Response: Sharply monitor for each learner to do the musical task or for actions *in the direction* of the correct musical task.

3. Reinforcing Feedback: Let singers know which specific actions represented the correct musical task or were in the direction of the correct musical task; this also will *let singers know that you know how well they have done*. Feedback does not end a task but instead is intended to lead in a choice of directions.

    - Cycle back to step 1 as a clarification of the task presentation, as to recycle the task to make intentions clearer and until better results are achieved.

    - Bridge to the next task in a larger sequence of tasks, aimed toward a complex pattern of musical behavior or toward higher levels of learning.

    - Move on to an entirely new task in a new teaching cycle, with feedback on the previous task presenting an anticipation of the same level of success in the new task, as in "that was well done, now let's see that you do as well on this one."

    - The completion of the task for the day, closure to a job well done, and yet as a signal that this is the level of musical behavior to continue in the future and to become habit, as in "keep up the good work."

A more complete discussion of this cycle of effective teaching is found in my book *Music Teaching Style* (Gumm 2003a) and is summarized in poetic form in *The Music Director's Cookbook* (Gumm 2005). Also, though intended for band directors, see Duke's (1994) depiction of the recurring nature of a *frame*, which suggests metaphorically that you stay within the frame of the same musical picture to add color and detail until the picture is complete. The point is how well singers do in the end and not just that they went through the motions as directed. Your interest is in their *best efforts, not their first efforts*. You go back to task until the task is done well. Doing well means to fully sense and therefore fully get results.

Difficult Vowels

Exercise Sequence. The next step is to move beyond primary vowels to tackle those that are more difficult to open up and resonate fully.

1. The AE [æ] typically gets stuck in the mouth, but instead of modifying it to an AH [ɑ]:

    a. Start with an AH [ɑ] in the Figure 3.13 exercise and retain the height into the AE [æ].

    b. Start with an EE [i] and retain forward and upper resonance into the AE [æ].

2. The EH [ɛ] typically gets stuck in the front, behind the top teeth and through the hard palate.

    - Start with an OH [o] and retain the back and rounded resonance into the EH [ɛ].

    - Start with an AH [ɑ] and retain the lift into the upper resonators in the EH [ɛ].

3. The IH [ɪ] is typically just "icky" in that it closes off with the tongue, forming a shallow tone in the mouth and against the hard palate, coming out rather brash and edgy.

    a. Start with EE [i] to keep the higher resonators open for the IH [ɪ].

    b. Start with AH [ɑ] to keep the soft palate open and the tone lifting into the IH [ɪ].

4. The UH [ʌ] is typically just "ugly" in that it is muddy and lacks direction. Instead of modifying the pronunciation to AH [ɑ]:

    a. Start with AH [ɑ] and work the height into the UH [ʌ] while shifting the vowel color.

b. Start with OO [u] to provide a forward focus to the UH [ʌ].

c. Start with EE [i] to make sure the UH [ʌ] does not remain stuck back and low in the resonators.

d. Start with OH [o] to give width and roundness to the UH [ʌ].

Background Information. There are two general schools of thought on how to make difficult vowels more resonant. The first is to modify difficult vowels to sound like a resonant vowel, which in effect changes its pronunciation. For example, the words "sad" /s æ d/ and "mud" /m ʌ d/ would be modified into "sod" /s a d/ and "mod" /m a d/ to take advantage of the easy resonance of AH [a]. Another example is to modify all vowels in higher range toward UH [ʌ] to create the resonant space needed, a method based on findings that all vowels tend toward an UH [ʌ] timbre in extended ranges anyway. This approach is also tied to an extreme drop of the jaw to anchor the larynx down as the UH [ʌ] stretches space open above. Perhaps the most extreme approach to vowel modification is presented in *The Sounds of Singing* (Coffin 1987) with his findings on different voice type tendencies laid out in a highly structured chart. A problem with vowel modification is the merging of vowel color and resonant tone color as one and the same sensation—to change resonance is to change the vowel. Another problem, pointed out by Axel Theimer of the Voice Care Network, is that vowel modification—what he calls "special shaping," "coloring of vowels," and otherwise "manipulating our articulators"—covers up "habitual tone quality inefficiencies" instead of helping to learn the foundations of vocal efficiency (Theimer, 2006). Even so, the different approaches to vowel modification have led to outstanding choirs and successful professional singing careers, and remain in prevalent use across the profession.

The option presented in this extended exercise is to retain vocal efficiency and correct pronunciation of vowels but change the resonance. The solution still begins with vowels that resonate more easily, but instead of changing the pronunciation of difficult vowels the singer learns a more permanent lesson—to *resonate all vowels fully*. Resonant tone color and vowel color are kept separate, not fused. The challenge is to keep each vowel color distinct and yet work for a uniformly resonant tone color. This challenge is addressed further in Chapter 5.

The Most Beautiful Vowel-Pitch

Exercise Sequence. As the previous exercise works through different vowels to develop a unified experience of resonance, this exercise works through individual singers' different habits of singing to discover the single most naturally resonant tone, which is unique to each individual singer.

1. Sing through various scales and arpeggios on a variety of vowel combinations—such as the examples listed two exercises previous under For the Voice Teacher and Choir Director.

2. Listen for the overall freedom of resonance and look for the relaxed manner used in producing the tone.

3. Find the tone that rings most beautifully and looks most healthily produced.

4. Figure out the vowel and pitch combination that was sung at that moment of natural resonance.

   - Some produce their most natural resonant tone on an AH [ɑ], some on an OH [o], some on EE [i], and so on, but on different pitches or ranges of the voice.

5. Memorize this sensation and apply it methodically across all vowels and pitch ranges of singing.

Background Information. Used as a core approach by one subgroup or school of voice teachers, this sequence came to my attention through my retired colleague Roland Bentley, whose students always sang with such easy, consistent, and vibrant tone. It follows principles of multisensory learning in that one sensation is aimed to connect to other sensations.

However, the method is only as good as the best tone that is identified and only as good as the ability of the singer or teacher to detect the best instant of singing. Its success depends on the existence of healthy singing at least somewhere in a singer's habits, and by itself does little to improve the best of a singer's habits. On the other hand, in efforts to improve singing, all it takes is one breakthrough moment and this exercise points the way to developing consistent resonant tone in a singer's every effort.

Vowel-Register Influence

Exercise Sequence. This exercise, observed in Janet Galván's work with children's and women's choirs, first establishes a resonant sensation on a chest-voice OH [o], and retains the sensation through the transition into a head voice OO [u]. AH [ɑ] is not used here because of its strong association with chest voice and an overly open mouth, and EE [i] is avoided to keep from experiencing any tightness or spreading of tone in head voice.

1. Following the pitch pattern in the last measure of Figure 3.13, sing the first pitch A at length on an OH [o].

a. Get a good sense of the relaxed resonance of the chest voice, lower pitch, and rounded vowel as the sensation to retain into head voice.

2. Make a smooth transition into head voice to the second pitch on an OO [u], throat still open, tone still flowing, and the lower roundness of the OH [o] still part of the sensation.

3. Move to each descending pitch in turn, very slowly and unpredictably to avoid any anticipation of the next lower note or any sense of gravity pulling down on the tone.

   a. Retain the light character and lifting sensation of the head voice as the voice makes a transition back into chest voice.

   b. Maintain a focused, upper-resonant tone that is natural to head voice and that also maintains the original round OH [o] resonance that started the exercise.

4. Repeat the pattern a half step higher or lower at a time within the range that keeps the starting and ending pitch in chest voice and the highest pitch in head voice.

For the Choir Director. Just as there are different schools of thought about whether to modify vowels or learn consistent resonance regardless of the vowel, there are different schools of thought about resonance in a choir. One is to refine tone by limiting the resonance of the choir. Head voice is often the model for the lean and focused tone desired, and a lip-puckered OO [u] is favored for its focus and its lack of strong overtones. Warm-up exercises bring the head-voice quality down into chest voice and place OO [u] resonance behind everything that is sung. The problem is that such resonance-limiting approaches leave singers with a limited concept of tone production, one that varies greatly from solo singing. This perpetuates a divide between voice teachers and choir directors as teachers of singing, the voice teachers having to deal with the tension and other consequences of an overly refined "choir voice." The opposite school of choir directors seeks a fuller tone with richer resonance, using an AH [a] vowel in chest voice as the model for the underlying resonance. A natural opening of the mouth, rather than puckered, is preferred in this approach.

A bridge between these two schools is presented in this exercise. Singers take the advantages of the natural resonance in a chest voice OH [o] into head voice, and take the advantages of the refined and focused head voice OO [u] down into chest voice. The result is that all tones, regardless of register or vowel, have an easy-flowing refined resonance. The choir learns a tone that is natural to the individual singers in the choir. The result is a healthy and strong approach to singing, one that is flexible and consistent between choral singing and solo singing and adaptable to a greater variety of musical styles.

Effects of Posture on Resonance

Rope Pull Over a Cliff

Exercise Sequence. Imagination plays an important role in sensing a posture that affects resonance. Be playful enough to enjoy the full benefit of the experience.

1. Imagine that you are up on a high cliff, standing at the edge ready to pull a bucket up and down the cliff by a rope (Figure 3.14).

2. Maintain a center of gravity to keep your balance.

   - Keep the feet shoulder width apart and one foot slightly behind the other.

   - Bend the knees slightly to stay flexible.

   - Balance the body's weight on the balls of the feet with the weight off the heels.

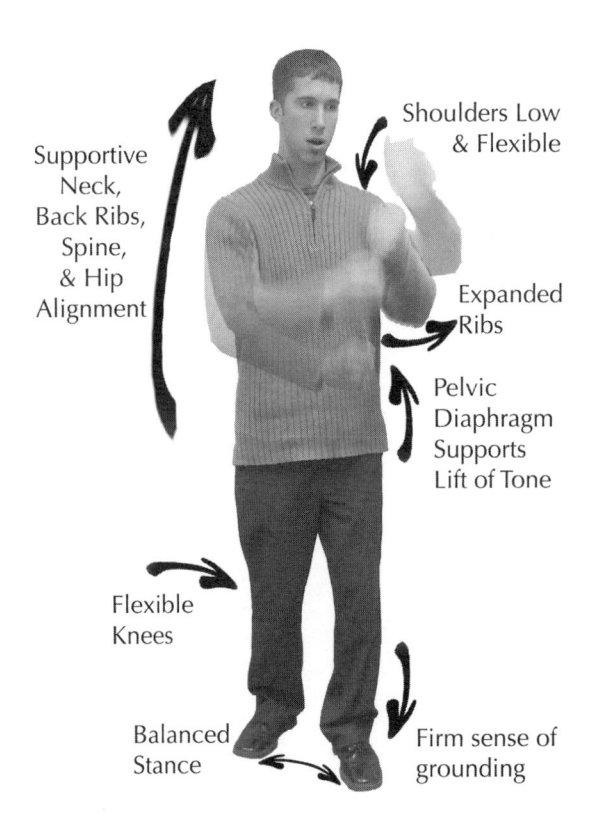

FIGURE 3.14 Imagining pulling a bucket up by a rope brings balance and deep supported tone.

Supportive Neck, Back Ribs, Spine, & Hip Alignment

Shoulders Low & Flexible

Expanded Ribs

Pelvic Diaphragm Supports Lift of Tone

Flexible Knees

Balanced Stance

Firm sense of grounding

- Expand and rotate the ribcage to align the spine, actively involve costal and back muscles, and bear the weight across the entire body down into the legs.

- Keep the body flexible, alert, and ready to shift the weight to counterbalance any sudden movements.

3. Hold the imaginary bucket by the rope with arms extended out over the cliff edge, and lower the bucket down the face of the imaginary cliff, hand over hand with one hand at a time lowering the bucket.

    - Feel how steady breathing operates on its own, separately from the efforts to lower the bucket.

    - Feel the entire body respond to maintain balance as one hand takes the weight of the bucket and the other hand lets go.

    - Feel the ribs expand out wide to help expand the power behind the arm movements.

    - Feel how the spine responds flexibly, buoyantly, and separately from muscle efforts.

    - Sense how the back muscles assist not in pulling the rope but as a unit in the safe and balanced use of the spine.

4. During this hand-over-hand bucket lowering, with the efforts firmly planted through the feet and the body flexible and responsive, sing a slow ascending scale on a choice of vowels.

    - Feel the connection of the body to the tone from deep down, even from the feet, up and through with a full resonant tone.

5. Hand under hand now, pull the bucket back up the cliff edge, holding it out far enough to keep it from scraping against rock.

6. Sing a slow and steady descending scale.

    - Sense the consistent source of energy from down deep in the center of the body.

    - Feel the relaxed and low larynx and release of tension in phonation.

    - Hear the rich, dark, supported tone that results from this posture and effort.

Background Information. This exercise is another upside-down experience that borrows the sensation of downward movement to sing ascending pitches more securely, and borrows the sensation of lifting to descend in pitch more securely. Added to this upside-down experience is a deep sensation of balance and wonderfully supportive posture caused by distributing weight across the body. This buoyant and flexible sensation of posture is far from the notion that posture is to remain stiff and unmoving. The body stays flexible and responsive and is deeply rooted from the feet on up. The pelvic diaphragm is positioned beneath the internal organs, the ribcage expands, the spine is placed in a healthy position, and the shoulders find a low and natural position.

Separation of movements in different systems is also a target. Arm movements must become detached from the rest of the body or else the weight of the bucket and movement of the arms will throw the body off balance and forward. Breathing, which must continue during the lengthy rope-pull effort, comes to function separately in perhaps a more deep and free manner than in everyday experiences.

Because the majority of our senses revolve around the head, a lot of singers focus on efforts from the neck up. The limited perceptions of neck-up singing is seen in shallow chest breathing, a lack of involvement of lower breathing muscles, a forward leaning head and posture, sound aimed out the mouth to the outer ears, an overly open mouth as the main way for sound to get out, raised larynx and eyebrows, and a lack of sound being sent to any distance away from the immediate space in and around the head. Check for such signs of neck-up singing, and work to extend the senses beyond the head and get the rest of the body involved in the process.

This exercise returns to a starting point in Chapter 1, that posture affects vocal techniques related to each chapter in the book and provides a foundation for all of singing. Physiologically, the function of posture in singing is to keep the *feet* under the *pelvis*, the pelvis under the *diaphragm*, the diaphragm under the *vocal cords*, the vocal cords in line with the *resonators*, and the resonators free to *project* sound out and beyond. Singing posture starts from the ground up, with the placement of the feet and flexible knees providing balance, responsiveness, and buoyant lift all the way up through each system. Without balance, tension creeps in other places of the body; therefore, an effective posture keeps the rest of the body from tensing to make up for lost balance.

This summary of the alignment of internal functions coincides with the externally visible alignment of the ear, shoulder, hip, knee, and ankle down a central vertical line—the proper body alignment prescribed and pictured in books ranging in topic from general kinesiology (Oatis 2004) to body mapping (Conable & Conable 1995, Conable 2000, Conable & Conable 2000) to voice (Dayme 2004). Not so much mentioned in other sources is that by lining up these observable points, the internal functions of singing also happen to come in line. This alignment creates a more dynamic and hydraulic action in breathing and singing. It is more dynamic because of the flexible movements across several systems that together provide more energy into singing than possible with individual systems. It is hydraulic in the sense that the lift in one system is transmitted to other systems that collectively give rise to a larger force. The larger collective force is greater than the lone efforts of neck-up singing.

Important Principle for All Learning. Imagination is a powerful tool in learning. As said by Albert Einstein, "Imagination is more important than knowledge, for knowledge is limited while imagination embraces the entire world." It allows singers to experience situations that cannot otherwise be reproduced in the classroom, brings meaningful past experiences into the classroom, and builds new shared experiences that add meaning. It uses familiar images to get singers to sense something new and places singers in an environment perhaps never experienced before. Imagination can draw all of the senses together into a vivid experience of singing. This cliff's-edge experience draws upon imagination to develop a whole-body experience that is otherwise not experienced in traditional voice lessons or choir rehearsals. Find other past experiences from which to learn a stronger sense of the body's involvement. Be creative and imaginative in finding appropriate situations in which new and more effective sensations can be experienced.

Extended Exercise. An imaginary situation can become less effective when repeated. The initial response to the image can become less vivid, less interesting, and too commonplace to excite the intended response. Therefore, new situations may be needed to focus attention and effort more sharply. Here are two more options to get your own imagination started.

7. Sing with the *tone cradled in the forearms* like carrying an armload of firewood, knees flexible, ribcage rotated and expanded, spine tall, larynx lower, airway open down into the body to the tone cradled in the arms.

8. Keeping the upper body upright, bend the legs to reach down and *pick up imaginary buckets of water* on either side, one bucket for each hand. As the buckets are lifted, feel the low position of the shoulders, the rotation of the ribcage, the separation of arm movements in response to separate buckets, and flexible balance throughout the body in the attempt to balance and not to spill water.

Tilted Posture to Affect Tension and Gravity

Exercise Sequence. Efforts to find an effective posture need to lift and release a resonant tone against the downward forces of gravity. This exercise demonstrates what singing feels and sounds like with the effects of gravity taken off of posture and instead working in favor of resonant tone. A teacher or trusted helper is required for this sequence, someone strong enough to hold a lot of the singer's weight; permission of the singer needs to be acquired for this.

1. Stand with feet together and toes pointed in and touching.

2. Put one hand in a fist and the other hand wrapped around it, the two hands locked together.

3. Extend the arms straight out front into the palm of the teacher's or helper's hands.

4. Ready to trustingly bear the weight of the singer, the helper tilts the singer forward by the arms, the singer's feet staying put with heels off the floor and weight on the toes and balls of the feet (see Figure 3.15).

5. As the singer sings a pitch, the helper pushes with small, unexpected shakes that move through the arms and into the singer's body.

    a. The tongue and muscles of the jaw, throat, neck, face, and possibly even the sinuses should shake free of tension and hang in a relaxed manner simply by the new angle of gravity and especially due to the extra shaking (see the Figure 3.15 arrow going up from the shoulder).

FIGURE 3.15 A tilted position releases tension and allows a deeply supported release of resonant tone.

b. The ribcage, costal muscles, diaphragm, and shoulders should shudder in response to the pushes from the helper, causing bursts of tone to flow more loudly and freely out from the chest up through the head (see the Figure 3.15 arrow going down from the shoulder).

6. In repeated attempts, copy the sensation experienced at the height of the pushes and produce the fullest tone consistently across a long held tone, with the helper shaking only on occasion to keep tension from coming back.

  a. Sense the experience holistically without analyzing its details, simply holding on to the total experience at once.

  b. Sense the experience sequentially, detecting specific parts of the body that release tension and get out of the way to allow tone to come out freely and fully.

7. Sing scale patterns and melodies in this tilted position with the helper shaking tension out a moment before it typically occurs, such as at a peak pitch or on a rising interval, until each tone is equally relaxed, deeply supported, and resonant.

8. Stand upright and sing, producing the same tone and maintaining the same sense of freedom from gravity as in the tilted position.

Background Information. In Chapter 2, an upside-down technique of singing high with a low-pitch sensation (Figure 2.7) was used to maintain relaxed phonation at all pitch levels. The tilted-posture exercise (Figure 3.15) is not upside-down but gets the body to sense singing in the same manner—by *throwing off the body's reaction to the force of gravity*. The exercise points out the connection between the physiology of the body and the acoustical sound that the body is capable of producing. All it takes is to put an upside-down sensation into your upright posture.

Extended Exercise I: Centrifugal Force and Upside-Down Gravity. Other upside-down and off-tilt exercises are possible in finding a fuller resonance and relaxed manner of singing.

9. Bend at the waist, flop over like a *rag doll* with arms falling forward and down ahead of the upper body, and sing in a way that keeps the outward and downward force experienced in the flopping motion.

10. Bend at the waist with hands on the knees and head dangling down freely and bouncy like a bobble-head toy, sing a tone that follows the relaxed sensation out the face and head, and listen for sound to sweep the floor. Stand up during a long

held tone to check that resonant tone continues in the same manner by the time you are standing.

11. Get on hands and knees with head dangling down like a bobble-head toy and listen to sound resonate and fill the space under the body and across the floor.

12. Ride a spinning playground merry-go-round, lying down with the head toward the outside, and sing with tone flowing with the centrifugal force.

13. Swing forcefully on a playground swing, and sing at the upward peak during the sense of weightlessness.

Extended Exercise II: Shaky Alternatives. Besides the effects of gravity, shaking also has its effects on the sensation in the tilted-posture exercise. These alternatives keep the shake but remove the off-balance tilt. These are all done in a standing position during singing, with a teacher or trusted helper providing unexpected movements that establish (a) a lower center of gravity, (b) a firmer sense of connection to the ground, and (c) a posture that is flexible, responsive, and full-bodied.

14. Hold the hands out in the same manner as step 2 for a helper to send movement through the arms and into the ribcage and head; use an unexpected pull forward to draw out additional sensations of posture and tone production.

15. Hold one arm out front or to the side with a fist in the palm of the helper's hand for one-sided pushes and pulls that keep the body alert, poised, and responsive.

16. The teacher or helper pushes gently forward on the spine between the shoulder blades for the singer to aim efforts back and taller away from forward singing, and to affect lower abdominal breathing.

17. With the singer's hands to the side in normal standing position, the helper alternates with a series of unexpected pushes to the back, upper arm, or a shoulder on one side or the other to keep the singer from holding any tension in the upper body that could disrupt the full resonance of the tone.

Sensory Experience: How Many Directions Can Sound Travel?

Exercise Sequence. This exercise uses hand positions mostly as out-of-sight mental targets to direct sound back and up before moving forward. It works like the sonar-hand sensory experience that began this chapter, only now the sound does not bounce back off the hand.

1. Place a hand palm down straight above the head. As you sing, direct sound through resonant spaces in the direction of the hand (Figure 3.16). Draw the hand upward as if drawing sound out of the top of the head. What sensation is felt:

   a. Down the nose?

   b. Throughout the nasal cavity and sinuses?

   c. Across the palate?

   d. On the top side of the palate?

   e. At the roof of the sinuses?

   f. Through the brain cavity?

   g. Other places vibrations are felt?

2. Place a hand, palm toward the head, diagonally above and behind the head. As you sing, direct sound in a line past the ears and out of the head in the direction of the hand. What sensation is felt:

   a. Down the nose?

   b. Throughout the nasal cavity and sinuses?

FIGURE 3.16 Targeting sound different directions out of the head.

c. Inside the ear, in the inner ear?

   d. On the ear tips?

   e. Through the brain cavity?

   f. On the scalp?

   g. Other places vibrations are felt?

3. Place a hand, palm toward the head, directly behind the back of the head. As you sing, direct sound through the head in the direction of the hand. What sensation is felt:

   a. Down the nose?

   b. Throughout the nasal cavity and sinuses?

   c. On the lower scalp?

   d. In the upper spinal column of the neck?

   e. Other places vibrations are felt?

4. Hold a hand out by one ear and as you sing direct sound out the side of the head toward the hand.

   a. Can you actually create a sense of vibration on one side and not the other?

Background Information. There is no reason to limit resonance to traditional ideas about singing, whether the idea is that sound comes out through the mouth or through the sinuses. Sound waves can travel through other surfaces and spaces as well, including the brain cavity in an upward and backward direction that can tingle the scalp. It can vibrate the neck and spine down into the shoulders. These so-called sympathetic vibrations can even go down into the body, given the right posture and attention.

For the Choir Director. In the discussion of forward singing at the end of Chapter 2, one cause of this problem was the constant attention to a conductor at the podium. Use this how-many-directions exercise in a rehearsal situation to teach singers to direct resonance up and out while maintaining visual contact with the conductor. This extends thinking in two directions—unity of performance through the conductor and unity of resonant tone up and into the room. The following steps provide an alternative way to focus attention to other directions other than forward toward the conductor and audience.

1. As the choir rehearses a learned song, have singers turn round and round in place, which gets them to perceive sounds from all directions around them and to blend and balance their singing to what they hear as they turn.

2. Signal for singers to face forward as they continue to singing.

    - Notice improvements in resonant choral tone such as increased warmth or breadth of tone projected out into the room.

    - Share your perceptions with the choir to reinforce their improved awareness and new sensations.

    - Develop the rule for singers to focus attention forward to the conductor and yet draw from sounds around them to focus it upward, out, and beyond.

This issue of getting sound out into a room is discussed at greater length in the upcoming Chapter 4 and is shown visually in Figure 4.8. For now, write down any exercises of your own that may have come to mind as you worked through this chapter.

Name of Exercise

Exercise Purpose:

Exercise Sequence:

Background Information:

CHAPTER 4

PROJECTION AND RELEASE OF SOUND

In this chapter are movement and mental imagery exercises that help the singer perceive sound outside the body and into and across space. Awareness is shifted to the result of singing beyond self. With this shift in awareness, singing becomes more a sense of release than of pushing and shoving sound out of the body.

Acoustics: Amplitude

Sensory Experience: How Does Singing Get Louder?

Exercise Sequence. The purpose of this exercise is to find out where efforts are made to project a louder vocal tone.

1. Sing an AH vowel on a medium-range pitch, first at the volume of a conversation voice and then at a loud dynamic level. Repeat as needed to answer questions in step 2.

2. Which of each choice below best describes your efforts to sing louder?

    - Do efforts feel tighter, or more relaxed and freer?

    - Is more sound produced inside of you, or outside of you?

    - Does more sound come out a smaller space, or out a larger space?

    - Does it feel like sound is compacted into a smaller space, or like sound is expanded into more spaces?

    - Does the center of vibration stay in the same spot or change to a different spot?

    - Does it feel like sound is being squeezed out, or like more sound is being released up, around, and out?

    - Is sound pushed forward harder, or spread around more with ease?

3. Sing different vowels across both dynamic levels, explore step 2 questions once again, and compare whether the sensation changes on different vowels.

4. Talk loudly and then sing loudly.

    - Does the center of sound change when talking is changed to singing?

    - Does tension and effort change between talking loudly and singing loudly?

Background Information. There are several misconceptions that singers have about singing louder. Louder sound can be attempted by pushing pressure against an object in the body, by forcing it through a surface, by channeling it like a megaphone through the mouth, by compressing it or compacting it tighter in the available space, and by closing off space to compress the available tone into a smaller space. Sound can be forced into the nose, through the hard palate, in the mouth, or in the throat. Such efforts may take a lot of muscle and seem more powerful, but the body does this through tension instead of release. The sound may seem louder in the immediate space of the singer, and more vibration may be felt as a result, but sound produced this way does not travel far or sound loud very far away.

It is the opposite of these misconceived efforts that needs to happen—sound needs to open up to more space and be released from the body more freely to be louder and more resonant. The correct conception of sound is to make it taller, not compress it smaller. Loud is primarily the result of a taller sound wave; the height of a sound wave referred to as its *amplitude* (Figure 4.1).

Because of the various problems that result from the use of the word, "louder" is perhaps one of those words that could be done away with when it comes to singing. As with any other misunderstood word, however, it does not hurt to say "louder" if associated with appropriate sensations and techniques for getting loud. Directions that better match acoustical properties of sound are:

- Make the vocal tone *taller*.

- Find more *space* for sound to vibrate and come out.

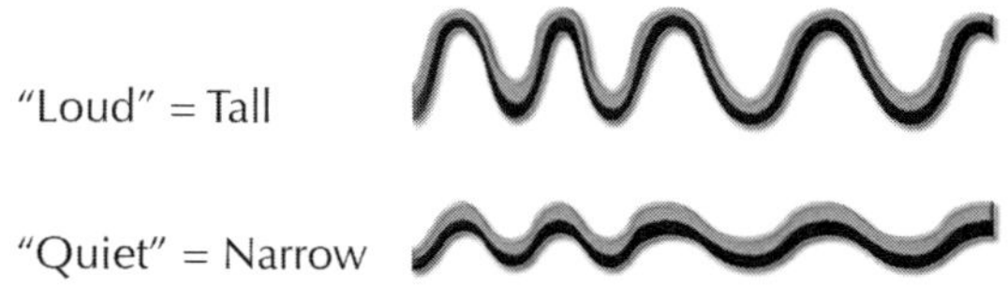

"Loud" = Tall

"Quiet" = Narrow

FIGURE 4.1 The height of the amplitude of a sound wave determines loudness.

- *Release* more sound from more places in the body high to low.

- Allow more sound to *escape*.

These properties of projection are explored in the following exercises.

Narrow to Tall Hands

Exercise Sequence. This exercise focuses on making the vocal tone taller, with the result of a more relaxing release of resonant tone across a wider range of dynamics.

1. On singing any pitch, pattern of pitches, melody, or choral part, hold the hands out front, one hand above the other, palms facing the center as if holding a ball in front of the face (Figure 4.2).

2. As if holding the size of sound between the hands, move the hands shorter or closer together and then taller or farther apart, and fill the space between with the size of sound held by the hands. Use all of your senses:

   a. Watch the hands as the distance between increases.

   b. Hear the changes in sound in the air around you.

   c. Hear the sounds inside the head, whether muffled, hollow, nasal, or piercing.

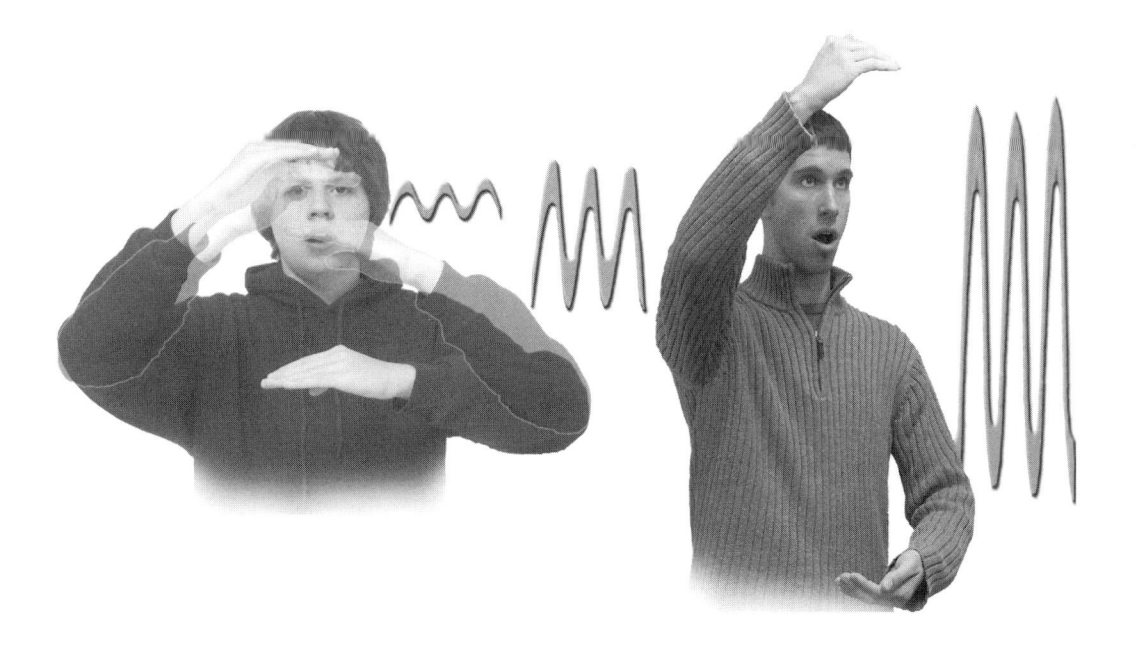

FIGURE 4.2   Narrow hands for a quiet tone and tall hands for a loud tone.

d. Feel vibration in the portions of the body outlined by the hands.

e. Feel the vibrations inside the head.

f. Feel the vibrations on flesh and bone.

g. Imagine the size of tone in front of you—give it color, shape, texture, and weight if it helps make more sense.

h. Picture the insides of your body filled with sound—give it a color or texture if it helps.

3. What had to physically change for sound to fill the space between tall hands?

Background Information. Like a speaker in a sound system, when the volume is turned down the small center of the speaker vibrates most, and when the volume is turned up the vibrations move out from the center to the outer ring. Therefore, sound gets louder by being taller and broader, not by forcing more energy into the compact space at the center. In a sound system, it is the amplitude that increases to change the loudness of the sound; therefore the more technically correct name for the volume knob is "amplitude knob" because it turns up the amplitude or height of the sound wave.

The voice turns up the amplitude by resonating, or literally by re-sounding, in more spaces of the head and chest. To resonate, more space needs to open up and echo the sound that originates from the vocal cords. These spaces are the focus of the exercises in the following sections.

Extended Exercise: Dynamics Markings. Crescendo and decrescendo markings in music indicate changes in dynamics in an acoustically correct way. Lines extend farther apart, or taller, for the music to grow louder and draw closer together, or shorter, for music to get quieter. However, dynamic markings such as *p* for *piano* or *f* for *forte* are arbitrary symbols on the page that do not visually represent the nature of short-to-tall dynamics. Use these extended uses of the short-to-tall hand motions to help maintain an open and resonant tone as attention is focused on dynamics markings in the music.

1. Use short-to-tall hand movements to physically follow the relative distance between lines in *crescendo* and *decrescendo* markings on a classroom board and in a selection of music (Figure 4.3 a).

    a. Steady hand movements help singers correct a typical sudden drop in dynamics at the start of a decrescendo, and instead assist a smooth and steady reduction in sound across the length of the marking.

2. Add vertical lines that visually divide the crescendo and decrescendo markings into equal segments for more precise points of reference (Figure 4.3 b).

3. Add numbers at each vertical line to provide a numerical order to each degree of dynamics (Figure 4.3 c)

4. Under each line that was added in step 5, add individual dynamic markings from *p, mp, mf,* to *f* and back again (Figure 4.3 d), moving the hands an appropriate distance apart for each marking.

5. Sing different dynamic levels *p, mp, mf,* and *f* with the gradual crescendo/decrescendo markings removed, using the same width between hands and the same sensation of release of tone at each level of loudness (Figure 4.3 e).

6. Bring more sense to the exercise by changing the intent of dynamics from loudness to colors or character words.

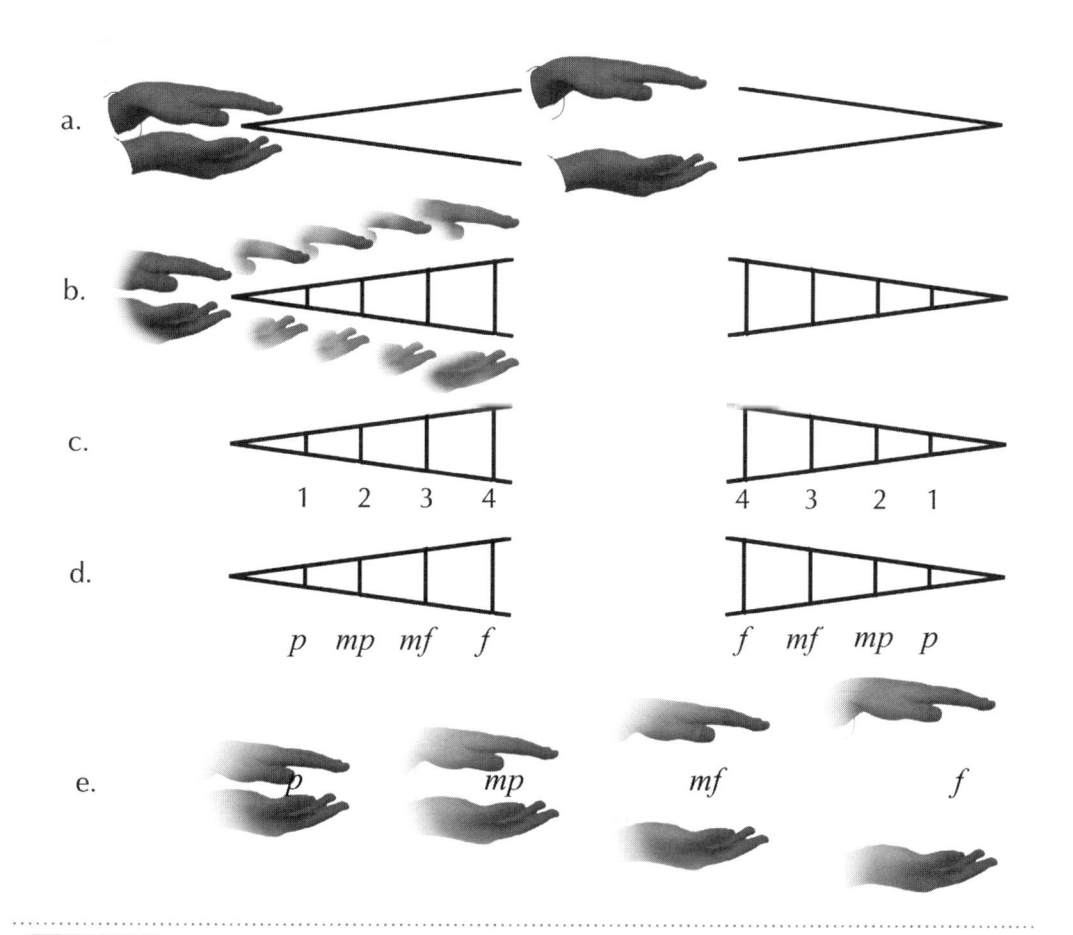

FIGURE 4.3 Tall and short hands used to execute dynamics accurately and freely.

- Turn a *forte* dynamic from being "loud" to being a radiant red or "convincing" with tall and confident hands.

- Turn *mezzo forte* into a vivid green or "everyone can hear me" with hands open to the distance of the farthest possible audience member.

- Turn *piano* into a brilliant blue or "attention-getting hush" with hands as a focused beam that carries sound freely to any distance across a room.

The goal is to be heard by all members of an audience at all dynamic levels. Singing should not be weak or lifeless at any dynamic level. Also dynamics should be adjusted to the size of the room and should always be executed with proper tone production within the limits of the individual voice.

For the Voice Teacher and Choir Director. Having singers use short-to-tall hand gestures verifies their attention to dynamic markings in the music. Though it is more typical to assess dynamics by simply listening for students to sing louder or quieter as markings change in the music, the hand movements add a kinesthetic, hands-on sense, and allows the teacher to "see" the singer "think."

For the Choir Director. The use of short-to-tall hand gesture to show dynamics is an effective assessment tool in a choral situation of many singers. The teacher can detect individual student attention and music reading skills across the entire group. Results can be used for summative judgments for grades, but better is to use results for formative evaluation, which is to evaluate on the way to helping students become better music readers. You can learn who makes quicker and slower decisions by the speed of reaction, who tends of follow other singers rather than the music by the change in gaze, or who stays focused or is easily distracted away from music by eye movement. An ideal goal is to teach all singers to be as quick as the quickest and as focused as the most focused; a practical solution is to mix different strengths in the standing order of each section to the advantage of the entire choir.

Technically it is best to keep dynamics within the capabilities of each individual choir. Presenting an image of a mature choir's *forte* to a young or untrained choir is inappropriate. Expecting a choir to produce a tone at an extreme dynamic beyond their control is like telling a beginning skier to point the skis straight down the hill and just try not to fall—disastrous! Keeping the range of dynamics within the capabilities of the choir is like telling a skier to go sideways on a hill at a controllable speed until techniques have been learned that allow a more mature approach.

Moving Sound Beyond the Resonators

Peek-a-boo Hands

Exercise Sequence. As when playing this age-old game with a baby, this exercise first hides the tone and then lets it come out in a joyous sound.

1. To get a sense of trapped tone, place the hands in front of the face and eyes and sing an AH [a].

   - Is there a sense that the sound is blocked, not only by the hands but inside as well?

   - Does the throat feel narrow?

   - Do the tongue and jaw close the mouth space.

   - Does the head want to back up?

2. Take a breath for singing, and just at the onset of singing tone release the hands away from the face and out, as in the release of the hands for a peek-a-boo.

   - Watch the hands move away from the face.

   - Let everything that wants to open follow the hands out and away.

   - Feel the sound vibrate across the face and out into the open space revealed as the hands move to the side.

   - Keep the sound flowing into the room beyond.

Background Information. Our perceptions of the surrounding space affect the physical way we attempt to sing into the surrounding space. This exercise is important for those who wear glasses, which can give the sense that sound is blocked just like the hands in front of the eyes blocked sound in this exercise. For those who wear glasses, take them off when you sing to perceive the sound releasing more freely beyond and into the room.

Extended Exercises. Better yet, explore the extended exercises below using glasses and other common experiences and objects.

1. Take eyeglasses by the side bows, and in singing a long tone move the glasses off and forward, watching them as they move away.

- Notice anything that opens up to allow sound to follow the forward movement of the glasses.

- Feel the open throat and the release of pressure to allow sound to flow more freely out and away.

2. Wearing a baseball cap, echo the sound off the brim above the eyes.

3. For singers with long bangs over the forehead, put a hand under the bangs and as you sing, draw the bangs or flip them out and upward for a physical sense of where sound can be released.

4. Find other common experiences that could be adapted for this sound-releasing sensation.

Draw Tone Out Beyond the Resonators

Exercise Sequence. Like the peek-a-boo hand motion, this exercise helps draw tone forward out of the resonators, but adds a sense of space and time as sound travels forward.

1. On a single pitch or for each pitch sung in a scale exercise or melody, move the hands in a motion that draws tone out of the face (Figure 4.4); use two hands, one after the other, for a quicker series of pitches.

2. Start with fingers toward the face in a position used to grasp a baseball, as if gently grasping the front end of the tone about to come out.

3. Move the hand away from the face during singing with a slow, graceful, relaxed, and flowing motion.

FIGURE 4.4 Draw-tone-out hand gesture.

4. Extend the motion, and the tone, out to the full reach of the arm.

5. Release the hand's grasp on the tone, and allow the sensation to continue beyond the reach of the arm.

Background Information. The hand motion suggested in this exercise is very similar to the one suggested in Chapter 1, Figure 1.7 to trace the path of tone. The difference is that instead of a palm-forward motion that feels its way through the path of tone, this motion originates at the point that sound leaves the body and instead draws tone out. The sense that sound originates at that point is heightened by a slight grasp of tone by the fingers, which adds a round shape, a light weight, and soft consistency to the tone. The steady movement forward adds sensation to the invisible molecules of air from the face forward. Sound is so difficult to understand because it is invisible, which is solved by *giving sound a sense of direction, size, weight, speed, color, and other properties* using a simple hand motion.

To understand the importance of making more sense of the space in a room, take this example of two choirs singing in a same concert hall on the same program. One choir consists of mature, semi-professional singers who can resonate a powerful and deafening sound. They intensely focus on the conductor with fire in their eyes and emotion in their faces, and their bodies move responsively to every breath, attack, enunciated word, change in dynamic, and emotion of the music and text. In other words, their movements reveal a deep and intricate understanding of vocal techniques, but for lack of one thing. Their efforts are all aimed toward the immediate space around them, mostly down, at the person in the row ahead, into the music held in front of them, and at best as far out as the conductor. The other choir is a novice choir of young adults with but one advantage, a sense that sound is to travel with ease out into the concert hall. Their eyes are equally focused on their conductor, they also hold music in their hands, their vocal technique is as thorough though less seasoned, and their articulation of words is comparable. However, one of the key exercises in their preparation is this draw-tone-out exercise and others like it to gauge the effort needed to release sound up and out until it extends the full distance of the hall. The review in the local newspaper reveals the difference. At the start the music critic complains about the acoustics of the hall and the difficulty he had in hearing the adult choir, and yet he went on to describe details of the beautifully effortless tone, the clarity of each word, and ease with which the younger choir could be heard. The first choir seemed to be singing loud and yet too little was heard for any favorable comments to be offered by the critic for that choir. The issue of projection is this important from the audience perspective. By the way, this is a true story.

Extended Exercise: Backward Projection. Counteracting the attention to forward projection, hair can provide a concrete sensation of the path of sound out the back of the head. This extended sequence is only fully possible by people with long hair. Those with short hair can sense the hair at the start and otherwise only have the hand movement and imagination to help.

1. Reach the hands around the back of the neck and under the hair (or touching the tips for those with short hair), with one hand on top of the other.

2. As you sing, move the hands back, out, and away from the head, pulling strands of long hair along for a sense of length as sound is drawn along the path of the hands.

    a. Allow the head and body to follow the hands backward only slightly, if at all, without throwing off balance.

3. Repeat the move, alternating between quick and slow movements to find which one results in the greatest sense of relaxed openness and greatest release of tone out and beyond the resonators.

Telescope Hands

Exercise Sequence. This exercise puts the singer's focus even further beyond the space reachable by an extended arm.

1. Make a circle with the fingers and thumb on each hand and as if holding a long spyglass or telescope, line up one hand close in front for an eye to see through the circle, and extend the other hand out away from the body in a position that the eye can see through that circle as well (Figure 4.5).

1. Focus the gaze through the circles of both hands on an object at a distance across the room, and sing a tone through the imaginary telescope so that it projects to the distant object.

2. Check the accuracy of the sensation.

FIGURE 4.5 A telescope-hands position gives a sense of direction and shape to tone across open space.

- Did the tone shrink in size to fit through the small hole? That is not intended, so open up and send a full sound in and around the holes of the hand until the sound makes it to the point across the room.

- Did the throat, lips, and sinuses all open up like the tube of a telescope? This is one possible positive sensation that can result. Be careful it is not only the mouth that rounds—the hands are at eye level to coax sound out of open sinuses.

- Were the abdominal and costal muscles active underneath the effort to sing out and through the hands?

- What got out of the way so that sound could travel the distance?

3. If first efforts do not work to project a focused and resonant tone across the room, then shift the gaze farther.

    - Focus out the window, across the yard, into the next building.

    - If no window is in the room, focus on someone imaginarily on the other side of the wall, across the hall in the next room, or farther until the body opens up and sends a focused tone out and beyond.

4. Add a sense of movement to the view through the telescoped hands by moving the hands back for inhalation and forward for phonation.

    - Forward motion during singing also adds a sense of movement of sound across the immediate space, as with the draw-tone movement shown in Figure 4.4.

Background Information. This exercise is not as touch-sensitive as others, but is more for the visually oriented learner. Space if so open and seemingly without substance, energy, or direction that its fuzzy effects on singing are typically ignored. Sound needs an energetic sense of direction, and because air is invisible and space so intangible, the best solution is to place the hands or other objects across the space to fill the void.

For the Voice Teacher. The result of this telescope-hand exercise can be heard from across a room, but can be better guided and assessed when the teacher is the object at the other end of the telescope gaze. Not only listen for the sound arriving but also get a sense of the energy and vibration behind the tone at the target spot. The focus to the tone can be sensed by hearing and feeling whether it is centered at head level or drops to the floor. Use this strategy for more effective control and response to singer efforts.

1. Hold your hands in the position of holding a telescope just like the singer's position (Figure 4.5).

2. From a distance across the room, move the circles of both hands in line with the singer's hands, and look back through the four hands at the student's eye.

3. As the singer sings, back up, extending the length of the "telescope tube" and causing the singer unexpected additional effort in order to project farther yet. It also gives a sense of movement of sound at the farther distance.

4. Listen for sound at eye level, and if not projected at that level then estimate how far the sound traveled and redirect efforts farther until it is heard at eye level.

For the Choir Director. The bigger the size and space of a rehearsal or concert hall, it seems, the more singers tend to spread tone in more directions. This misguided effort is logical but incorrect. The more sound spreads, the less energy there is behind its path, and the less sound actually travels out to be heard.

On the other hand, a focused tone has the energy to travel out the distance, and to keep traveling until it reaches all corners of the room. To redirect efforts to fit the size of any room, focus singers' attention to a distant point. Use the movement of this or other exercise to add more sensation to the direction of sound through an open space. Continue working to project sound out until it is heard to vibrate in the distance. Better yet, set the sights further than the other side of the room until sound echoes back your way. In every effort to project, avoid forward pressure on the vocal cords and forward tilting or leaning. Maintain eye contact to the conductor, but put the mind's eye on moving sound up and across the distance.

Learning to Hear Sound in a Room

Sensory Experience: Can You Echo Sound at Different Levels of the Room?

Exercise Sequence. This exercise could be one to use in every lesson, practice rehearsal, and concert situation because it focuses on the acoustical results of singing. In every effort to sing, the sound in the room tells you how well you will be heard and where.

1. Standing with effective posture for singing, aim sound to the floor, sing, and stop sound by inhaling silently to hear the echo in the room. Add a kinesthetic and visual sensation to the effort by gesturing a sound wave (as in Chapter 2, Figure 2.3) that sweeps across the floor and by visualizing a squiggly sound wave that follows the path of the hand.

- Did the sound of the voice echo across the floor?

- What happened in the resonators to direct sound to the floor?

- Was any tension involved in the effort to sing to the floor? Try this step again until no tension is experienced as sound is aimed toward the floor.

2. Aim sound at head level against the wall at the other end of the room, again stopping sound suddenly with an inward flow of breath. Add other senses by waving the hand at head level and imagining a squiggly sound wave vibration being drawn across the room by the hand gesture (again with Figure 2.3 as an example).

- Did sound echo back to you off the wall?

- What occurred in the resonators in order to direct sound forward?

- How did breathing efforts differ from singing to the floor?

- Were you able to project with ease?

3. Without changing posture or the direction of stance, aim sound to echo off the ceiling and not the floor, in one corner of the room and not another, behind you and not in front of you. Gesture to each targeted area of the room and imagine a colorful sound wave echoing in each area as you sing.

4. Go back to Chapter 3 and compare this experience of projection with efforts to sing in many directions out the head (Figures 3.1 and 3.16). How do internal efforts coincide with echoes in the room?

Background Information. Acoustics work the same no matter the size of the room, just to the greater or lesser extent possible within the given space. Comparing the resonators to a room, efforts in Chapter 3 were like echoing sound off the floor of the chest cavity, off the back wall of the pharynx and forward out through the mouth, off the ceiling of the sinuses and nasal cavity, and even through the brain cavity and out the back of the skull. The acoustics of the head and body are a miniature of the acoustics of a room.

Comparing sound at different levels of a room with resonance in and around the head, the similarity of acoustics between the two spaces becomes obvious. Chest resonance tends to go to the floor, mouth-oriented resonance tends to hit flat against the wall, and resonance above the palate tends to rise to the ceiling to be heard across a room. *Where sound vibrates in the head is where sound will travel in a room.* In this way, the head is a miniature of a room.

Extended Exercise. The effects of this exercise can be better heard in a reverberant space, one with hard surfaces that echo the sound clearly. To get a better sense of how the spaces in the head and body leads to the sound in a room, sing in different rooms and spaces.

- Sing in a good choral rehearsal room or practice room with a balance of hard and soft surfaces that allow sound to be heard at different levels.

- Sing in a walled-off shower or bathroom stall, which allows the amount of sound inside the stall to be compared with the amount outside the stall, with more sound outside revealing how easily sound projects up and across a distance.

- Sing in an isolated stairwell in a public buildings to compare whether singing tone travels down or up.

- Sing in a handball court or small gymnasium so the resulting sound can be heard and analyzed over longer stretches of time.

The distance and level at which sound echoes is a concrete and accurate measure of the effectiveness of singing efforts, and the sound in a room is a neutral and trustworthy teacher for learning how best to resonate and project.

Testing the Effect of Posture on Projection

Exercise Sequence. Returning to previous exercises in posture, this exercise now focuses on the acoustical results of ineffective and effective posture.

1. With the head leaning forward (Chapter 2, Figure 2.16, left), sing a tone and breathe in silently to listen to the echo in the room, especially listening to corners where sound concentrates long enough to be sensed.

    a. Did the tone travel close to you or farther away? Half way across the room? All the way across the room?

    b. Did the tone travel to the floor? Lower walls? Bottom corner of the room? Waist high in the room? At head level? Above the head?

2. Compare the bent-posture results by singing a tone produced with a poised and lifted posture (Figure 2.16, right; Figure 3.9; Figure 3.14).

    a. How did the distance of the tone change? Farther away, closer, or no change?

b. How did the level of the tone change? Did it rise, lower, or stay at the same level throughout?

3. Repeat the comparison between steps 1 and 2 until a posture is found that allows vibrations to easily travel to the far side and top level of the room.

Background Information. The desire to project to an audience makes singers tend to lean out toward the audience as if physically trying to get sound closer to the audience. As discussed in Chapter 1, leaning throws off balance and causes tension to hold the body upright, perhaps even borrowing from pushing muscles and thereby sending a danger signal for the vocal cords to close. As discussed in Chapter 2 bending the neck can cause strain that traps air pressure below the vocal cords, or it can cause an airy sound as too much air is allowed to escape. As discussed in Chapter 3, bending also limits the path of sound to go out of the mouth more than out through the resonating spaces in the upper half of the head. In terms of projection, sound coming from the mouth falls quickly to the floor or travels harshly forward at or below mouth level. But don't take my word for it. Try this exercise to find the optimal posture that allows sound to leave the head and project into a room more easily.

Extended Exercise. In the effort to find the optimal posture for easy projection of tone, review the various hand positions used in the book for other purposes than projection.

4. As you sing in the direction of the hand positions in the following list, listen for where sound projects and echoes in the room.

    a. Figures 1.5 to track breath noise and in Chapter 2 to explore resonant spaces.

    b. Figure 2.7 downward arm movement for feeling a low pitch.

    c. Figure 2.10 funnel hands for opening up on high pitches.

    d. Figure 2.13 arm push game to feel tone lift easily.

    e. Figure 3.1 sonar hands to find the center of resonant tone.

    f. Figure 3.8 palate hands to channel tone above the palate.

    g. Figure 3.9 hands in front of ears to direct tone into the nasopharynx.

    h. Figure 3.10 to excite the sense of smell and draw tone to the olfactory area.

i. Figure 3.11 to draw tone across the maxillary sinuses.

j. Figure 3.16 for directing resonance in new different directions out the head.

5. Notice any slight shifts in the body's poise and alignment due to the mind focusing on different directions of singing.

- Which efforts led to a poised posture that allows tone to easily project?

Choral Applications: No One is Heard, Everyone is Heard

Sensory Experience: Who is the Loudest in the Choir?

Exercise Sequence. How can a conductor know how singers hear each other? Have singers point it out for the conductor to see.

1. As the choir sings a unison pitch or melody, have singers point to the person heard the most.

   a. Look for those *pointed to by many people*; these are either the leaders to whom everybody listens, overzealous singers who need to learn to balance and match the rest of the choir better, or singers who could benefit from Chapter 3 exercises to learn to resonate less abrasively.

   b. Look for those who *point to each other*; these are either singers who work together beneficially or a clique whose exclusive effort works against the unity of the choir.

   c. Look for those to whom *nobody points*; these could be singers who need to learn to boost their tone to match the rest or simply be encouraged to sing out, but they may otherwise be loners and outcasts who need help finding their place in the choir, avoiders and loafers who need motivation to find reason to contribute to the choir, or singers who are too ill or out of shape to produce a strong tone.

   d. Look for those who *point neighbor to neighbor* either side-to-side or front-and-back; these are singers who are listening and coordinating locally but not singing beyond their immediate surroundings.

2. While singing a chord or chord progression, have singers point to the person heard most in their section.

a. Look for the same as before, many hands to one person, hands pointing to each other, those to whom nobody points, and hands pointing neighbor to neighbor.

3. While singing a chord or chord progression, have singers point to the section heard most.

    a. Look for the number of singers pointing *across the choir to a distant section*, which indicates either that quieter sections need to match the projection of the loudest section, or that the loudest section needs to match the efforts of the rest of the choir.

    b. Look for the number of *singers* pointing *to their own section*, which indicates that singers may be singing more than they are listening and matching other sections.

    c. Look for the number of *sections* pointing *to their own section*, which allows the comparison between sections that need to boost projection and sections that need to reduce their projection, and helps point out the difference between listening within and across sections.

    d. Look for those who point *to the next section*, which is a fairly uniform result.

4. Have singers all point to one section for the rest of the choir to match.

    a. Listen for whether or not the choral sound matches their pointing, that the one section can be heard a bit over the rest of the choir.

    b. Switch sections until the choir learns to balance with each section and each section learns to project above the rest of the choir.

5. Have singers all point to a single person for the entire choir to match.

    a. Listen for whether or not the one person is heard above the rest of the choir.

    b. Switch to other singers to find the effect of individual singers' tones on the entire choir.

Background Information. With this exercise, vocal technique, motivation, and behavior management come together as possible reasons for a lack of unified tone projection among the choir. Motivation and behavior management problems include the phenomenon of social loafing (Gumm 2006) but may require a more comprehensive set of solutions (Gumm 2003a). Added to the list of possible solutions are these multisensory vocal techniques that help solve the psychological and physiological problems that keep singers from reaching their potential.

A good rule of thumb in solving unequal projection problems among singers and between sections is that singing involves 60% listening and 40% singing, a rule shared in a convention presentation by Simon Carrington, the co-founder and past member of The King's Singers who later served as a choral professor in the United States. Others have exaggerated this to 80% or 90%, but this would seem to cause weak singing in everybody. Whichever ratio is used, efforts to sing should be in line with the tone heard in the rest of the surrounding choir and into the surrounding space.

Going beyond this exploratory sensory experience is a set of exercises that purposefully develops the ability to project and hear different characteristics in a choir. First is the ability to project equally across the entire choir, which is a natural next step to this sensory experience. Second, presented in two exercises, is the ability for each section to project a unique tone quality so that each section is heard distinctly. Third is the ability to detect subtle differences within the choir, surrounding the choir, and at a distance away from the choir. These are things that affect the audience experience in a concert, but also things that a conductor can learn to anticipate and solve both in rehearsal and in concert.

Quartets to Whole Ensemble

Exercise Sequence. This exercise starts with the natural clarity of one person singing each note as the model for each section of the choir to sing as one. Sound is projected equally across all singers by matching the acoustics and physical efforts of individual singers. Use this sequence in unison singing, chord progression warm-up exercises, and in selections of music.

1. Choose one person from each section of the choir, and assign each to sing one pitch in a chord when directed to start (Figure 4.6).

2. Prepare the rest of the choir to be ready to add their voice when signaled, without changing dynamics or character of the tone.

    a. Individual singers are to take a breath when needed, as in staggered breathing, in a way that does not interrupt or cause a "hole" in the overall sound of the section.

3. Signal the small group of singers to sing their assigned pitches in a chord—a four-note chord for SATB, a three-note chord for SSA, and so on.

FIGURE 4.6 Highlighted quartet starts the process, each singer matches until all sing as one.

4. Point to one additional singer at a time to join the singers already singing.

   a. Listen for each added singer to match in pitch/frequency, loudness/amplitude, resonance/timbre, and vowel color.

   b. To keep singers listening to singing and not to talking, use nonverbal feedback instead of verbal feedback to assist in the efforts of each singer added to the choral sound.

   - A nod or shake of the head.

   - Thumbs up or down.

   - Smile or frown.

   - Appropriate facial expressions.

   - Any multisensory arm or hand movement that would change the direction, energy, and freedom needed for each singer to match—such as a sound-wave hand wave (Figure 2.3) or narrow-to-tall hands (Figure 4.2).

5. Besides listening for voices to not change the overall timbre and loudness of the choral tone, also listen that each added singer's tone *can be heard*.

a. Use the draw-tone-out hand signal (Figure 4.4) from the point of view of the conductor drawing tone from the singer.

b. Like a catcher's mitt catching a ball, signal to the singer that the tone has reached the conductor's hand, with a nod or thumbs up to signal success.

Background Information. Beyond verbally directing singers to "blend" and "balance," this exercise puts these directions into tangible action. In this exercise, blend is the result of each singer matching pitch frequency and resonant timbre. Notice that no particular timbre was defined, because the particular choral tone chosen or preferred by the conductor is not the issue here. Blend means that everybody's sound mixes together so that no singer is noticed. Balance means that no single singer or choir section can be heard and yet every singer and choir section can be heard. Balance can either be aimed toward equal amplitude or toward sections balanced at different amplitudes for musical purposes—such as bringing out a melody or special musical feature. There is also pyramidal balance with the lowest voice the loudest and each higher voice a bit quieter.

For the Choir Director. Notice that by this point in the book a vocabulary of meaningful hand and arm gestures has been built up. In a choral situation, once singers have been guided in their singing by their personal use of gestures and movements, by using these same gestures the conductor can nonverbally and visually "reach" into a singer's vocal technique and guide singing efforts without a word. Such gestures can be incorporated into traditional meter patterns to invigorate precise physical efforts in the singers. Have singers practice the following:

1. Expand the ribcage during an upbeat gesture.

2. Engage abdominal muscles on the down beat or entrance gesture.

3. Breathe in to stop sound at the cutoff or release gesture

    a. Avoid the typical crimping "cut off" gesture, which may cut off space in the throat or mouth to stop sound. Instead, use a gesture more appropriate to inhalation such as a releasing, lifting, or expanding-hand gesture.

Beyond these modifications of traditional conducting gestures, also use specific gestures from this book—or developed on your own—for a powerful set of communication tools between the conductor and singers. This powerful communication is possible because of the deep multisensory experiences shared by everybody in the choir. Shared experiences allow many short cuts in communication to be taken, with one slight move affecting the technique and tone of every singer. Take this nonverbal communication into a concert, and singers can be kept alert to any issue signaled by the conductor. One quick reminder ignites new energy into the performance.

Important Principle for All Learning. Whenever a group of people shares an experience, there develops the possibility for shorthand communication. Shared experiences in multisensory vocal techniques allow for quick and deep communication by a simple gesture that ignites strong sensations in each singer.

The power of shared experiences in group learning puts a new spin on attendance policies for school, community, church, and professional choirs. To miss a rehearsal is to miss deep meaning that may affect the final concert. Suppose the rehearsal that was missed included this particular exercise, and then at the choir concert one singer's tone stuck out above the rest. Guess who stuck out? Chances are it was the singer who missed the rehearsal. Compound this across the entire season of rehearsals and you have holes in the unity of tone due to any number of singers missing any number of shared experiences.

Choir attendance practices that make no sense in light of the power of shared experiences include: (a) when singers are allowed to attend choir rehearsals as they please, (b) when attendance exceptions are made for one singer or another, and (c) when more talented singers are brought in as last minute "ringers" to supposedly boost the quality of the performance. When singers are not at rehearsals, they have not sensed the intimate details of preparation—which is why these attendance practices "make no sense." To be a member of a choir or any ensemble means to share in the experiences that allow a choir to have the same, shared, multisensory experiences.

Making up an absence also takes on new meaning in light of the issue of shared experiences. Absences do occur in choirs for good and legitimate reasons, but the experience still has been missed. Make-up policies that do not make sense are (a) having singers with excused absences do make-up work but those with unexcused absences not make up missed experiences, (b) require extra written work, chores, and isolated time out or detention that are unrelated to the experiences missed, and (c) a free number of absences before consequences or make-up work is applied. By focusing on the experiences shared by a choir, make-up work should (a) apply to all who miss a rehearsal, (b) be an attempt to experience what the rest of the choir experienced, (c) encourage a sense of ownership and responsibility to the ensemble, (d) involve others in the choir who were there to interpret how the experience was perceived, and (e) be a rewarding and uniting learning experience rather than punishing and divisive. An ensemble is a group of people who come together in shared experience to move the same, think the same, see the same, hear the same, and sound the same, so why not also feel the same positive ownership and responsibility when it comes to attendance?

Separation of Harmonics by Resonance Assignment

Exercise Sequence. A strategy that helps develop a vivid choral tone is to assign each choral section to resonate in parts of the body that highlight different overtones of the harmonic series. All singers are to keep the resonators open, relaxed, and accessible to sound, regardless of the central focus of resonance.

1. Filling out the bottom of the harmonic series, the basses are the "floor sweepers" in the choral tone. Basses focus resonance in the chest cavity to enhance wide and slow-moving sound waves. Hold the hands out round at ribcage level to openly draw the tone into the chest cavity and out into the surrounding space.

2. Coming in acoustically above the basses, the tenors fill out the lower middle overtones. Tenors ring the tone across the width of the sinuses (see the exercise shown in Figure 3.11) for a high cheekbone tone that rings clearly in the region just above the fundamental.

3. Altos sing with low resonance much like the basses, close in range to the tenors yet with a distinct color that rings the upper middle overtones.

4. Sopranos sing with high resonance much like the tenors, yet ring the highest overtones.

Background Information. The problem that this strategy solves is the invasion of sections into each other's acoustical territory. When basses sing with high resonance placement, the fundamental does not sound as loud as do the overtones; as a result the choir's overall tone sounds thin and lacks depth, and the audience cannot easily distinguish bass pitches from tenor pitches. When tenors sing with a low baritone or bass quality, their quality is perceived to be closer to the fundamental, overtones clash in the same acoustical space as the basses, the choir's tone sounds muddy and heavy, and the audience cannot easily hear tenor pitches. The same goes with altos and sopranos, that even though pitches are in different ranges, the overtones overlap in acoustical space, pitches are difficult to distinguish, and the overall tone quality is thrown to one extreme or another. The better solution is to have each section ring overtones in separate ranges of the harmonic series.

Separation of Harmonics by Vowel Assignment

Exercise Sequence. In this exercise, low to high choral sections are assigned a different vowel that focuses their resonance around different harmonics. If needed before this sequence is attempted, go to Chapter 5 to develop distinct vowel colors each with resonant tone.

1. Assign basses to sing on an AH [a], tenors on an OH [o], altos on an EE [i], and sopranos on an OO [u].

    a. For a five-voice choir, AY [e] can be assigned to the middle voice between OH [o] and EE [i].

    b. For choirs with other voicings, assign vowels in the same order from the lowest voice section to highest.

    c. Choirs with sections in the same range can still benefit by assigning different vowels.

2. Sing an open chord with each voice part singing the assigned vowel.

3. Listen for each section's tone to travel across the room at different levels (Figure 4.7), the bass/lowest tone across the bottom of the room, the tenors/mid-low above, altos/mid-high next, and the soprano/highest tone above the rest in the room.

4. Sing a chord progression, with each voice part singing the assigned vowel.

5. Sing through a choral selection of music on the assigned vowels instead of on the text, listening for continued separation and clarity between voice parts.

6. Sing through choral selections with text while maintaining the resonance of the assigned vowel as the underlying sensation of tone production. Sing each word distinctly but with an underlying sensation of the assigned vowel.

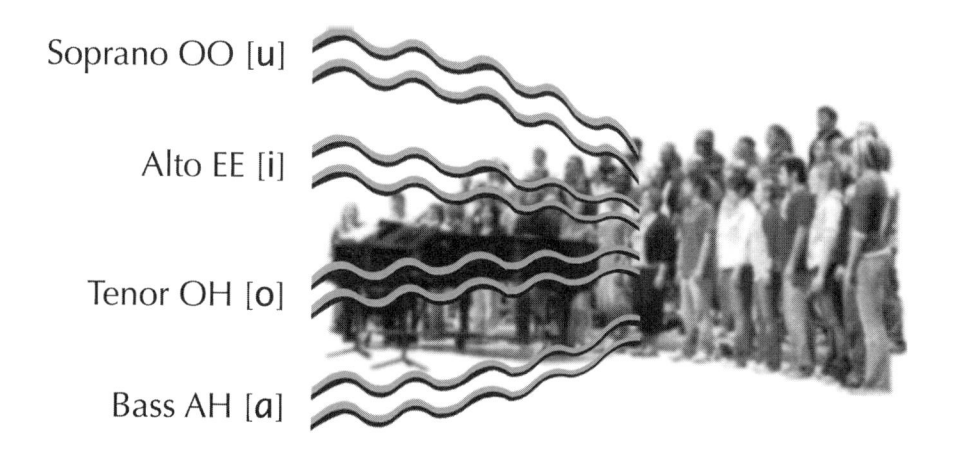

Soprano OO [u]

Alto EE [i]

Tenor OH [o]

Bass AH [a]

FIGURE 4.7 Making choir sections audible by using the resonance and overtones of different underlying vowels.

Background Information. The natural resonance of different vowels enhances and divides the harmonic series across sections of the choir much the same as in the previous exercise. However, this exercise may be easier to accomplish than learning to resonate in different levels of the body, something especially difficult to check individually in large groups. The use of vowels also relates this exercise to the Chapter 5 topic of vowels, where evidence is presented that shows how different vowels highlight different overtones. The distinct point made here is that vowels help each section's tone to project and be heard.

Waves, Dips, Holes, Bubbles, Arrows, Lines, Squiggles, and Circles

Exercise Sequence. In this exercise are presented ways to hear acoustical problems close within the choir, in the surrounding area of the choir, and at distances away from the choir. Have the choir sing a pitch, a unison scalar exercise or melody, a chordal exercise, or any selection of choral music for extended lengths as you work through steps in this sequence.

1. Listen for the following acoustical conditions directly within and around the choir, imagine an appropriate visual image of sound on top of the real image of the choir (Figure 4.8, top image), and use motions that reflect and guide singers' efforts.

    a. *Beats*, the collision of two mismatched frequencies in acoustical space, and *absence of beats*, which means singers are in tune with each other.

    - To represent beats, imagine two or more interweaving sound waves colliding in space; and for in-tune singing, imagine two wavy lines moving parallel to each other.

    - With sound wave hand motions (Figure 2.3), gesture two colliding sound waves with two hands that whisk each other as they pass in the air; when beats go away, gesture a parallel wave motion with both hands moving together as one.

    b. The *absence of sound* in an area, which indicates a lack of balanced projection or that singers in the area are not on the same pitch and not producing a unified tone.

    - Imagine arched lines over and through the choir that would outline the envelope of its tone, with dips and holes where there is an absence of sound.

    - Gesture a dip or a circle around the hole, signal for individual singers to project and "plug the hole" use the drawing-tone-out gesture (Figure 4.4) or other appropriate gesture.

c. Individual voices or areas *projecting beyond the rest of the choir*, as in a sense of "denser," "more," "farther," or "elsewhere" compared to the rest of the choir.

- Imagine a bubble protruding above the otherwise straight line or curve of the choir's tone.

- Gesture the contour of the choir's tone with a hump above the area where sound protrudes, show a quizzical look or shake the head in search of the source of the sound, and signal a smooth curve, head nod, or a thumbs-up okay when singers correct the balance.

2. Listen for the following *acoustical conditions in the larger spaces surrounding the choir*; visualize sound with an appropriate image (Figure 4.8, middle) and guide and show the result of the choir's efforts using appropriate gestures.

    a. The *direction* and *distance* that sound travels, whether focused and unified in a single direction or scattered and spread.

    - Imagine a circle that unifies the choir's tone above the conductor or further beyond; imagine arrows in the direction and at the distance that sound is heard to travel.

    - Trace a circle in the air to establish a lofty target for singers, gesture poor directions of sound in the air with a shake of the head and a unified path toward a better target with an affirming nod of the head.

    b. The level at which tone projects, from low to high in the room, whether unified or at different levels from different areas of the choir.

    - Imagine the area in which sound is heard alive with squiggly sound waves.

    - Gesture toward the level that sound is heard with a shake of the head and then gesture an up-and-out path to redirect singers' efforts.

    c. Listen for *acoustical conditions of sound in the far corners and walls* where sound reaches, collects, and echoes back in the rehearsal or concert space.

    - Imagine sound-wave squiggles in corners and against walls where sound is heard to echo (Figure 4.8, bottom).

    - Show with appropriate gestures where sound is heard and where sound is desired, and have the choir breath a release of tone to listen for the results of their efforts.

FIGURE 4.8 Multisensory synesthesia-like perceptions: seeing choral sound within the choir (top), around the choir (middle), and at distances away from the choir (bottom).

Background Information. Precise hearing in a choir is a prized skill that gives instant respect to a choir director. To be able to point out the person who sings a wrong note and tell what note was incorrect is not a common skill and often is simply impossible because of the complex wave forms produced by a choir. The psychology of music perception does not allow the brain to capture such precise differences in pitch in such a large group. Singers sing just a bit off from each other in pitch, but the brain stereotypes this complex mesh of pitches and perceives the whole as one harmonious sound. There is a point at which pitches and tone colors are close enough that there results a "chorusing effect" that links each individual sound into one choral tone.

By this point in the book, you must have grown accustomed to seeing directional arrows and other markings on top of photographs of people and the spaces around them. The goal is to develop the ability to see what is heard and felt, hear what is seen and felt, and feel what is seen and heard. In this exercise, this ability is put to the test. Bubbles in choral tone, lines and dips and squiggles in front of a choir, and arrows in the direction of tone—these are examples of *synesthesia*, the synthesis of different perceptions in your experience of sound.

Now, go ahead and add one of your own exercises that relates to this chapter.

Name of Exercise

Exercise Purpose:

Exercise Sequence:

Background Information:

CHAPTER 5

FREEDOM OF ARTICULATORS FROM OTHER FUNCTIONS

The role of the articulators—teeth, tongue, jaw, lips, and cheeks—is to shape the sounds that distinguish one vowel, consonant, syllable, word, or phrase from the next. As with resonance, the role is to color the tone, yet whereas resonance colors the overall vocal tone, articulators add specific colors, noises, and sounds identified with the text. The exercises in this chapter aim to allow the articulators to carry out this role freely without changing the voice's characteristic resonance or inhibiting other functions of deep breath supported vibrant tone.

Clear and Distinct Vowels

Arm-Shape Guided Vowel Shapes

Exercise Sequence. This exercise uses distinct arm movements to help develop distinct vowel colors. The exercise is thanks to Weston Noble, distinguished Luther College choral director for 57 years.

1. Say "ah."

2. With arms rounded and hands up over the head (Figure 5.1), follow the arm shape in saying "AH!"

    - This is the sensation to be memorized for every pronunciation of [ɑ].

3. Say "oh."

4. With arms rounded and hands down by the hips (Figure 5.1), now say "OH?!"

    - This is the sensation to be memorized for every pronunciation of [o].

5. Say "oo."

6. With hands in a position as if holding a telescope (Figures 4.5 and 5.1), move the circle forward away from rounded mouth as you say "OO!?!"

   • Memorize this sensation for every [u] in your singing.

7. Say "ee."

8. With the same rounded hands as if holding a telescope, move the hands away from eye level and say "EEEE."

   • Memorize this tall yet focused sensation for every time you sing [i].

9. Say "eh."

10. With the draw-tone gesture of Figures 4.4, now say "EH?!"

    • This is the vibrant and beautiful taste to be pronounced in your every [ɛ].

Background Information. More than a one-effort exercise, using the arms to guide vowel shapes can set a new standard for all future sensations of vowels. Do not take new experiences and throw them away, make them habit by repeating them. Use these vowels every time they are sung. An [ɑ] or an [i] is not simply a pronunciation that stays the same across all languages, each vowel becomes a sensation that is to stay consistent across all instances of singing. The sensation of lifting the arms over the head when pronouncing the [ɑ] carries with it a kinesthetic lift of the soft palate, the ribcage, the cheek

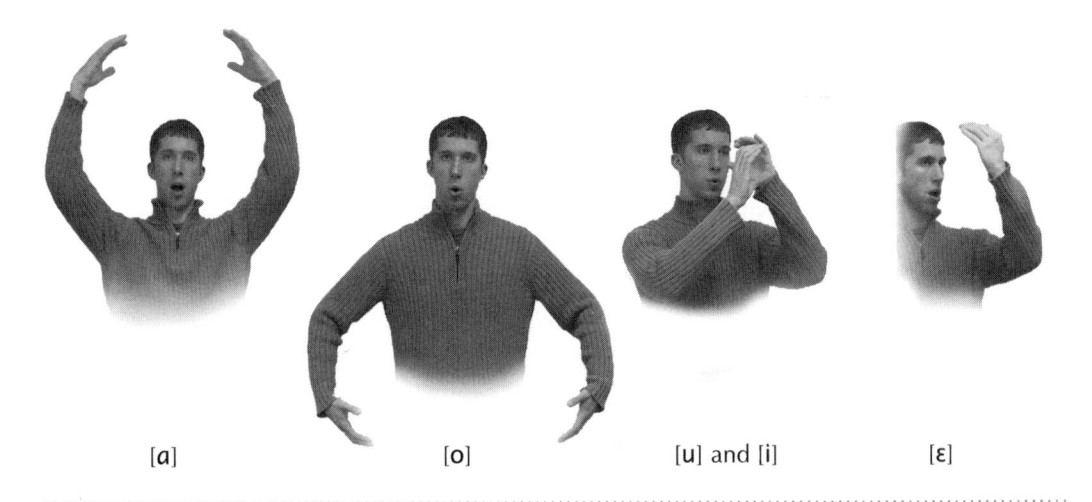

[ɑ]   [o]   [u] and [i]   [ɛ]

FIGURE 5.1   Arm shapes to guide vowel shapes and colors.

smile muscles, and along with it all a lifted and resonant tone. It also carries with it an emotional feeling to help vivify the color and experience of the [a]. Focusing on the lift may also help cancel out the movement of an overly dropped jaw or depressed tongue, both of which often have the habit of trying to help out in making the [a] tall. This entire sensation occurs at once with the expressive and bodily-shaped [a] that is intended in this exercise. And so it goes as you experience the fuller shape of each vowel with the help of arm movements. Though the first curious experience of this exercise can never be duplicated, the exercise can be invigoratingly repeated to allow the sensations in the body to guide the sensation of each vowel.

Pant-sing on Changing Vowels and Syllables

Exercise Sequence. This exercise completes a longer sequence of panting exercises that began in Chapter 1 with simply learning to breath deeply, openly, and relaxingly. To summarize, panting helped guide relaxed breathing, relaxed breathing helped guide relaxed phonation on one pitch, relaxed phonation on one pitch helped guide relaxed phonation on pitches both low and high, and now relaxed phonation is to stay consistent regardless of changes in vowel and syllable. If the previous steps have not yet been made into habit, go back and review the pant-breath, pant-sing, and pant-sing-on-scales exercises (Figures 1.6 and 2.4) before proceeding to this exercise.

1. Pant-breathe four times to relax the jaw, open the throat, relax the larynx low, and feel the sensation of low breathing.

2. Sing scale patterns with changing vowels, as in Figure 5.2, top lines of text.

    - Feel the free and easy movement of the articulators in a way that does not change the sensation in the breathing muscles, larynx, and resonators.

FIGURE 5.2   Pant-sing exercise on different vowels and syllables.

3. Sing scale patterns with changing syllables, or combinations of different initial consonants with different vowels, as in Figure 5.2, bottom lines of text.

- Again, feel the free and easy movement of the articulators in a way that does not change the sensation of breathing, phonation, resonance, and projection.

Background Information. You can always tell a novice singer by the way the resonance of the voice changes along with the movement of the articulators from one vowel or syllable to the next. Not only the color of vowels and consonants change, but the entire character of the voice closes down and opens up with each closing and opening action of the teeth, tongue, lips, and jaw. Such mouth-oriented changes in tone are like a plunger mute being placed over the bell of a trumpet and then off again to create a wah-wah effect, or the dampers in front of an organ's pipe chamber closing and opening to change dynamics. Say the words "wah-wah" with the sound trapped in the mouth and you get the idea.

Perhaps the most obvious quality in common between successful singers in any style of music is the presence of a resonant tone apart from the movement of the articulators. Perhaps the most obvious quality that differs between singers and between styles of music is the type of resonance used. Therefore, perhaps *the most universal skill to successful singing is for resonance and tone quality to stay consistent regardless of the movement of the articulators*. Each singer can sound quite different, but the singer's tone stays consistent and distinct regardless of the work of the articulators.

The joining and separating of functions in different systems of singing is the focus of this entire book, and in this particular exercise the focus is on the separate functions of the articulators. The articulators have a habit of trying to help out in other systems involved in singing. The *tongue* depresses in the back or curls down the center in an attempt to shape the space of the resonators. However, the tongue is an articulator that shapes vowel color and should play only a slight role, if any, in creating space for resonant tone color. Besides, involvement of the tongue in resonance merely traps sound in the mouth, stuck below the palate. Another bad habit of the tongue is to move with too large of motions in shaping vowels, even though vowels can be shaped very distinctly without such exaggerated and tense movements. A bad habit with the *jaw* is to bite or clench down on vowels, tensely trapping sound in the mouth as with tongue tension. Tension in the *lips* also serves to trap sound in restricted areas, which likewise harms the resonant tone. Muscles involved in biting also get overly involved in articulation, so conflicting functions of these same articulators must be separated out of the process.

The solution provided in this exercise is to first experience deep breath-supported tone up and through the entire set of systems, and then to add vowels and consonants in a way that does not alter the resonance of the tone. The breathing system plays its separate role, the vocal cords play their separate role in response to breathing, the resonators color and amplify the tone produced by the vocal cords, and the articulators enter the picture without interfering with these other systems.

Beyond the simple examples shown in Figure 5.2, there are many common vocalises and exercises that serve the same purpose—to start with good resonance and then add articulation. Search out other examples that follow the same multisensory pattern and add them to the list of exercises in this chapter.

Stretched Open Hand

Exercise Sequence. This exercise continues the separation of vowels from resonance, but works further to separate the different functions of the articulators themselves. The height of a stretched open hand is used to keep the singer alert across different consonant and vowel combinations. The hand also signals for tone to be equally resonant in the most difficult vowels or when vowels are followed by a nasal consonant.

1. Hold the hand to the side of the face, just within view of peripheral vision, with palm in, thumb by the jaw, fingertips by the eye as if reaching up inside to lift the soft palate. Let the sensation of the stretched-tall hand send the signal to stay open and resonant.

2. Move the hand forward to draw vowels out to their full resonant height across the time the vowel is sung. Let the forward movement signal the length of time from the start of the vowel to the finish.

3. Use this hand motion for each of the following situations.

    a. Sing *vowels that are difficult to resonate*—IH [ɪ], AE [æ], EH [ɛ], UH [ʌ]—to maintain resonance in each (Figure 5.3 a).

    b. Sing vowels followed by *nasal consonants* [m], [n], NG [ŋ], [r], and [l] to keep nasality from creeping into each vowel, before the nasal resonance of the consonants contaminates the resonant tone around the vowel (Figure 5.3 b).

    c. Sing *diphthongs* AY /ei/ or /ɛi/, OY /oi/, EW /iu/, IE /ai/, OH /ou/, and OW /au/ (Figure 5.3 c) to keep the nasal [i] or closed [u] from contaminating the resonance of the primary vowel; curl the fingers as the secondary vowel is sung; note that the primary vowel is the second vowel in EW /iu/.

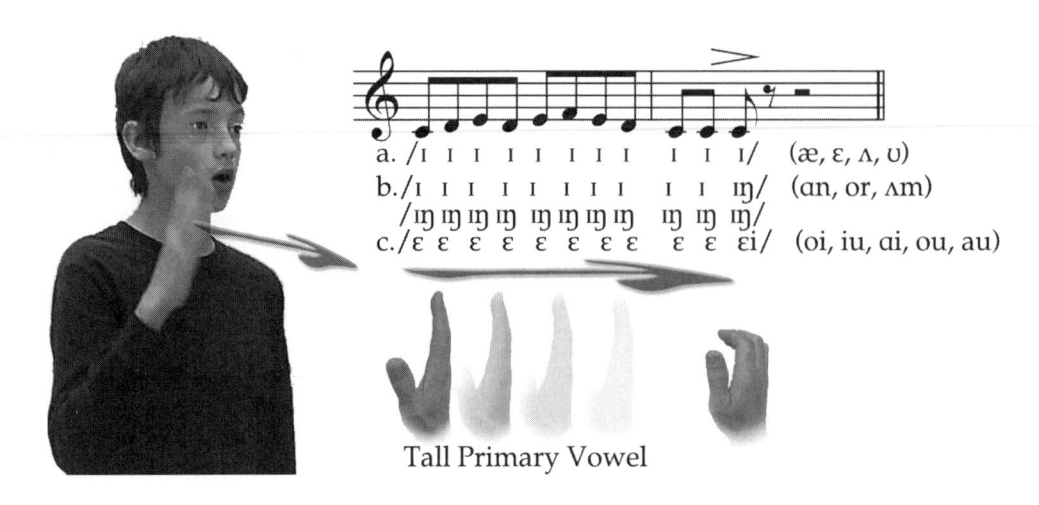

FIGURE 5.3 A tall hand signals the resonators to stay open across the length of a vowel.

Background Information. As discussed in Chapter 4, two practices exist in pronouncing vowels that are difficult to resonate. Either modify the pronunciation of words by choosing vowels that already have a resonant tone, or use correct pronunciation and learn to resonate all vowels. In the second approach, the pronunciation of song texts can be looked up in a dictionary and written out in IPA. It is now common practice for class voice textbooks and vocal music anthologies to conveniently transcribe texts into IPA for you. In these IPA transcriptions, look for vowels that are difficult to resonate, vowels that are followed by nasal consonants, and diphthongs, and then use the tall-hand motion or other choice of solutions to maintain resonant tone across all vowels.

Extended Exercise. The following steps are provided as practice in identifying and solving problem vowels.

4. Look for problem vowels in the IPA transcription of the text "Oh say, can you see by the dawns early light." This example would translate as /o sɛi kæn iu si bai ɵʌ danz ɝli lait/.

5. The transcription points out:

    a. The difficult vowels AE [æ] and UH [ʌ].

    b. The vowel/nasal-consonant combinations of AEN /æn/, AHN /ɑn/, and UR /ɝ/.

    c. The diphthongs AY [ɛi], EW [iu], and IE [ai].

6. Use the forward moving tall-hand gesture to maintain resonance tone across each of these situations.

Sensory Experience: Which Word Am I Singing?

Exercise Sequence. To verify the contaminating effect of the vowel or consonant that follows a current vowel, sing these word combinations to find out if the word that is sung can be predicted by the vowel that is sung. A teacher or friend can listen and predict the word you are singing as the vowel is sung at length.

1. On a single pitch or melodic pattern, sing either "mock," "mall," "monster," or "marble."

    a. Sing the MAH /mɑ/ without finishing the word.

    b. Predict the word based on the color of vowel.

    c. Choose and sing the same or another word in unexpected order until each choice is sung at least once.

        • Were guesses correct?

        • Were there noticeable differences in the nasality of vowels due to the movement of tongue and jaw in anticipation of the [l], [n], and [r]?

2. Find other combinations to test how purely you can sing the same vowel in different situations.

    a. To test the purity of [ɪ] with nasal consonants that follow, sing "thick" in comparison with "thin," "thimble," "thing," and "thrill." Did you sing the same vowel or different colors?

    b. To test the purity of the [ɛ], sing "Ted" in comparison with "temperature," "tender," "tear," and "tell." In a diphthong situation, check the primary vowel sung in "take."

    c. To test the difficult AE [æ], sing "pad," "pal," "Pam," "pants," and "pang." Which is the purest and most resonant in these combinations?

    d. To test the purity of vowels with nasal consonants, sing "Todd" compared to "Tom," "tall," tonic," and "tong." Did you sing the same [ɑ] for each?

e. To test that the nasal vowel in a diphthong does not creep in to contaminate the primary vowel, sing "odd" compared to "eye," and "owl;" sing "food" compared to "few" and "fuel;" sing "toad" compared to "toe, "toy," "toil," and "tone;" and sing "pod" compared to "pie" and "pow-wow."

f. Repeat each list until each vowel is the same as in the first word of each list, not contaminated by the movement of the tongue and jaw, the resonators stay consistently open for each vowel, and until the helper cannot tell the difference between words.

3. Besides repetitive practice in different combinations of words, find which of the following multisensory solutions is most helpful in singing equally resonant vowels in the words in each list in steps 1, 2a, 2b, 2c, and 2d.

   a. Start singing the first word in each list, but in the instant before finishing the word, complete a different word in the list instead. For instance, sing "mock" but at the end of the sustained vowel change your mind and finish the word "marble" instead. In repeated trials, was the first word consistently guessed?

   b. Use the arm shapes from the Figure 5.1 exercise in this section, repeating the same arm sensation as you sing the vowels in each list of words. Did the arm movements help guide consistent vowels?

   c. Use pant singing from the second exercise in this section, panting the vowel at least four times before finishing each word. For instance, sing PAH-AH-AH-AHEE /pɑ ɑ ɑ ɑi/ with the secondary vowel being pronounced only as the fourth primary vowel dies away. Did the repetition of supported tone purify the vowel in each word?

   d. Use the forward moving stretched-open hand gesture from Figure 5.3 in this section as each vowel is sung. Did the sense of height and length help maintain the same resonance in the vowel as each word in the lists was sung? Does this help keep you alert and sensitive to the resonance across an entire word?

4. Find other combinations of difficult vowels, nasal consonants, and diphthongs in music being learned and use your choice of solutions.

Separate Function of the Tongue

Palate Hands and Freedom of Tongue

Exercise Sequence. This exercise is an extension of the palate-hands exercise in Chapter 3 in which the hands block sound from going directly from the mouth to the ears.

Throughout the sequence, keep sound coming out through the head from above the hands instead of from the mouth below the hands.

1. Place hands across the face as in Chapter 3, Figure 3.8.

2. Sing on one pitch a sequence of vowels, EE-EH-AH-OH-OO /i ɛ ɑ o u/, and then EE-IH-AE-OH-UH /i ɪ æ o ʌ/.

3. Sing syllables that combine different vowels and consonants—NOO-NOH-NAH /nu no nɑ/, LAH-LAY-LEE /lɑ le li/, ZEE-ZOH-ZAH /zi zo zɑ/, NGEE-NGAY-NGAH /ŋi ŋe ŋɑ/, and other combinations.

Background Information. A common sequence in this book is to start on a neutral vowel on a single pitch, change pitches on the same neutral vowel, change vowels and syllables in a pattern of pitches, and then sing a melody with text. This sequence detects problem in simpler situations of singing before adding difficulties related to the movement of articulators. In this exercise the final problem to solve is to keep the resonators open and vibrant above the palate as the tongue responds to changing vowel shapes and consonant articulation. By isolating the sound coming out above the palate hands, it is easy to detect which vowels and consonants cause problems. The exercise does not provide a direct solution except to keep whatever gets in the way out of the way of sound getting above the palate. The following exercises provide more tangible solutions.

Sensory experience: Is the Tongue Involved Where It Does Not Belong?

Exercise Sequence. This exercise asks you to do what your mother may have told you as a child, to "hold your tongue," except this time it means literally to hold your tongue with your fingers.

1. Gently grasp the tip of the tongue with the fingers and thumb and bring the tongue partly out of the mouth (Figure 5.4).

2. Sing a pitch.

   - Does the tongue stay relaxed when tone is produced or does it grab and tighten?

3. Change the "sing" into a "honk," and honk the same pitch out the relaxed and open spaces of the head.

FIGURE 5.4 Hold your tongue to detect and release tension.

- Does the act of honking the tone help the tongue stay out of the way?
- If so, then never "sing" again; instead always think of honking or phonating.

4. Sing an ascending five-note *do-re-mi-fa-so* scale on an AH [ɑ] or EH [ɛ].

   - Does the tongue stay relaxed and in place, or does it tense and pull back as pitch rises?
   - If it continues to tense, bring the tongue farther out, including the back of the tongue out of the throat.

5. Sing up and down a five-note *do-re-mi-fa-so* scale on an AH [ɑ] or EH [ɛ].

   - Does your tongue want to yank back into your mouth as you sing higher and relax as you return to lower pitches?

6. Sing up and down a five-note *do-re-mi-fa-so* scale on AH-EH-EE-OH-OO /ɑ ɛ i o u/, with two pitches for each vowel.

   - Does the tongue pull back any harder for certain vowels?
   - Can you keep the tongue relaxed on each vowel?
   - How much movement is necessary to shape each vowel?
   - If the tongue is being held and therefore not heavily involved in shaping vowels, what else is involved in vowel shape than the tongue?

Background Information. As explained in the first section of this chapter, the tongue tries to help out in other functions of singing. This sensory experience points out in many singers that the tongue wants to help in singing higher. Like a violin string being stretched to tune higher, the tongue pulls at the larynx to tighten the vocal cords on higher pitches. This is the wrong conception of how the vocal cords work—not by tightening, but by oscillating back and forth, relaxed and free enough to move more quickly on higher pitches.

Once this interfering movement of the tongue is revealed, the tension needs to be replaced with a new sensation and function. One solution implied in the sequence is to grasp the tongue to sense its relaxed position before singing, memorize the sensation, and maintain it during singing. Second is to keep holding the tongue during singing to alert the singer to the presence of tension and remind the singer to relax the tongue muscle. Third, pulling the tongue farther out of the mouth gives it a stronger movement forward to counteract the old backwards pull.

Another solution presented in the exercise sequence is to change the way you think about singing. Box the old habits into a parenthetical "sing" as if a cliché that has lost its effectiveness, and replace it with a new word or term that is associated with the more effective way to produce tone, such as the technical term "phonate" or an everyday term such as "honk." When you think of singing as sound-making or tone-producing rather than "singing," you allow your sound to flow relaxingly behind the tongue, beyond the mouth, and into the sinus chambers above your palate. What word best describes the sensation to you?

In answer to the final question in the sequence, with the tongue out of commission to shape vowels, you may find how vowel color is shaped by the resonators as well as by the tongue. With the tongue's exaggerated vowel-shaping movements tamed, tone rises into the nasal cavity where very small movements color vowels with more consistent resonance.

Important Principle for All Learning. Different problems of terminology in multisensory learning have been described in this book starting in the Introduction. In this exercise, the problem is that a word can come to be associated with an entire out-dated way of behaving. Continued use of the word conjures up the old habits that have been worked out in separate exercises. Old habits suddenly come back to cancel out new efforts with a simple mention of the old terminology. This is further reason why to use the terminology that singers use to describe a successful experience. Honk happened to be the word that made sense to me as a student singer; pay attention to your own words that best capture experiences of successful singing.

Tongue Curl and Fat "L" Tongue

Exercise Sequence. This exercise provides alternative solutions to holding the tongue.

1. Touch the tip of the tongue to the gum line behind the front lower teeth and curl the middle of the tongue up and out (Figure 5.5, left), pulling the back of the tongue out of the throat and filling most of the mouth cavity.

2. Sing a chord arpeggio pattern of *do-mi-so-do-so-mi-do*.

    a. Was the larynx able to stay in low position with the pull of the tongue out of the way?

    b. With the tongue mostly filling the mouth cavity, where did sound come out?

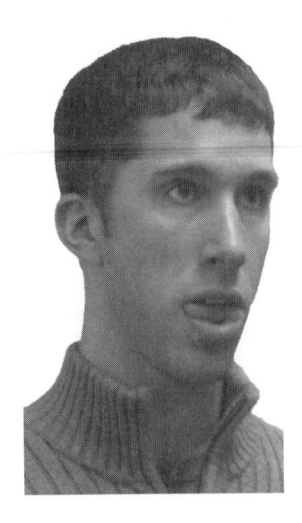

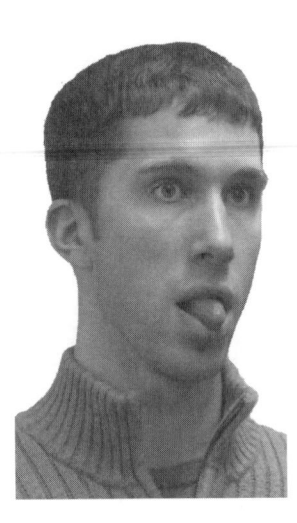

FIGURE 5.5 Tongue curl and fat "L" tongue positions.

   c. As the intensity increased as pitches sped up higher, how did the sensation of resonance change?

3. Point the tongue forward out of the mouth and rest the teeth closed against it about half way along its length (Figure 5.5, right), keeping the tongue round and full as if saying an L [l].

4. Repeat step 2.

Background Information. Two optional tongue movements are included in this exercise in case a singer has trouble with one or the other. Both fill the mouth cavity and therefore more likely channel tone through the resonators. Both bring the tongue away from the back of the throat where tone and air pressure may have been trapped before. Both movements allow tone to flow more freely through the pharynx, and both make it easier for the larynx to find a lower position.

By filling the mouth cavity with the tongue, sound must find another way out. Even with a small space above or around the tongue, it is easier to release the air pressure upward than to force it past the tongue. Besides, with the tongue engaged in a very involving move, it has less chance to trap sound through the mouth. If either choice does not work at first, make a bigger sensation of the movement by bringing the tongue farther out of the mouth, especially on the highest notes of the pitch pattern.

Bubble Hand Above Rocking-Tongue Hand

Exercise Sequence. This exercise uses both hands, one to guide the subtle movement of the tongue and the other to keep the tone resonant.

1. As you sing AH-EE /ai/ back and forth, as in /aiaiaiaiai/, on a single pitch, move one hand palm down in a gentle rocking motion to guide the tongue in an unintrusive action, and place the other hand over the first hand in an upside-down-U shape like a bubble, as if holding the resonance consistently open and vibrant (Figure 5.6).

   a. On AH [ɑ] the wrist is lower and the fingers are higher.

   b. On EE [i] the wrist is higher and the fingers are lower.

      - The hand rocks back and forth as the tongue follows in search of the minimum movement needed for a distinct change in vowel colors.

2. Identify the sensation of resonant tone consistently floating over the tongue; elevate it higher into the resonators with a lift of the bubble hand; project it out and beyond with a fling of the hand up and out ahead of the resonators, all with the tongue still gently rocking and not interfering.

3. Sing different combinations of primary vowels such as AH-EE /ai/, EE-AH /ia/, OO-AH /ua/, AH-OO /au/, OH-EE /oi/, OH-AH /oa/ and the like.

   - Feel for a uniform resonance to develop above the movement of the tongue, keeping vowel colors distinct and yet holding this consistent resonance in place.

4. Sing combinations that move into more difficult vowels of IH, AE, EH, UH, such as OH-IH /oɪ/, AH-AE /ɑ æ/, OO-EH /uɛ/, EE-UH /iʌ/, and the like.

5. Sing across several vowel combinations, such as EE-AY-AH-OH-OO /ieɑou/.

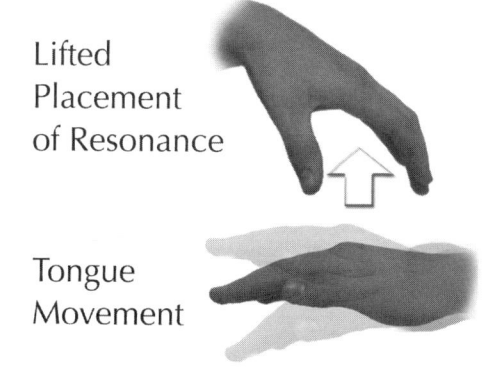

Lifted Placement of Resonance

Tongue Movement

FIGURE 5.6 The bubble hand on top guides resonance, the rocking hand on bottom guides the tongue.

Background Information. One of the tongue's most natural roles in singing is to shape vowel colors. However, this role is often overly done, using exaggerated movements that are not necessary. The tongue needs only to shift the space slightly to change from one vowel color to the next. In addition, the tongue is not solely responsible for coloring vowels—the resonators also play a role in shaping vowel color.

This exercise may be the one that gets a singer to find where resonance exists separately from the changing space around tongue movement. There is a rich, ringing quality that floats up and over the tongue action, a central focus of tone that stays put regardless of tongue shape. The sensation of this central resonance is heightened by the floating bubble sensation in the upper hand. Wrap your hand around it and you may find that it can be inflated and moved about as a separate entity. It exists as a separate function of singing.

When a singer learns to move and inflate this bubble at the center of resonant tone, a new benchmark in singing has been reached. With the separate existence of resonant tone now discovered, the singer is free to get rid of a lot of excess movement and effort that was used to build each system of singing. Suddenly, the strong efforts to breathe can let go and be drawn upon only in the amount needed to keep the tone buoyant and full. Tension around the larynx suddenly lets go to allow the vocal cords their free and effortless vibration in the lighter breeze and leaner column of air. Strong muscles involved in articulation suddenly let go, unneeded to pull on the pitch and squeeze the space in search of a resonant tone. A vibrant tone travels easily out from the singer with less effort.

Extended Exercise I: Word Pronunciation. To test for consistent resonance across vowels, extend this exercise by phonating through combinations that lead to words.

6. Compare the resonant tone when singing one vowel to the next with how vowels are sung once the word is glimpsed and in mind.

    a. AH-IH-EE-OH-OO-UH /ɑɪiouʌ/, which is roughly the pronunciation of the state of Iowa.

    b. OO-IH-L-EE-OO /uɪliu/, which is "Will you?"

    c. OO-EH-UR-AH-UR-EE-OO /uɛrɑriu/, which is roughly saying "Where are you?"

    d. OH-AH-EE-N-OH-OO-N-AH-OO /oɑinounɑu/, or "Oh, I know now!"

Extended Exercise II: Placement. A new sensation can come about through the separation of resonance from vowel color, a central focus of resonance called *placement*.

However, because resonance can be inflated and expanded, it is not a sensation of being stuck in one *place*. Therefore, placement is too limiting of a term. Also, because the central focus of resonance can be moved around, the use of the term placement does not guarantee a uniform experience of placement from one singer to the next. The term is best used only to describe that the *center* of resonance can be made to focus consistently in one place. Explore the sensation of moving placement in this extended exercise.

7. Sing combinations of vowels as before, moving slowly from one vowel to the next across the following steps.

8. Move the upper "bubble" hand upward as if floating higher above the lower "tongue" hand, feeling the nasal cavity open and vibrations rise up higher in the head with no change in the movement of the articulators.

    - Which placement along the path feels and sounds most natural and free?

    - Which placement feels most comfortable and sustainable?

    - At what point is placement so high that it limits the surrounding resonance and sounds hollow or artificial?

9. Move the upper hand forward, feeling placement move across the forehead, down the bridge of the nose, and into the nasal passages of the nose from above.

    - At what point is placement too far forward that it limits the surrounding resonance and sounds too nasal?

Extended Exercise III. Overtones. Besides finding that the central placement of resonance can move, a second changing phenomenon can be experienced—overtones. With the surrounding resonant space able to stay open regardless of tongue shape and vowel color, the slight shifts in space and color can be made to accent different overtones.

10. Sing EE-AY-AH-OH-OO /ieaou/ slowly over and over, maintaining the same pitch throughout.

11. During the slow movement from one vowel to the next, feel the slight shift of vibration across the tongue and back of the throat; guide movements and perception using slight motions of the lower "tongue" hand.

    - Listen to the residual resonance echoing in the mouth and floating in front of the mouth and nose area.

12. Listen for a pitch change as vowels change, not in the pitch being sung but in the residual resonance ringing in the mouth and outside the mouth and nose area.

13. Look at the sonogram/spectrograph of the author performing this exercise (Figure 5.7, top) or look at Figure 3.3 to track the overtones visually as they rise and fall with subtle changes of vowel color and tongue/pharynx shape.

14. Amplify the sensation of overtones by shifting the center or placement of resonance to ring in the mouth while maintaining full and vibrant resonance, trapping resonance yet with a free sensation of phonation and no tension (Figure 5.7, bottom).

For a more extensive and detailed look at the acoustical effects of changes in resonators during articulation, see *Voice-Tradition and Technology* (Nair 1999) or *The 21st-Century Voice* (Edgerton 2004).

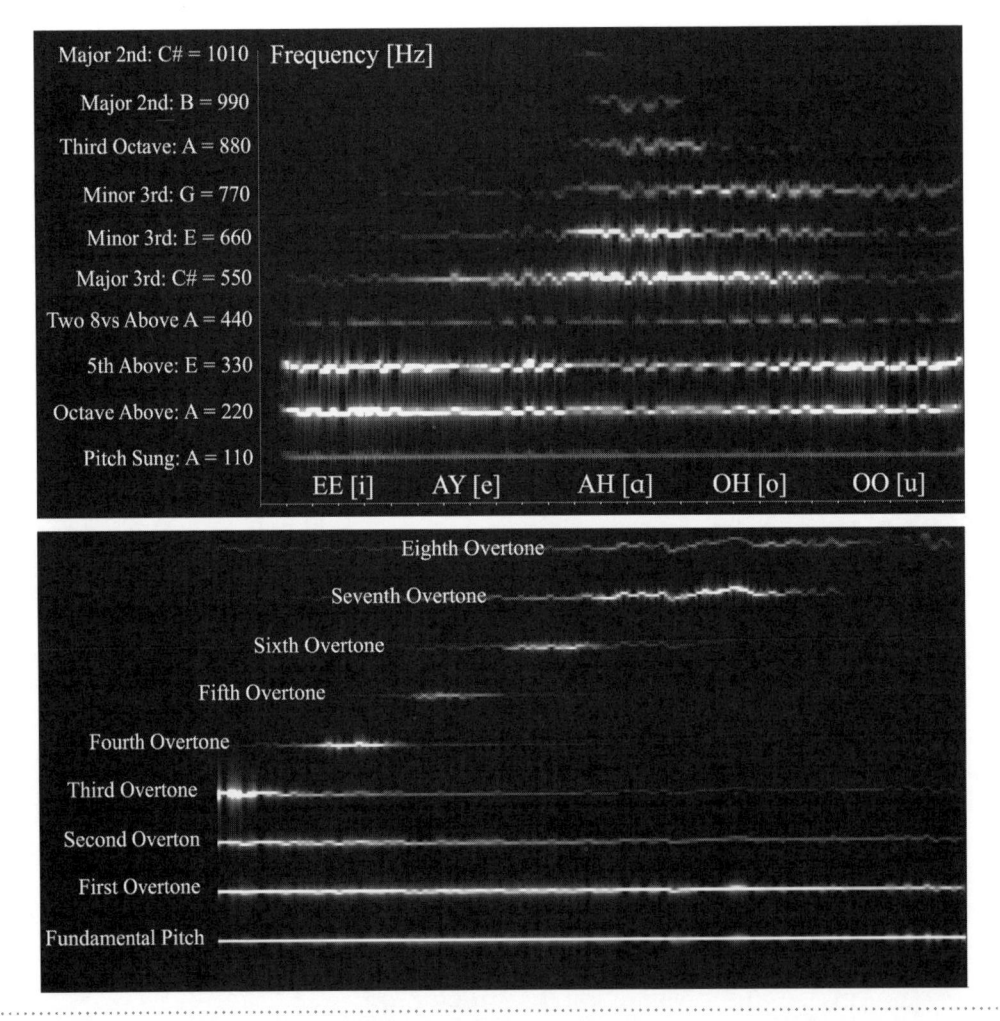

FIGURE 5.7 Different overtones are highlighted due to vowel shape (left) and slight changes in the shape of the oropharynx (right).

Important Principle for All Learning. If an exercise does not help make more sense of how to sing, be patient and keep working through the sensations of different topics and exercises. As the old proverb attributed to Augustus says, "Make haste slowly," or as said by the jazz musician and composer Hoagy Carmichael, "Slow motion gets you there faster." Slow explorations can lead to quick and unexpected discoveries. Allow discoveries to occur in their own time and they will happen sooner than if expected to happen.

Free and Quick-Moving Jaw

Finger-guided Relaxed Jaw

Exercise Sequence. Tension in the jaw is released by simple external control in this exercise.

1. Place an index finger lightly on the chin.

2. Allow the gravity of the hand to lower the jaw with a release of muscle tension and control (Figure 5.8), keeping the jaw from jutting out (left) and instead rotating it down and back (right).

3. Sing YAH /ja/ with the gravity of the hand releasing the biting muscle control of the jaw.

   - Did jaw tension increase with singing? Release the grip to the control of the hand weighing it down.

4. Sing YAH-YAH-YAH /ja ja ja/ on a rising *do-mi-so* with the hand leading the lowering of the jaw.

FIGURE 5.8 A jutting position of the jaw (left) changes to correct rotation (right).

- Did jaw tension increase with rising pitch? Again, release the grip to the control of the hand's weight.

5. Sing syllables that require jaw movement, helping the jaw to move freely by guiding movement with the weight of the hand, for example YAH-BUH /ja bʌ/.

Background Information. Jaw tension is a particular problem in certain types of people. The hard work ethic of a Type-A personality, the abrupt movement of a hyperactive, the meticulous detail of a perfectionist, and the protective motions of those who have had braces are distinct sources of tension in the jaw. Telling a person whose tension is based on physical effort to stop being tense does not work. There needs to be a replacement of effort, something to work at, something to perfect. This exercise provides such an effort. The effort presented here is to take charge of movement with gravity and external weight. This allows muscle tension related to the jaw to relax and give control over to external control. With the jaw and face allowed to relax, the sound will pop out up above, effortlessly. The effort, then, is to be effortless.

Yah-jaw Hand Flop

Exercise Sequence. This alternative exercise focuses on the correct rotation of the jaw joint.

1. Place the thumbs in the joint where the jaw meets the skull. Check for proper placement by lowering the jaw and feeling for the thumbs to be pushed out of the joint.

2. With fingers together, rotate the hand down to place the index fingers on the top of the chin (Figure 5.9).

3. Open the jaw in a way that the thumbs rotate as the hands follow the chin down and rotated back. This is in contrast to a downward movement of the jaw that stretches the joint.

4. Sing a YAH /ja/ or MAH /ma/ on a single pitch and then on a rising *do-mi-so* pattern on /ja ja ja/ or /ma ma ma/, guiding the free rotation of the jaw with the hands.

   - Especially check to release any biting action on the initial Y [j] or [m] and to keep biting tension from restricting the movement of the jaw.

FIGURE 5.9 Correct jaw rotation.

5. Sing songs or patterns that require combinations of jaw and lip movement (Figure 5.10), using this yah-jaw hand movement to detect situations in which the jaw wants to lock up and to instead guide continued free movement.

- Especially check when rapid movement of the lips locks the jaw closed; keep lip and jaw movement separate.

Background Information. A problem in jaw movement is the incorrect stretching of the jaw joint. Stretching of the jaw out of joint can be a sign of TMJ syndrome, which is often detected by a dentist more so than a doctor. TMJ is an acronym for the name of the jaw joint—Temporomandibular Joint. The syndrome associated with the jaw joint is the incorrect movement out of joint instead of rotating within the joint.

For the Voice Teacher. Because voice teachers work so closely with jaw movements, we can perhaps detect signs of TMJ syndrome. Check for proper rotation of the jaw joint. Look for hyper-extension of the jaw out of joint, a sudden protrusion around the joint, or a sense that the joint is switching gears to allow a more extremely open mouth. Listen for popping at the point the jaw shifts out of joint. Also check for limited movement, which means that the singer may be protecting from possible pain or popping in the jaw. Suggest that the singer check with a dentist or doctor on a regular checkup or visit.

For the Choir Director. Choir directors are infamous for giving commands to open the mouth wide. As explained and tested out in Chapter 3, the mouth does not need to open so wide for sound to come out. Sound vibrates through the resonators and out through the flesh and bone of the entire head and chest. An overly open mouth can pull tone out of the resonators and cause more problems than it solves. An open mouth is merely an external indication that the soft palate *may* be raised; the soft palate can be raised without an open mouth. Finally, the requirement to open the mouth leads to any number of movements of the jaw, including hyper-extension of the jaw out of joint. Therefore, fervent calls by a choir director to open the mouth wide may unknowingly cause or accelerate the occurrence of TMJ syndrome. In developing a raised soft palate and resonant tone, use other techniques than opening the mouth. Or if extended jaw movement is used, such as on extreme high pitches in the singer's range, then practice proper jaw rotation and not out-of-joint stretching.

/la la la la mi mi mi mi la la la la mi mi mi mi la/
/ja ja ja ja li li li li ja ja ja ja li li li li ja/

FIGURE 5.10   The combination of wide intervals and changing syllables develops quicker and freer movement of articulators.

Loose and Responsive Cheeks and Lips

Sensory Experience: Do the Cheeks Stay Plump During Singing?

Exercise Sequence. The external touch of a finger on the cheeks helps maintain upward lift of tone in this exercise.

1. Place a finger on the upside of a cheek muscle, just below the eye. See the finger out of your lower peripheral vision as you look out across the room.

2. Smile, and feel the cheek plump up like a fluffed pillow (Figure 5.11). Better yet, tell a joke or think of something funny to feel what the cheek does during a natural laugh.

3. Open the mouth and sing an AH [ɑ].

    - Did the cheek pillow flatten and lower with the downward movement of the jaw?

    - If so, did the tone follow the jaw downward?

    - If not, did the tone flow more easily through the resonators at cheek level or higher?

4. Plump up the cheeks again with a smile and keep it plumped up as you sing.

    - Were you able to freely release the jaw and keep the cheeks plumped up?

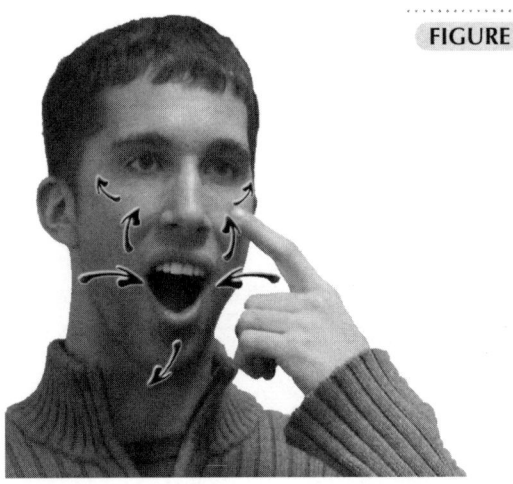

FIGURE 5.11 Separation of a lift in the cheek muscles and a relaxed rotation of the jaw.

- If not, use the other hand to guide free jaw movement using one of the previous two exercises.

- Did the tone lift with the lift of the cheeks?

- Was the mouth shape more vertical, with the corners allowed to freely and naturally stay in?

- Feel the relaxed movement of the side cheeks on either side of the mouth.

5. Use this cheek touch to verify that the cheeks stay plump while singing scale patterns and songs you have learned.

- Discover situations of rising or falling pitch intervals, and vowel and consonant combinations that lock cheek and lip movement to the downward pull of the jaw.

- Work to separate the lift of the cheek from the movement of the articulators, keeping an eye on the finger on the cheek. It takes concentration as the mind pays attention to so many different movements in the process.

Background Information. One multisensory principle laid out in the Introduction was that sound goes to whatever moves. The problem with jaw movement is that a stressful downward opening of the jaw pulls sound down with it. Even when maintaining free jaw motion, the attention is still on downward movement and may still tend to draw tone down with it unless there is a counteracting upward movement. This upward movement is provided by the cheeks. By separating the movement of the jaw with the cheek muscles, the tone is free to lift into the resonators. This cheek pillow-plumping exercise helps keep the tone aimed into the maxillary sinuses and above, regardless of the activity of the articulators in the other direction. For a more extensive exploration of the effects of facial movement on tone production, see Larra Browning Henderson's (2001) *How to Train Singers*.

When a person laughs in a crowd you can usually hear the sound from across a room above all other noise. Is it because of the wide-open mouth? No, not everybody laughs with the mouth so open, so it must be something else that makes a laugh project across a room. It is resonance and deep breathing that make it project. Typically a laugh is supported down low. Why do you think they call it a belly laugh? On the topside, *the raise of the cheeks into a smile lifts tone into the resonators*, through which tone is amplified tall and sent easily across the room. Laughing also releases tension, which keeps sound from being trapped. This is a shorthand description of the process of singing: deep supportive breathing, the throat and other systems in the middle free of tension and out of the way, and tone lifted into the resonators and projected out. Laugh a little, and discover the natural strength of breath support and easy lift of tone. The rest stays out of the way.

Mouth Corner Touch

Exercise Sequence. This exercise helps sharpen attention to the vertical movement of the mouth, particularly keeping the corners from spreading outward.

1. Touch the index fingers to the corners of the mouth.

2. Sing a scale pattern on YAH [ja] or a song with words that causes changing mouth actions.

3. Use the fingers to sense any tendency to move the mouth outward, and to remind the corners to stay in instead.

    - Notice the jaw and other face muscles relaxing as the corners of the mouth relax and stay in.

    - Check that cheek muscles stay plump in their effort to draw tone behind the palate and into the sinuses.

Background Information. Voice teachers and choir directors often tell singers to keep the corners of the mouth in. More than a verbal direction, this exercise takes action to sense the activity of the corners of the mouth. Physically checking the presence and absence of muscle tension alerts the muscles to stay loose and free, out of the way of other upward lifting efforts of singing.

Putting It All Together

Flop and Stir Arm Hold

Exercise Sequence. This exercise sums up all efforts of this chapter in one rich sensation that is guided by a teacher or helper.

1. With the singer standing, the helper holds with one or two hands the weight of one of the singer's arms, gently stirring and waggling the arm in unexpected motions until the singer lets go of the weight of the arm and hand and lets them move freely (Figure 5.12, top).

2. Connect the sensation in the arm and hand with the muscles at the back and base of the neck, shoulders, upper back, and up into the throat, jaw, tongue, and face.

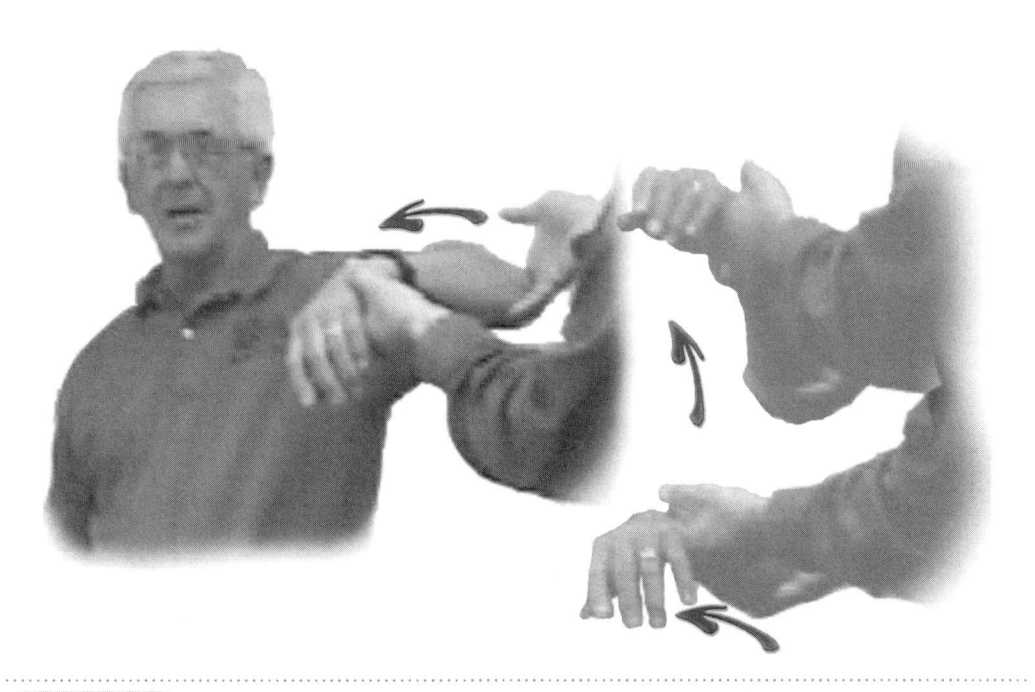

FIGURE 5.12 Release of the arm to external control guides release of tension in singing.

3. Sing a melody or exercise with mixed vowels, such as EE-AY-AH-OH-OO /i e a o u/, or syllables, such as LEE-LAY-LAH-LOH-LOO /li le la lo lu/, during which the helper counteracts tension with extra large movements of the arm until articulation occurs with the same freedom as felt in the held arm (Figure 5.12, bottom).

   a. Feel for instances that the arm lifts, tenses, or takes back control from the helper, which are signals that systems involved in singing are tensing up as well.

   b. These instances of tension may be on a rising pitch interval, peak pitch in a pattern or melody, a rigidly bitten EE [i], or a difficult rhythm that may grab in the throat instead of coming from low breath support.

4. When the singer comes to produce a consistent relaxed and resonant tone during singing, release the arm unexpectedly (Figure 5.12, top).

   - At the point of release, did the singer grab for tension, continue with freer movement and freer release of tone, or suddenly release even more tone in a relaxed release of energy as the sensation sweeps over the entire body?

Background Information. As professionals and practitioners in fields as diverse as physical therapy and yoga meditation will tell you, tension in one part of the body is linked to tension in another part of the body. In the same manner, letting go of tension in one part of the body helps release tension in another part of the body. The trick in this exercise is to selectively open up a path from the arm to the articulators without causing loss of effort elsewhere in singing. Notice that the arm-hold movement can start out as a holistic sensation that is linked to most every sensation from the neck up, and yet can be selectively linked to specific points as habits of tension are identified in the singer.

The advantage of this exercise is also the external control that allows sensations to be guided and detected by a problem-solving helper. Singers are not always aware of the existence of tension. Singing does require effort that leads to sensations of muscle activity. It is a puzzle to find out which muscles need to flex, how much they need to flex, and which muscle activity is considered tension that interferes with the processes of singing. This is when a teacher is required to help select appropriate sensations of singing. The point here is to provide options for how to activate appropriate muscles and release those that get in the way.

Tasting Each Component Sound

Exercise Sequence. Adapting and combining hand movements from earlier exercises, this exercise draws attention to each vowel and consonant in the text that is sung.

1. Transcribe the text of a selection of choral or solo music into IPA.

a. Underline each consonant that can be sung, which are called *voiced* consonants. Pronounce each consonant with a slight vibration in the fingertips of curled fingers (Figure 5.13, left)

- *Plosives*: [b], [d], hard G [g], soft J [dʒ]

- *Sustaining*: [l], [m], [n], R [r], [v], and [z]

- *Vowel Formation*: W as [w] or [u], Y as [j] or [i]

b. Put a check mark (✓) above each consonant that starts with sound stopped behind closed articulators and then is followed by a release of air, so-called *explosive* or *plosive* consonants. Pronounce each consonant with a quick flick of the index finger off the thumb to guide a quick release of air after each (Figure 5.13, middle).

- Voiced: [b], [d], [g], J [dʒ]

- Unvoiced equivalents: [p], [t], [k], CH [tʃ]

c. Identify sustaining consonants, add a check mark (✓) above each to keep articulation as brisk as a plosive instead of letting air out like an air leak, and use a combination of the voiced gesture (left) and plosive gesture (middle).

- *Voiced*:   [l], [m], [n], R [r], [v], [z], ZH [ʒ]

- Unvoiced equivalents: [f], [s], SH [ʃ]

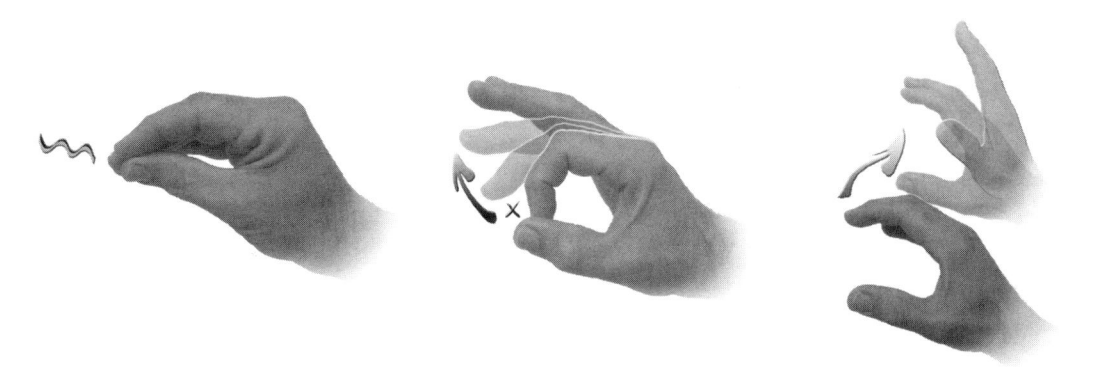

FIGURE 5.13   Hand and finger gestures help guide consonants: voiced (left), plosive and brief sustained (middle), and aspirated (right)

d. Identify consonants that are formed with air escaping unvoiced, so-called *aspirated* consonants: [h] as in "hello" and WH [hw] as in "where" or "when." Gesture the aspiration of air with a short forward twitch of a curled hand by the mouth, ready to stop and spring open with a tall-hand gesture for any vowel that follows (Figure 5.13, right).

2. Perform the entire text slowly with a distinct gesture for each type of consonant and a forward moving tall-hand gesture for each vowel (as in Figure 5.3), curling the hand at the end of diphthongs.

3. Perform the entire text more rapidly, using appropriate movements only for vowels or consonants that require a release of tension, extra attention to detail, or shift in function.

Background Information. Diction is the process of breaking down the component sounds in the text and articulating each accurately. The purpose of this chapter or exercise is not to provide a complete manual on diction, but rather to make diction more multisensory. To learn the different types of consonants provides knowledge but not function. To pronounce each as they are supposed to function is better, but still not as tangible as needed for deeper sensory learning. The use of hand gestures and other movements heighten attention to details of diction, heighten the sensation of diction, and make diction movements more memorable. In this exercise, hands and arms provide strong visual and kinesthetic sensations that guide the smaller movements of the articulators and override their old lazy habits. The improved sensation and sounds are then repeated and internalized until the hands and arms are no longer needed as external controls over the articulators.

Important Principle for All Learning. At this point, the body would be on overload sensing abdominal and costal muscle movement, bringing attention to the movement of the diaphragm, sensing resonance in different spaces, and so forth all at once. It becomes a juggling act in which more and more balls are thrown into the pattern—one dropped ball and the entire pattern may fall to the floor. To learn to juggle, you usually start by making the movements of one ball into a habit and then adding one ball more at a time until the entire pattern is coordinated and habituated. And so it is with learning to sing, that too many exercises should not be attempted in short time—it can overwhelm and confound rather than help efforts to learn. Or as said by the 19th-Century American author Nathaniel Hawthorne, "We go all wrong by too strenuous a resolution to go all right." There must be enough habit and coordination in some areas to allow new challenges to be introduced in other areas without the entire set of systems losing control.

For the Choir Director. Gestures to guide articulation can be used to excite attention to each unique noise and vibration involved in diction. Choral diction is an important topic for any choir to learn. The more unified the diction, the more unified the rhythm and tone of the choir. Realize, however, that beyond attention to sound is the possibility to *get the articulators* *of many singers to move at once*. In a multisensory way of putting it, the conductor's gestures not only guide sound, they visually signal movements in singers' bodies. A move of the hand and 80 singers touch the tongue to the roof of the mouth to form a consonant, which then makes a unified sound. For a choir to sound as one, singers not only need to know when each sound is to occur but also when to articulate a voiced consonant or shape a vowel. Gestures from this exercise and chapter can line up the movements of the articulators, remind singers to articulate with relaxed movement of the jaw and tongue, and shape vowels to the same height at the same time. There is something quite beautiful in a choir singing a pure primary vowel in a diphthong and then shading the color with a slow united closure into the secondary vowel. Top it off with a tasty final consonant, and the audience will taste the effect, too.

Now to complete this book, add an exercise that is related to this chapter, and continue to make this multisensory approach your own.

Name of Exercise

Exercise Purpose:

Exercise Sequence:

Background Information:

REFERENCES

Apfelstadt, Hillary (1986). Learning modality: A potential clue in the search for vocal accuracy. *Update: The Applications of Research in Music Education, 4(3)*, 4-6.

Braiker, Harriet (2001). *A Disease to Please*. New York: McGraw-Hill.

Bunch, Meribeth, & Cynthia Vaughn (2004). *The Singing Book*. New York: W. W. Norton.

Caldwell, J. Timothy (1994). *Expressive Singing: Dalcroze Eurhythmics for Voice*. Englewood Cliffs, NJ: Prentice Hall.

Coffin, Berton (1987). *Sounds of Singing: Principles and Applications of Vocal Techniques with Chromatic Vowel Chart*. Metuchen, NJ: Scarecrow Press.

Conable, Barbara (2000). *The Structures and Movement of Breathing: A Primer for Choirs and Choruses*. Chicago, IL: GIA Publications.

Conable, Barbara, & William Conable (1995). *How to Learn the Alexander Technique: A Manual for Students*. Portland, OR: Andover Press.

Conable, Barbara, & Benjamin Conable (2000). *What Every Musician Needs to Know About the Body: The Practical Application of Body Mapping & the Alexander Technique to Making Music*. Portland, OR: Andover Press.

Cooksey, John (2006). Kinesthetics and movement in the choral rehearsal. In Alan J. Gumm (Ed.), *The Choral Director's Cookbook: Insights and Inspired Recipes for Beginners and Experts* (pp. 22-23). Galesville, MD: Meredith Music Publications.

Cooksey, John (1999). *Working With the Adolescent Voice*. St. Louis, MO: Concordia Publishing House.

Dalby, Bruce (2005). Toward an effective pedagogy for teaching rhythm: Gordon and beyond. *Music Educators Journal, 92(1)*, 54-60.

Dayme, Meribeth Bunch (2004). *The Performer's Voice. Realizing Your Vocal Potential*. New York: W. W. Norton.

Dowling, W. Jay, & Dane L. Harwood (1986). *Music Cognition*. San Diego, CA: Academic Press.

Duke, Robert A. (1994). Bringing the art of rehearsal into focus: The rehearsal frame as a model for prescriptive analysis of rehearsal conducting. *Journal of Band Research, 30(1)*, 78-95.

Edgerton, Michael Edward (2004). *The 21st-Century Voice: Contemporary and Traditional Extra-Normal Voice*. Lanham, MD: The Scarecrow Press.

Eskelin, Gerald (2005). *Lies My Music Teacher Told Me: Theory for Grownups*. Woodland Hills, CA: Stage Three Enterprises.

Ester, Don P., John W. Scheib, & Kimberly J. Inks (2006). Takadimi: A rhythm system for all ages. *Music Educators Journal, 93(2)*, 60-5.

Feldenkrais, Moshé (1972). *Awareness Through Movement: Health Exercises for Personal Growth*. New York: Harper & Row.

Gumm, Alan J. (2003a). *Music Teaching Style: Moving Beyond Tradition*. Galesville, MD: Meredith Music Publications.

Gumm, Alan J. (2003b). Musical and technical sources of choral dynamics. *Choral Journal*, 43 (10), 27-39.

Gumm, Alan J. (2005). Well-rounded teaching and balanced learning outcomes. In Garwood Whaley (Ed.), *The Music Director's Cookbook: Creative Recipes for a Successful Program* (p. 52-53). Galesville, MD: Meredith Music Publications.

Gumm, Alan J. (2006). Leaven to counteract loafing: Developing a self-responsible and collaborative choir. In Alan J. Gumm (Ed.), *The Choral Director's Cookbook: Insights and Inspired Recipes for Beginners and Experts* (pgs. 49-50). Galesville, MD: Meredith Music Publications.

Heirich, Jane Ruby (2005). *Voice and the Alexander Technique: Active Explorations for Speaking and Singing*. Berkeley, CA: Mornum Time Press.

Hibbard, Therees Tkach (1994). The use of movement as an instructional technique in choral rehearsals. DMA, University of Oregon, DA9418994.

Hoffman, Richard, William Pelto, & John W. White (1996). Takadimi: A beat-oriented system of rhythm pedagogy. *Journal of Music Theory Pedagogy*, 10, 7-30.

Holt, Michele Menard (1992). The application to conducting and choral rehearsal pedagogy of Laban Effort/Shape and its comparative effect upon style in choral performance. DMA, Music: University of Hartford, DA9214439.

Klein, Joseph J., & Ole A. Schjeide (1981). *Singing Technique: How to Avoid Vocal Trouble*. Tustin, CA: National Music Publishers.

Lessac, Arthur (1997). *The Use and Training of the Human Voice: A Bio-Dynamic Approach to Vocal Life*. Mountain View, CA: McGraw-Hill College.

Lessac, Arthur (1979). *The Body Wisdom: The Use and Training of the Human Body*. Hollywood, CA: Quite Specific Media Group Ltd.

McKinney, James C. (1994). *The Diagnosis & Correction of Vocal Faults*. Nashville, TN: Genevox Press.

Nelson, Samuel H., & Elizabeth Blades-Zeller (2002). *Singing With Your Whole Self: The Feldenkrais Method and Voice*. Lanham, MD: The Scarecrow Press.

Oatis, Carol A (2004). *Kinesiology: The Mechanics and Pathomechanics of Human Movement*. Philadelphia, PA: Lippincott Williams & Wilkins.

Paton, John Glenn (2006). *Foundations of Singing: A Guidebook to Vocal Technique and Song Interpretation*. Boston, MA: McGraw Hill.

Ristad, Eloise (1982). *A Soprano on Her Head*. Moab, UT: Real People Press.

Sanders, Paul David (1991). An exploratory study of the relationship between perceptual modality strength and music achievement among fifth-grade students. Ph.D. dissertation, The University of Oklahoma, AAT 9210487.

Stanton, Royal (2000). *Steps for Singing for Voice Classes*. Prospect Heights, IL: Waveland Press.

Stanton, Royal (1979). *The Dynamic Choral Conductor*. Delaware Water Gap, PA: Shawnee Press.

Tsatsouline, Pavel (2003). *The Naked Warrior: Master the Secrets of the Super-Strong Using Bodyweight Exercises Only*. St. Paul, MN: Dragon Door Publications.

Theimer, Axel (2006). The perfect blend: Every choir director's dream. In Alan J. Gumm (Ed.) *The Choral Director's Cookbook: Insights and Inspired Recipes for Beginners and Experts* (pp. 106-108). Galesville, MD: Meredith Music Publications.

Vennard, William (1967). *Singing: The Mechanism and Technic*. New York: Carl Fischer.

Ware, Clifton (2004). *Adventures in Singing: A Process for Exploring, Discovering, and Developing Vocal Potential*. Boston, MA: McGraw Hill.

Waring, Fred (1951). *Tone Syllables*. Delaware Water Gap, PA: Shawnee Press.

Zikmund, Annabell B. (1988). The effect of grade level, gender, and learning style on responses to conservation type rhythmic and melodic patterns (Doctoral dissertation, University of Nebraska). University Microfilm No. 89-04, 520.

ABOUT THE AUTHOR

ALAN GUMM is Professor of Music Education at Central Michigan University, where he directs the Women's Chorus and teaches choral and music education courses. Gumm is the author of *Music Teaching Style: Moving Beyond Tradition*, editor and contributor to *The Choral Director's Cookbook: Insights and Inspired Recipes for Beginners and Experts*, and contributor to *The Music Director's Cookbook: Creative Recipes for Successful Programs*, each published by Meredith Music Publications. Articles by Gumm are also published in the *Choral Journal*, *Music Educators Journal*, *Journal of Research in Music Education*, *Bulletin of the Council for Research in Music Education*, *Southeastern Journal of Music Education*, and *Visions of Research in Music Education*. Applying the techniques detailed in *Making More Sense of How to Sing*, Dr. Gumm helped propel the MountainTown Singers to international competition, and his own choir was recognized in a *Saginaw News* concert review for its "clear sound, excellent vocal technique and magnificent tuning. The musical lines were beautifully shaped. This was expressive singing at its finest." Gumm has also been recognized with numerous awards for teaching excellence.

Prior to coming to CMU, Dr. Gumm was director of choral music activities at McPherson College, where he chaired the music department, managed a full voice studio, led eight U.S. and European choir tours, and co-founded and conducted the McPherson Chamber Orchestra. Dr. Gumm also previously taught at Ithaca College, University of Utah, and in Kansas public schools. He holds the doctor of philosophy from the University of Utah, a master of music from Fort Hays State University, and a bachelor of arts from McPherson College, is a member of Music Educators National Conference, American Choral Directors Association, Society of Research in Music Education, and the National Education Association, and is a past member of the National Association of Teachers of Singers and the Barbershop Harmony Society.